Conceptual, Social–Cognitive, and Contextual Issues in the Fields of Play

Recent Titles in
Play & Culture Studies
Stuart Reifel and Jaipaul L. Roopnarine, Series Editors

Volume 1: Diversions and Divergences in Fields of Play
Margaret Carlisle Duncan, Garry Chick, and Alan Aycock, editors

Volume 2: Play Contexts Revisited
Stuart Reifel, editor

Volume 3: Theory in Context and Out
Stuart Reifel, editor

Conceptual, Social–Cognitive, and Contextual Issues in the Fields of Play

Edited by Jaipaul L. Roopnarine

Play & Culture Studies, Volume 4

Ablex Publishing
Westport, Connecticut • London

Library of Congress Cataloging-in-Publication Data

Conceptual, social-cognitive, and contextual issues in the fields of play / edited by
Jaipaul L. Roopnarine.
  p. cm.—(Play & culture studies, ISSN 1096–8911 ; v. 4)
  Includes bibliographical references and index.
  ISBN 1–56750–647–X (alk. paper)—ISBN 1–56750–648–8 (pbk. : alk. paper)
  1. Play—Psychological aspects. 2. Play—Social aspects. I. Roopnarine, Jaipaul L.   II.
Series.
BF717 .C66 2002
155.4'18—dc21   2001022794

British Library Cataloguing in Publication Data is available.

Library of Congress Catalog Card Number: 2001022794
ISBN: 1–56750–647–X
        1–56750–648–8 (pbk.)
ISSN: 1096–8911

First published in 2002

Ablex Publishing, 88 Post Road West, Westport, CT 06881
An imprint of Greenwood Publishing Group, Inc.
www.ablexbooks.com

Printed in the United States of America

The paper used in this book complies with the
Permanent Paper Standard issued by the National
Information Standards Organization (Z39.48–1984).

10 9 8 7 6 5 4 3 2 1

Copyright Acknowledgments

The author and publisher gratefully acknowledge permission to use the following material:

Chapter 2, "Huizinga's Contributions to Play Studies: A Reappraisal," is reprinted in part from
Homo Ludens, by Johan Huizinga, copyright © 1950, Roy Publishers. Reprinted by permission of
Beacon Press, Boston.

Contents

Part V. Adult Play

Editor's Note

It is a distinct honor to assume the role of series editor of *Play & Culture Studies*. The Association for the Study of Play (TASP), through the research and theoretical contributions of an international, multidisciplinary group of scholars, has been at the forefront of delineating the role of play in advancing our understanding of evolution and behavior. Theoretical and conceptual advances, scientific investigations, and discourse about applied issues and different dimensions of play are richly chronicled in the last three volumes of this relatively new series and several prior volumes published by TASP. A common practice has been to publish papers that report on both qualitative and quantitative studies within the broad disciplines of education, psychology, anthropology, sociology, leisure studies, and primatology. Within this multidisciplinary genre, the goal of the series has been to publish manuscripts that cover play in humans and animals in wide-ranging contexts (see Reifel's introductory remarks in Volume 1 of this series).

Taking note of the exemplary work of the previous series editor, Dr. Stuart Reifel, and in keeping with the multidisciplinary focus, Volume 4 presents an eclectic compendium of 15 peer-referred chapters. True to the mission of the series, the chapters cover a range of topics—some are conceptual, others are data-based. In the conceptual chapters, the authors provide excursions into the adaptive, cultural, and social significance of play. The data-based papers fall into four categories: the role of age, gender, and ethnicity in play participation, social-cognitive connections to play, fighting and playfighting, and play and process in adulthood.

I am very grateful to Stuart Reifel, Jim Johnson, and Priscilla Snell-White for the guidance and support in getting Volume 4 ready for publication. I look forward to working with the authors and editors of forthcoming volumes and with the people at Greenwood Press in getting a high-quality series published in a timely fashion.

Jaipaul L. Roopnarine, Series Editor
Brooklyn College and the Graduate Center
The City University of New York
and *Syracuse University*

Part I
Conceptual Issues Regarding Play

1

Recapitulation Redressed

Brian Sutton-Smith

INTRODUCTION

Twenty-five years with the Association for the Study of Play confronts the participant with the difficulty that its members are scholarly as classicists, literati, historians, anthropologists, psychologists, sociologists, biologists, leisure theorists, and so on, but nevertheless, they often appear to be talking about quite different subject matters and using quite different theories to explain their intent. My recent book, *The Ambiguity of Play* (Sutton-Smith, 1997), was my own attempt to come to terms with this interdisciplinary fecundity. It was a deconstruction of social science play theory and was intended to demonstrate that the bulk of contemporary psychological and cultural play theories have hidden ideological assumptions as well as conscious scientific ones. The ancient play theories of gambling were framed as rhetorics of fate; the theories of sports as rhetorics of power; the theories of festivals as rhetorics of identity; the theories of frivolity as rhetorics of inversion. The modern play theories of childhood were framed as rhetorics of progress; rhetorics of the imagination, rhetorics of creativity; and rhetorics of the self as secular individuation. Unfortunately, having arrived at that kind of deconstructive synthesis, one was still left with the need to search for some more fundamental and universal account of play function and structure. An evolutionary pursuit beckoned as likely to be the most worthwhile, and I relied upon S.J. Gould (1977, 1996a, 1996b) to derive a conception of play in biological terms as a form of adaptive (random) variability (Sutton-Smith, 2001). While this seemed to be a useful hypothesis to partially account for forms of play functioning, it did not speak cogently to the very similar structures of play that occur throughout history as well as cross-culturally. The intent of this chapter is, therefore, to address these structural issues in play, and then to return through that discussion to a reevaluation of the adaptability hypothesis as a functional account.

BATESON'S PARADOX

The single most important and widely agreed-upon structural thesis brought forward about play in the 20th century is Bateson's (1972) contention that play is a kind of paradox. By that he means that play always is and is not what it displays itself to be. The child playing "mother" both is and is not a mother. Or a dog playfighting will use a nip to connote a bite but not what a bite connotes. The nip means a bite, but it does not mean it is tearing something to pieces, which is what the word *bite* usually means. By word ("Is this pretend?") or gesture (a play face or exaggerated and stylized moves), or by taking place in stadia, on a stage, or in playgrounds, playrooms, or playpens, with sports equipment, costumes, or toys, play always metacommunicates the message that "this is play." It is not the real thing, whatever that is. Bateson's discoveries have led to a wealth of information about play signals in both animals and humans and about the kinds of virtual reality that constitute play.

What we additionally want to know, however, is why anyone (indeed, why everyone, animal and human) should bother to be playing in the first place. Bateson suggests that play is a crucial step in the evolution of communication. Using Freudian concepts of the unconscious and the conscious, he suggests that there is in the evolution of communication first a primary process kind of thought where no discrimination is made between a map and its territory, between a symbol and that to which it refers, and second, there is a more advanced secondary process kind of thought where such discriminations are made, where pretense is pretense and reality is reality. He says, "In primary process map and territory are equated. In secondary process they can be discriminated. In play they are both equated and discriminated" (1972, p. 185). The problem with this formulation, however, is that we do not know when or where, if ever, such a primary-secondary thought process shift occurred in the evolution of the species.

DAMASIO'S PARADOX

Recent writing in neurology makes it possible to hypothetically reframe Bateson's brilliant thoughts about play's metacommunicative evolutionary function in neurological terms. The major source here is Antonio R. Damasio and his book *Descartes' Error* (1994), in which he attempts to show that body and mind are never as separate as Descartes had originally announced. The rational mind does not alone create one's conscious existence as in Descartes's classic expression "cogito ergo sum." There are instead primary and secondary emotions that accompany different kinds of reflexiveness and consciousness from the very beginning of species evolution. Damasio talks of *primary emotions* as resident mostly in the more archaic or limbic parts of the brain, which give rise to primarily reflexive emotions and actions. These primary emotions are involved in the immediate and instinctive actions of fight and flight, which secure survival because of the speed at which they occur. In reptiles and fish, whose survival depends on constant rapid scanning for predators, this is their main brain system. These emotions still occur for ourselves when we are suddenly startled or threatened and our heart beats faster, or when we tremble, perspire, are enraged, or are suffering a painful loss or, alternatively, when we are suddenly overwhelmed by feelings of surprise, triumph, joy, or love. These primary emotions propel us into action when emergencies arrive and, when properly applied, have saved lives throughout early species history so that they are now embedded in all of us, although perhaps are now only used by humans largely in emotional crises.

However, some 65 million years ago (Smith, 1984), with the advent of mammals, larger neocortical areas were selected, these involving the *secondary emotions*. These developments in the frontal lobes of the neocortex required more contemplative decision making in thoughts and actions and were associated with attempts to secure survival through careful delays and reconsiderations. The difference between the two emotional systems seems to be something like the difference between passion and perspicacity, or between intense emotional extremities and more controllable emotional fictions, aesthetics, and imaginings. What is important to register is that mammals still have both of these emotional forms functioning within themselves. In general, however, it is the function of the secondary emotions to modulate or simulate the more extreme character of the basic primary emotions, so as to protect us from the stress that they might occasion, and to entertain instead the multiple flexible alternative possibilities that consciousness now permits. It might be said that civilization is basically an attempt to live such a secondary emotional life without too much direct fear, disgust, sadness, and rage, though without thereby also neglecting the ability to react effectively with feeling and rapidity in times of emergency, and without also losing the ability to shriek with triumph, surprise, and happiness in moments that do not do injury to others. The paradox may be that without the primary emotions humans are likely to lag in vitality, but without the secondary emotions they are likely to lose control of, and be endangered by, these relatively uncontrollable sources of their own vitality.

What is important to recognize, according to Damasio (1994), is that the more rational emotional processes occur in this way within the more general and fundamental framework of the primary processes. They are not totally separate from them neurally. On the other hand, the structures in the limbic system (in particular the amygdala) are not alone sufficient to support the experiential processes of the six cortical secondary emotions. Therefore, there is a juxtaposition of the two conjoined systems. In some cases, the secondary emotions can concoct images and simulations that are relatively distant from the primary emotional forms. Of particular ludic interest here is that Damasio speaks of *as if* neural loops in which "the brain learns to concoct fainter images of an 'emotional' body state, without having to reenact it in the body proper. . . . Thus there are neural devices that help one feel 'as if' they were having an emotional state, as if the body were being activated and modified. Such devices permit the mind to bypass the body and avoid an energy consuming process" (p. 155).

THE LUDIC EMOTIONAL PARADOX

What Damasio is saying is that the *as if* loops become a critical part of the novel secondary emotional system at this point in evolutionary history. But it is also believed that it is only with the appearance of the mammals that playing also becomes widespread in evolutionary history. Admittedly it is not known whether play is present with the most ancient forms of mammals, though it is conjectured that it is to a lesser degree (Burghardt, 1998). The present thesis is that these two events, the emergence of secondary emotional systems and the emergence of play, are linked in evolutionary history.

At this point we return to the issue of why play as a paradox might be especially representative of Damasio's emotional dichotomy. What he is essentially arguing is that mammals profited and succeeded because of their ability to use the insight gained from secondary emotions. The crisis that the mammals suffered by doing so, however, was perhaps how to maintain the vitality of these primary and reflexive emotions that could sometimes secure survival, within the carefulness that secondary emotions would dictate. This might be phrased as the internal emotional crisis of the mammalian neural revolution. It is through their response to this crisis, it will be argued here, that play emerged as an acted-out fictional type of response. Why this ludic representation of the bimodal emotional state might have arisen is suggested by neurologist Edelman when he says "the brain in forming concepts makes maps of its own activity, not just of external activity, as in perception" (1992, p. 109). What is probable, given modern research (Ledoux, 1992), is that such playful maps have their own location and neuronal pathways. And one might expect a linkage to the secondary systems' damper switches on primary emotions because play is likewise in part such a damper system, as is evident in the message "this is play not reality."

In these ludic terms Bateson's (1972) paradox can be interpreted as based on such a map, being relevant because it is representing the brain's own emotional dichotomy and the brain's own emotional management. That is, people engage in play not just because it is a paradox, but because that paradox represents the brain's paradoxical management of its own dichotomous emotional nature. The brain uses the emotional secondary system to control the primary emotional system while still giving the latter muted access to expression. Thus, play is always accompanied by routines, rituals, and rules in terms of which the neo-frontal cortex controls the structure, but the players are allowed to vent their primary emotions: squealing, avoiding, hiding, shoving, and so on. Play, whether in animals or humans, is thus formulated as an enacted fiction, which is a less desperate way of being excited by primary emotions. Which is to say that play gives access to the fundamental "liveliness" of primary emotions without gen-erally having to pay for the costs that might occur when these things are in-dulged in normally. To put it as Bateson does earlier, this is why play is directly about the "nip" but also indirectly about the "bite."

PLAY AS RECAPITULATION

The classic recapitulation theories foster the view that individuals in their development (ontogeny) go through stages similar to those gone through bio-logically by earlier species (phylogeny) (Gould, 1977, Ruse, 1996). There has been little scientific support for this formulation, but what can be admired about it is the fairly realistic sense that early scholars such as Gulick, Hall, Spencer, and others had about the somewhat primary emotional or "primitive" character of a great deal of human play, a primitivity well captured in children's play in the last century by the works of Gomme (1894) and in this century by Iona and Peter Opie (1950) and myself (1959, 1981), as well as for adults in many of the historical accounts of play (Bakhtin, 1984; Huizinga, 1955; Spariosu, 1989). In short, play continues today, as in earlier times, to encapsulate fictionally the regressiveness of the primary emotional life. In that lies its vitality and perhaps its "intrinsic" motivation. It recapitulates, in its own surprising form, the mam-mal binary emotional crisis, and that is why its reputation has been redressed here. This is a statement that as play was then, it is basically also now. The present play paradox continues to represent the fictional *as if* of the ancient relatively reptilian regressive primary emotions under the sway of the secondary, more rational cortical processes.

As Edelman might perhaps say, in these old circumstances, play became a neural map that allowed for the mollified expression of the primary reflexive emotions by fictionalizing them and metacommunicating that fact. In this fic-tional conception, in general, but not always, the secondary emotional system wins out over the primary emotional system. More importantly, as we shall see, it becomes possible today to distinguish between the kind of play fictions that are more resonant of the primary emotions and the kind that are alternatively more directly expressive of the character of the secondary emotional system, although both are always mutually involved to some degree. More importantly, if the most basic and universal structure of play is thus primarily reflective of this dualistic internal emotional system, and if this has been carried on this way for perhaps some 65 million years, it is not surprising that it has been so difficult for us moderns, committed as we are to the civilizing secondary system of emotions, to comprehend play's paradoxical character. If there is indeed any biological progress over time since then in this ludic phenomenon, it might be due to the increasing size of the cortex in some species, or to cultural progress in so many other phenomena. In our own human case, we have made enormous secondary emotional progress. But it is still true, as empirical and therapeutic studies show, that those who rest only on these resources and deny themselves the mitigated accesses of play to the primary emotions thereby take the risk of greater depressiveness. On the other hand, those who are psychotic, or maladjusted and victims of their own primary emotional processes, quite often cannot play. One depressive modern group needs, therefore, more willful play to reverse the dominant emotional secondariness of their lives, and the other pathological group, in contrast, needs play to harness the primary emotional extremities of their lives. The first needs more connoted "bite" and the second more connoted "nip." One is always supposing, that is, that these play forms of emotional remediation make a difference. But whether they do or not, they continue to symbolize and to enact this most fundamental evolutionary compromise, which lives on with us and within which we enjoy the reverberations.

THE PARADOXES OF FOLK GAMES AND PLAY

The different kinds of play can be arranged in terms of the kinds of emotional syntheses that they make possible. There can be ludic dimensions that vary between the archaic reptile resonance and the modern mammal resonance. If we take typical "folk" play concepts, then the above dimension of play forms can be shown to contain a variety of standard types that vary along the lines mentioned. It is important to realize, however, that these are discussed here as normative kinds of examples. It is quite possible for any form of play to be played in a nonstandardized fashion so that it would be more appropriate in one of the other categories. The interest here is in the possibility of seeing the range of cultural and individual play forms in a more evolutionary light, for example in:

1. Deep play

2. Contact sports

3. Celebrations

4. Monitored play forms

   (a) Adventures and explorations

   (b) Performances and mind play

PLAYS THAT SHOW A STRONG RESONANCE OF ARCHAIC FORMS

We presume, following Barbara Ehrenreich (1997), that the archetypal situation for these kinds of play may be that of the predator and its prey. Or, following Wrangham and Peterson (1996), the archetypal situation might be that of the alpha male against his competitors. Presumably all of the less critical winner-loser parallels in play forms could derive from either of these evolutionary archetypes.

Deep Play

The deep play concept was first presented by Geertz (1973), who focused on gambling in cock fighting in Bali. While there has been much criticism as to the ambiguities of his ethnography, the concept was, among other things, meant to cover a situation in which a player, entering into one of these games, could as a result lose all his possessions, including his home and his wife. Geertz states his position in a way that is directly consonant with the archaic, "emotional" explanatory points for play being presented here, particularly as we have italicized it in his quotation that follows:

Every people, the proverb has it, loves it own form of violence. The cockpit is the Balinese reflection on theirs: on its look, its uses, its force, its fascination. Drawing on almost every level of Balinese experience, it brings together themes—animal savagery, male narcissism, opponent gambling, status rivalry, mass excitement, blood sacrifice—*whose main connection is their involvement with rage and the fear of rage, and, binding them into a set of rules which at once contains them and allows them to play, builds a symbolic structure in which, over and over again, the reality of their inner affiliation can be intelligibly felt.* ... Balinese go to cockfight to find out what a man, usually composed, aloof, almost obsessively self-absorbed, a kind of moral autocosm, feels like when attacked, tormented, challenged, insulted, and driven in result to the extremes of fury, he has totally triumphed or been brought fatally low. (p. 27)

Therefore, deep play is the kind of play in which the closest exposure to the primary emotions is courted or risked in whatever are the prevailing cultural terms for such exposure. These are sometimes occasions where one may even doubt that the word *play* is appropriate because there seems to be such direct exposure to emotional trauma. Yet there are even more extreme "deep play"-like kinds than that of Geertz, for example, when war is carried out in a sporting manner, as is reported historically in some Melanesian and Polynesian cases. For example, the Dani in New Guinea occasionally make war as one village against another in adjacent valleys: "The war is surrounded with much pomp and circumstance, shouting and enthusiasm; it is fought according to a set of understood rules; and it is marked by a playful or sporting attitude that appears to take precedence over the idea that eventually someone must be killed" (Blanchard, 1995, p. 167). Yet in one village count, 28 percent of the men and 2 percent of the women died in such encounters. Given all the whooping and joking, shouting, and wittiness, at the expense of the opponents, who are quite well known, much of what is going on is clearly at least a kind of marginal playfulness.

Another interesting "deep" variant is the two-man tug of war using leather thongs tied around testicles among the Inuit people. These Eskimo males typically engaged in contests that caused considerable pain to both the players, but during which they were not permitted to express any emotions except smiling (Glassford, 1976). Here, the emotional response of fear or anger, which might be forthcoming, is explicitly denied by the game rules, while being perilously evoked. The existence of such "war" play forms is perhaps a validation of the view that the primary emotional extremities revealed negatively by fear, rage, despair, pain, dishonor, defeat, and sacrifice, or positively by victory, power, pride, triumph, and achievement, which are then couched in these secondary metacommunications of the above positive kinds (whooping, joking, smiling, etc.), support the position here that play is most fundamentally about providing maps for an arrangement that allows for both these primary and secondary kinds of emotion. The paradox lies in the contrasts between the extremities of danger and the protection of the rules, protections that in "deep play" cases are partial at best.

Contact Sports

There are many other kinds of sports that risk personal injury to some of the participants and these are widespread throughout the world and throughout what is known of the human history of combat. Often this is because the fighting is of a total kind, with few if any holds barred, as in the Greek Pankration or in the turn-taking slug fests, one blow each at a time, found among some Eskimo and some South American Indian groups. Again, there are, cross culturally, a host of physical contests in which accidents are quite frequent and this includes most major ancient sports: stick fighting, wrestling, kickball, football, boxing, spearfights, horse fights, ball games, shinty, lacrosse, and team play in general (Polikoff, 1987). Similarly, in modern sports there are high rates of accidents in boxing, kick boxing, bull fighting, football, ice hockey, wrestling, mountain climbing (in particular on Mt. Everest, where over a span of 100 years one out of five have perished in the attempt; Sutton-Smith, 1998), ice skiing, surfing, high-speed auto racing, as well as many of the extreme sports, such as snow-boarding, roller skating, and luging. All of these are also notable for their much advertised, if sometimes simulated, perilous possibilities (Rinehart, 1998). Given these examples, there is strikingly little change in the periodic joy for male contact and dangerous sports widely found historically and anthropologically in the human record. Here again, all these forms of play have in common some metamediation of the emotional extremes. The greatest enjoyment is of course in winning these contests; and of taking these extremities of encapsulated emotion and subsuming them to one's own team or individual valor. Apparently women's contact sports may go the same exaltative way, as when in the 1996

Olympics, after winning in women's soccer, the U.S. goalkeeper ran naked through the streets. The postludic negations of the opponent's triumphs vary from the opposition's heroic reserve to extensive weeping or sometimes what is called "poor sportsmanship." Even, on occasions, the secondary protections break down and the realm of play controls is totally bypassed by hooliganism and the wrecking of rival townships. Normally, however, obedience to the rules and rituals of virtue or humility is required by the larger organizations of which one is supposedly a loyal member.

In modern times there has been an enormous increase in the size of the groups that offer ever more access to contact sports (through television, media, and stadia). Approximately 2 billion people watched some parts of the 1998 World Cup, which is probably more people than have ever done anything in common before in history. Spectators also find that in these play situations they can scream and yell their approval or disapproval of what they see before them. I have had my female college students tell me that screaming at college basketball games was a primary form of fun for them because it was something that they had never been allowed to do anywhere else in their lives. The Olympics is another example of multiple sportspersons seeking world victories while masses of spectators follow their progress. All of which means that the management of these sporting contests has become ever more complex, and that although the contests themselves are still both framed in rules, they are still manifestations of the primitive emotions of joy and sorrow. The changes in history are largely ones of increasing complexity and increasingly symbolic forms. There seems, however, little change in this ludic mapping of the basic duality of the relationship between primary and secondary emotions, in which the secondary controls are the price for the indulgence of the primary emotions. Apparently we are destined to eternal recapitulations of this our mammalian invention and mammalian fate.

Celebrations

While victory or defeat (fight and flight) were the key emotional risks to be taken in the prior examples, the critical emotional paradigm with all celebrations, of which contests are often a part, has to be that of being a member of the group celebrating or of being an outcast. The fear, often more basic even than the violence of sports, is that of not belonging to a membership group and of not, therefore, having a group identity. And the major playful maps against this isolation are those that gather groups together to create a social contract through their multiple celebrations, including those of sports. Ancient forms are such events as Australian Aboriginal Corroborees, Soshone Fandangoes, dragon boat festivals, the Point Hope Whale Festival, Roman Carnival, Palio at Siena, Carnival in Rio de Janeiro, and so on. Modern forms are everything from ethnic parades, Rose Bowl and Macy's parades, the satirical Doo Dah Parade in Pasadena, cowboy festivals, Easter, Christmas, Thanksgiving, and July 4th, to personal forms of celebration such as birthday parties, Valentine's Day, Mother's Day, and honeymoons.

What is central playfully to all celebrations is the availability of one or more kinds of emotional license that allow members to deviate from normal or conventional circumstances or ways of behaving. While the license in sports is, as shown, various forms of contest, the license in the simplest forms of celebrations is maybe laughter, clowning, and eating, but in more extreme celebratory forms may become orgy, inebriation, gluttony, and all other possible kinds of deviation. Celebrations thus vary from Mothers' Day to Rabelais, with the license being gifts on the one hand and indulged barbarity on the other. But whatever the forms of license and the novel intensities that they bring to the gathering, the primary emotional risks add licensed vitality to the occasion, and yet abide by the secondary contexting of the event in terms of private or national sentiments, so that all this inversion of normality is also received as a civilizing contribution.

A RESONANCE OF MODERN FORMS

Monitored Physical Play Forms

Adventures and Explorations

What is central to all of the following monitored forms of play is novelty of some kind or other, whether threatening or not. While this is also true of the contestive and celebratory forms of play, it is somewhat less central there. The key to monitoring the following types of play, however, is mainly to reduce their physical, that is, emotional, dangers.

For example, in the individualistic athletics, which have developed so strongly since their initiation by the Greeks, most forms of contest have been without physical contact. There are the multiple athletic forms where the players do not touch each other physically, as in running, jumping, swimming, archery, javelin, discus, track and field, and so on, which do not imply any injurious contact. We assume here, however, that the exaltation of victory or the misery of defeat are still the emotions that these games have in common with the other, more direct forms of physical contest. These noncontact forms of play make it clear that injury and accident is not essential, although the issue of winning or losing still remains central. But in general it seems probable that there are now more forms of such monitored play than ever before in human history. That is, there are more ways in which persons can play with only a very remote chance that the licenses or novelties so granted them will be in any way dangerous. We would include here the classic forms of winning or losing through strategic conquest, such as chess, Go, Wari; or in games of chance, such as bingo, the lottery, and so on; or in games of strategy and chance, such as poker, bridge, and so on. In all of these cases, winning and losing, triumph and despair, are still critical, but in general there is no physical violation of the competing persons. In contemporary times there has also been a vast increase in video games and with it a steep escalation in the imagined envisagement of primary emotions—fear, horrors, disasters, and so on. But in all of these games the player is typically not in a social game but is sitting in his own bedroom or the video playroom or wherever. What these games gain in the intensity of the primary emotions that are portrayed, they also gain in the player's control over these external circumstances, which can be departed from at any moment by turning away from the game or turning off the screen.

The most obvious modern example of monitored play is the way in which the play of children has become increasingly supervised throughout this century, in terms of the provision of toys, of preschool playgrounds, of supervised play groups, of video and computer games. The earliest public school playgrounds of the last century were not so monitored and were often fairly wild places to be. But from about 1900, most of this changed and any such forms of violence were disallowed (Sutton-Smith, 1981). The most striking modern adult-monitored examples are to be found in the management of travel, exploration, outward-bound adventures, and in climbing or cycling athletics, which are now pursued by increasing numbers of persons. Ship, train, and bus vehicles take parties of all ages to explore famous places (such as Mayan temples) within which the members are in fact insured against negative physical consequences.

Monitored Imaginative Play Forms

Performances and Mind Play

In many ways modern civilization has become a culture of multiplicitous entertainments and some have written about modern life as increasingly a theater or movie (Gabler, 1998). Present-day culture has made celebrities out of professional players of many diverse kinds such as athletes, television hosts, comedians, film stars, film directors, novelists, dancers, songsters, musicians, sculptors, painters, dancers, and actors. These persons display themselves in terms of their own genres, and in general, whatever the contents of their enactments or of the audience roles, all are quite safe in what is expressed before them, although the content is sometimes quite peaceful and at others can be quite catastrophic. As Hall (1999) has said recently, "It is one of the paradoxes of our age that we have created entire economies around activating this fear system under safe conditions in the form of theme park rides and Stephen King novels and films which have us on the edge of our seats."

In dreams and fantasies, players can empathize with contests, celebrations, adventures, explorations, and performances. All play transformations are possible depending on the player's own mental health and range of life experience. Humor and playfulness are probably the most common modern expressions of mind play, in which the verbal and amusing violations of all standards of behavior and morality are taken for granted, either personally or socially, and the laughter expressed and received is, nevertheless, regarded as of considerable mental health value. These players go the furthest backward in their reptilian metaphors and yet are the furthest forward in their momentary delights in their immediate world.

QUALIFICATIONS

The present theory rests on a number of assumptions, some of which require more careful qualification. These are:

- That there is an evolutionary discontinuity of reptile and mammal behavior.
- That the treatment of all types of play can be similar.
- That the interpretation of play can be chiefly in terms of emotions.
- That the present recapitulatory theory is relevant to all types of play.
- That the mammal brain has a capacity to make simulative maps of its own activity.
- That play's simulation of the evolutionary emotional duality results chiefly in a revitalization of the players.
- That play is a binary ludic map that simulates the secondary emotional system engaging the primary emotions within a safe context provided by the secondary emotions.

The primary difficulty here is uncertainty about the lack of play in reptiles, and the lack of information about the most ancestral forms of play occurring in either species some 65 million years ago. With some exceptions (Burghardt, 1998), the data available from current forms does make the present reptile/mammal contrast feasible, and it has been widely assumed in the literature (Burghardt, 1984, pp. 32–33; Goleman, 1995, p. 23). It has been noted that mammals as compared with reptiles are warm-blooded, have higher metabolic rates, get prenatal and parental care and food and warmth, and have vigorous motor activity and surpluses of energy as well as neonatal periods for skill practice. These factors, however, underlie all the novel cortical activity in mammals; they are not specific to play forms.

It has also been suggested that motor play and object play may have different functions from social play, which is the major focus of this chapter. It is not impossible that these earlier two have indeed grown out of the general exploratory activity, which characterizes both reptiles and mammals, and that they represent somewhat different systems from the emotional system being focused on here. Our own preference, however, is to subsume these two forms of play to the kind of contrastive excitations we are claiming for social play. What may separate body motion as exploration from play is the increased excitation, form exaggeration, and mastery of simulated risk with the latter. What may separate object exploration from object play is the increased excitation and simulated mastery of risk and predation with the latter.

The key to the present evolutionary theory as contrasted with most others is the focus on the patterning of emotion as has been suggested by Damasio. In general, naturally enough, affective issues have not been central in most discussions of animals because they are not accessible to observers. There is also a further problem here—that in combining the several types of emotion as a part of the primary system, the issues are being oversimplified. Obviously rapid reflexive reactions of fight and flight, for example, are the basic kind. But in general this paper has also been including impulsive highly intensive emotional expressions as a part of this same primary zone (yelling, squealing, loud boasting, or dismal crying). Then again, beyond that, it is here also admitted that the deep play possibilities may include actions that involve total loss, total rejection, death, and even criminal levels of emotionality at the edge of what the play comes to mean. In short, at present, the category of primary emotions is something of a metaphoric "swamp" in this account. All that can be said at this point is that perhaps it could not be otherwise.

The information that is most unavailable in the present formulation, however, is that which postulates that the mind maps its own simulative ludic responses to the existential battle between the primary and secondary emotions. But how does it do that? Edelman states that the brain is more like a jungle than any kind of logical machine. Furthermore, it is about 80 percent concerned with itself and only 20 percent with the external world. Our only whisper of a theory is when Damasio talks of the *as if* emotions in his secondary emotional system. The word *fiction* has been used throughout this chapter, however, to keep in the forefront the fact that it is always only play that is being discussed. Edelman's map in this case is a fiction. The word *ludic* should suffice in scholarly life to imply such a separate frame and a different reality as does the word *fiction*, except the habit has developed in this century of subsuming the concept of play to some other kind of everyday reality (growth, power, identity, creativity, flow, etc.). These rhetorics of play are then taken as if they present play's major meaning. But the actions of play are themselves not primarily in those everyday spheres of reality. The maps of play are primarily in a fiction or virtual reality-like domain. On the other hand, the trouble with calling play "virtual reality" is that we fail then to distinguish realistic forms of virtual reality (training in weightlessness for space travel, for example) from the normal *fictional* play. We should perhaps speak of play as *virtual irreality* to distinguish play from other forms of irreality, such as "spiritual visions" or "schizophrenia," as well as from everyday life (Heim, 1993). The notion that the primary result from engaging in the playful emotional dualism is a temporary reinvigoration of the players, derived from the testimony these days of most players to their enjoyment, fun, flow, epiphany, ecstasy, escape, and so on, during the play itself. In many senses, play, often found as a part of religious rituals in earlier times, seems always to have been a kind of prereligious ecstasy through the high involvement of the players in these highly credible but limited irreal activities. In both cases there is a kind of redemption of the sense of the worthwhileness of being alive, whether it is in games or in church services. The other kinds of evidence for this revitalization effect can be found in the therapy literature or in the research on classroom play experiments, where those in the play groups as compared with the controls are more optimistic and confident in their activities. School activity or adult work without play is apparently an invitation to various forms of depression. Still, it needs to be noted that despite several million years of this hominid player enjoyment of the ludic manifestation of primary emotions controlled by the secondary emotional systems, there is still no shortage of wars, holocausts, pograms, genocides, ethnocides, and so forth. According to some, nothing has changed in that respect. The scale is just much larger (Keeley, 1996).

Finally, the view that play is a kind of binary system may perhaps be appropriate only for some limited kind of play; or, perhaps, while it is a useful analysis, it may be an insufficient one. It needs mention that I have long held a bias in favor of some kind of binary structural analysis of play, as indicated in articles on play as replication and reversal (Sutton-Smith, 1966), games of order and disorder (1977), games as the socialization of conflict (1973), and the dialectics of play (1978a, 1978b). Nevertheless, support for the view that animal effects do take on the binary quality that is being suggested by the present theory gathers some tentative support from Fagen's (1981) recording of the multiple elements in animal play. On the one hand, animal play features (primary emotional) *disorderly* behavior: (a) play sequences are highly fragmentary as compared with nonplay parallels; (b) they are often disorderly or reversive in character; (c) they include exaggerated movements; and (d) they share an atypical intensity of action and noise.

On the other hand, there are clearly also controlling behaviors providing an *orderly* (secondary emotional) context: (a) play is highly repetitive and at times quite orderly (not unlike the effects of the rules, rituals, and routines in human play); (b) there is typically the inhibition of harmful actions to other players and an inhibition of stressful encounters; and (c) there are explicit signals through face, sounds, gestures, and postures that indicate the message that "this is play" and that we can trust each other and cooperate.

A further indication that this primary-secondary duality of emotions may indeed be a fundamental way to think about the nature of play is the fact that play theories about humans also tend to show a preoccupation with the irrationality of the primary emotions or the rationality of the secondary emotions or some combination of both.

Primary emotion play theories are those in which the emphasis is upon irrationality and disorder and the way in which play is a vehicle for the less acceptable human emotions and irrational thoughts. Some of the notable play theorists present play as grotesque realism (Bakhtin); anarchic power (Spariosu); deep play (Geertz); inversion (Babcock); illicit play (King); dark play (Schechner); unsinn-wahnsinn (McMahon); nonsense (Stewart); panoply of tropes (Fernandez); disorderly, fragmentary, and reversive (Fagen); play of signifiers

(Derrida); a dialectic of safety and risk (Myers); dissidence (Scott); transgressive (Stallybrass); carnival (Falassi); fools (Fox); tricksters (Hughes); primordial negatives (Burke); unrealistic optimism (Bjorkland); denotative license (Fein); transitional objects (Winnicott); divergent thinking (Lieberman); wishful thinking and abreaction (Freud); desire (Hans); willfulness (Nietzsche); carthasis (Menninger); ecstatic actions (Fink); quirky variability (Gould); exaggeration (Miller); instinct (McDougall); recapitulation (Hall); improvisation (Sawyer); flexibility (Fagen).

Secondary emotion play theories are those in which the emphasis is upon the rationality and normality of the play actions as they contribute to the control of play. These include exploration (Berylne); assimilation (Piaget), subjunctivity (Vaihinger); imagination (Singer); symbolism (Bretherton); playfulness (Barnett); scaffolding (Vygotsky); mastery (Erikson), effectance (White); affect regulation (McDonald); relaxation (Patrick); intrinsic motivation (Rubin); flow (Csikzsentmihalyi); positive emotion (Lewis); autotelia and paratelia (Kerr); agentivity (Bruner); stress reduction (Bekoff); stylized behavior (Abrahams); symbolic interaction (G.H. Mead); bonding (Harlow); surplus energy (Schiller); practice (Groos); learning (Thorndike); performance (Bauman).

Obviously both of these sets of concepts are at times ambiguous and can fit into either the primary or the secondary category. (Note that these theoretical concepts and their bibliographical references are to be found in *The Ambiguity of Play* [Sutton-Smith, 1997, pp. 218–220].)

Further support for a binary analysis of play structure can be derived from a number of play theorists, other than Bateson, who have also considered play to have a paradoxical-like structure, for example, Handelman (1992) and Goldman (1998), play as private fantasy vs. cultural mythology; Stewart (1978), play as nonsense vs. sense; Myers (1991, 1992, 1998, in press-a, in press-b), play as risk vs. security; and McMahon (1999), play as nonsense vs. utter nonsense.

IMPLICATIONS

What this recapitulatory theory does for us, if valid, is to indicate that despite all our civilized progress, our play forms are still fundamentally what they have always been for mammals: contests (rivalry), celebrations (belonging), explorations (novelty), performances (display), and, for humans, playfulness (humor) and imaginings (mind play). They all continue, whether the old or the new forms, to recapitulate the novel balance between the primary and secondary emotions, which were a part of the mammal evolutionary passage. The many modern theories of play motivation discussed previously, while they seldom attempt to answer the ultimate evolutionary questions, may nevertheless serve as reasonably correct indicators of some of the proximate realities of all of this play. As shown above, a plethora of functions has been attributed to play. There are at least 100 play concepts in our most recent count, and there is no reason to doubt that, given the complex nature of the basic evolutionary and neurological reality, many of them have some relevance to the effects of this paradox on the world of those who are the players. The 20th century uses of human play—in play therapy, in play curriculums, in play as reinforcement, in personality play types, in play as make believe, in play as school sociodrama, in adventure playgrounds, in novel or electronic toys, in play as an evolutionary training in variability, and so on—all of it tells us something about the vitality of play in human life if nothing much about the basic paradox of play itself. As a recapitulation of past primitivities, this theory of play and evolution raises some skepticism about the relatively total idealizing of play that goes on in most modern child play theory and increasingly in adult play theory (Sutton-Smith & Kelly-Byrne, 1984). Play looks indeed as if it is a high priority for the life of some vitality, but it is seldom, therefore, necessarily an activity of any great delicacy; and there are plenty of "dark" or primary emotional forms of play as well as some light or secondary forms. Naturally, every civilized person would wish to increase the amount of participation in the latter, but as is clear from the play examples above, the evidence seems to say that the fruits of play (revitalization, etc.) are most likely only when there is some accompanying vicarious participation in the primary emotional, often horrifying, scenarios.

CONCLUSION

Despite 100 years of thought and research in the 21st century, the function of play has been largely inexplicable. What has been asserted in this document is that play might have been an outcome of the evolutionary change that occurred when the earth's species moved from the reptilian groups to the neurologically relatively more complex mammals. The additional cortex available to the latter led to conflicts in the management of the erstwhile emotional habits of the prior species. While the basic emotions of lust or hate, pride or shame, triumph or failure, continued to vivify the lives of the new species, the generally trigger-like and precipitous reactivity of these reptilian emotions threatened to endanger the complexities of mammal survival. There developed, in consequence, a conflict between the desire for the emotional vividness of the past and the need for emotional cautiousness within the new more cerebrated view of life's complex realities. Play, when it emerged in the more complex neocortex, represented a fiction-like representation or map of the new desire to remain emotionally lively but without losing lives in consequence. Play was the neurological ludic map of an existential and propagandistic compromise between emotional liveliness and emotional danger. It was more than just rationality against irrationality, as it is sometimes couched (Spariosu, 1989), or of superego against the id as in yet another famous theoretical framework. Play became rather the metacommunicational paradox that Bateson (1972) maintains, between unreality and reality because it reflects this underlying paradoxical neurological ludic compromise of being emotional without risking the consequences of such emotion. In some ways, the circus and its animals and clowns are an excellent metaphor of the basic ludic map construction. The animals symbolize the possibility of great danger, the clowns symbolize the disruption of conventions, while the acrobats symbolize the disruption of physical safety. And yet it all takes place in the great circus tent where hopefully nothing really dangerous or disruptive will occur to any members of the audience, even if they sometimes feel as if it might. Play is presented here then as an endless evolutionarily instigated drama. It is termed here a recapitulation, but perhaps should rather be called a phylogenetic fixation, because it is such a constant map of the mammal reality, the emotional dilemma of which never really changes, even though there are constant changes in individual and cultural deployment.

A final note refers to our earlier attempt to speak of play as adaptive variability (Sutton-Smith, 1997, 1999, 2001), in the Gould sense of emergent variation, which is of a random character but as such is the major resource for evolutionary change. That the present eternal recapitulatory ludic fixation can also be a structural source of such emergent variation is implied by all the variant concepts referring to types of play, types of emotion, and types of play concepts in the lists above. If there is any truth to the proximal causal attributions implied by any of these many terms, then present play indeed functions not only as an echo of our everlasting control and expression of emotional "primitivity," but also as a source of variable other behavioral and mental possibilities that sometimes filter through these ludic screens into everyday life. Play's function is most centrally that of emotional joy and emotional peace, but its variant actions must inevitably provide some trickle-down of functional transfers—a kind of functioning we have spoken of elsewhere as an adaptive potentiation (Sutton-Smith, 1975).

REFERENCES

Bakhtin, M.M. (1984). *Rabelais and the world.* Bloomington: Indiana University Press.

Bateson, G. (1972). *Steps to an ecology of mind.* New York: Ballantine.

Blanchard, K. (1995). *The anthropology of sport.* Westport, CT: Bergin & Garvey.

Burghardt, G.M. (1984). On the origins of play. In P.K. Smith (Ed.), *Play in animals and humans* (pp. 5–42). London: Blackwell.

Burghardt, G.M. (1998). The evolutionary origins of play revisited: Lessons from turtles. In M. Bekoff & J.A. Byers (Eds.), *Animal Play: Evolutionary, comparative and ecological perspectives.* Cambridge, England: Cambridge University Press (pp. 1–26).

Damasio, A.R. (1994). *Descartes' error: Emotion, reason and the human brain.* New York: Putnam.

Edelman, G.M. (1992). *Bright air, brilliant fire.* New York: Basic Books.

Ehrenreich, B. (1997). *Blood rites: Origins and history of the war.* New York: Henry Holt.

Fagen, R. (1981). *Animal play behavior.* New York: Oxford University Press.

Gabler, N. (1998). *Life the movie: How entertainment conquered reality.* New York: Knopf.

Geertz, C. (1973). *The interpretation of culture.* New York: Basic Books.

Glassford, R.G. (1976). *Application of a theory of games to the transitional Eskimo culture.* New York: Arno Press.

Goldman, L.R. (1998). *Child's Play: Myth, mimesis and make believe.* London: Berg (Oxford).

Goleman, D. (1995). *Emotional intelligence.* New York: Bantam.

Gomme, A.B. (1894). *The traditional games of England, Scotland and Ireland.* London: Constable.

Gould, S.J. (1977). *Ontogeny and phylogeny.* Cambridge, Mass: Harvard University Press.

Gould, S.J. (1996a). Creating the creators. *Discover, 17*(10), 42–54.

Gould, S.J. (1996b). *Full house.* New York: Harmony Books.

Hall, S.J. (1999). The anatomy of fear. *The New York Times*, magazine, February 28, pp. 42–91.

Handelman, D. (1992). Passages for play: Paradox and process. *Play and Culture, 5*, 1–19.

Heim, M. (1993). The *metaphysics of virtual reality.* New York: Oxford University Press.

Huizinga, J. (1955). *Homo Ludens: A study of the play-element in culture.* Boston: Beacon Press. (Original work published 1938)

Keeley, L.H. (1996). *War before civilization: The myth of the peaceful savage.* New York: Oxford University Press.

Ledoux, J. (1992). *The emotional brain.* New York: Simon & Schuster.

Lee, D.J. (1994). *Life and story.* London: Praeger.

McMahon, F.R. (1999)."Playing with Play": Germany's carnival as aesthetic nonsense. In S. Reifel (Ed.), *Play & culture studies* (Vol. 2, pp. 177–190). Stamford, CT: Ablex.

Miller, S.N. (1974). The playful, the crazy, and the nature of pretense. *Rice University Studies*, 60(3), 31–51.

Myers, D. (1991). Computer game semiotics. *Play and Culture, 4*, 334–345.

Myers, D. (1992). Simulating the self. *Play and Culture, 5*, 420–440.

Myers, D. (1998). Playing against the self: Representation and evolution. In S. Reifel (Ed.), *Play & culture studies* (Vol. 1, pp. 31–48). Greenwich, CT: Ablex.

Myers, D. (in press-a). Is play random?

Myers, D. (in press-b). Play and paradox: How to build a semiotic machine.

Opie, I., & Opie, P. (1950). *The lore and language of school children.* New York: Oxford University Press.

Polikoff, M.B. (1987). *Combat sports in the ancient world.* New Haven, CT: Yale University Press.

Rinehart, R.E. (1998). *Players all.* Bloomington: Indiana University Press.

Ruse, M. (1996). *Monad to man: The concept of progress in evolutionary biology.* Cambridge, MA: Harvard University Press.

Singer, J.L. (1973). *The child's world of make-believe.* New York: Academic Press.

Spariosu, M. (1989). *Dionysus reborn.* Ithaca, NY: Cornell University Press.

Smith, P.K. (Ed.). (1984). *Play in animals and humans.* London: Blackwell.

Stewart, S. (1978). *Nonsense: Aspects of intertextuality in folklore and literature.* Baltimore: John Hopkins University Press.

Sutton-Smith, B. (1959). *Games of New Zealand children.* Berkeley: University of California Press.

Sutton-Smith, B. (1966). Role replication and reversal in play. *Merrill-Palmer Quarterly, 12*, 285–298.

Sutton-Smith, B. (1973). Games: The socialization of conflict. *Sportswissenschaft, 3*, 41–46.

Sutton-Smith, B. (1975). Play as adaptive potentiation. *Sportswissenschaft, 5*, 103–118.

Sutton-Smith, B. (1977). Games of order and disorder. *TASP Newsletter, 4*, 119–126.

Sutton-Smith, B. (1978a). *Die dialektic des spiels*. Schomdorf: Verlag Karl Hoffman.

Sutton-Smith, B. (1978b). The dialectics of play. In F. Landry & W.A.R. Orbam (Eds.), *Physical activity and human well-being*. Quebec: Symposia Specialists.

Sutton-Smith, B. (1981). *A history of children's play*. Philadelphia: University of Pennsylvania Press.

Sutton-Smith, B. (1994). Memory of games and some games of memory. In J. Lee (Ed.), *Life and story* (pp. 125–142). Westport, CT: Praeger.

Sutton-Smith, B. (1997). *The ambiguity of play*. Cambridge, MA: Harvard University Press.

Sutton-Smith, B. (1998). Reviews of Jon Krakauer, "Into Thin Air," & B. Coburn, "Everest: Mountain without Mercy." *TASP Newsletter, 22*(3), 7–10.

Sutton-Smith, B. (1999). Evolving a consilience of play definitions: Playfully. In S. Reifel (Ed.), *Play and Culture Studies* (Vol. 2, pp. 239–256). Stamford, CT: Ablex.

Sutton-Smith, B. (2001). Reframing the variability of players and play. In S. Reifel (Ed.), *Play & Culture Studies* (Vol. 3). Westport, CT: Ablex.

Sutton-Smith, B., & Kelly-Byrne, D. (1984). The idealization of play. In P. K. Smith (Ed.), *Play in animals and humans* (pp. 305–322). London: Blackwell.

Turner, V. (1969). *The ritual process*. New York: Aldine.

Wrangham, R., & Peterson, D. (1996). *Demonic males: Apes and the origins of human violence*. Boston: Houghton Mifflin.

Huizinga's Contributions to Play Studies: A Reappraisal

Thomas Henricks

Isaac Newton once dismissed his own gifts by saying that if he saw farther than others it was because he stood on the shoulders of giants. In the field of play studies, modern scholars stand on the shoulders of Johan Huizinga. Now more than 60 years old, Huizinga's *Homo Ludens: A Study of the Play-Element in Culture* (1938/1955) remains a beautifully fashioned, if controversial, description of the cultural possibilities of play. For Huizinga, play was not some isolated portion of public affairs but rather an activity undergirding all culture. Indeed, play may be seen as one of the great engines that produced the societies of the West.

In this context, Huizinga's great essay has attracted its share of influential admirers. Cultural historian Theodore Roszak (1972, p. 94), for example, argues that "the work compares in scope, originality and profundity to the seminal works of Marx and Freud, a superb effort to create a comprehensive theory of human behavior and social life." Literary critic and theorist Jacques Ehrmann (1968, p. 31) claims that *Homo Ludens* "inaugurates an anthropology of play expressing views of remarkable scope and insight." In his important summary of play theories, Joseph Levy (1978, p. 57) argues that the book's "impact on the study of play is witnessed in every piece of scholarly writing on this topic." And most recently, prominent play scholar Brian Sutton-Smith (1997, p. ix) acknowledges Huizinga as one of "the three truly great 20th-century play theorists" who have changed forever our understanding of this subject.

Huizinga, who died in 1945 in occupied Holland, would have been pleased by the continuing acclaim for an eccentric book that spanned (and thus did not fit neatly into) the academic disciplines of the time or even the body of his own historical work. However, he would surely be perplexed by the selective reception of the book's themes. *Homo Ludens* has left its mark on the modern literature of play, games, and sport primarily as a distinctive conceptualization of play. Anthologies in these fields (see, e.g., Dunning, 1972; Hart, 1972; Morgan & Meier, 1995) routinely include some passages from Huizinga's book as a paean to play's elusive and contrary qualities, in particular, to its mixing of the orderly and essential with that which is chaotic and fleeting and insubstantial. Beyond this, Huizinga's warnings about the decline of the play-spirit in modern civilization (a concern he shared with Freud) have been heard if not always heeded. However, it is striking that the thesis of *Homo Ludens*—that play has performed a significant role in human history as a culture-creating activity— largely has been rejected, forgotten, or ignored.

Amidst this selective veneration, Huizinga has found his share of critics. In perhaps the best-known extension of Huizinga's ideas, Caillois (1961) argues that Huizinga unaccountably emphasized the social contest ("agon") at the expense of other types of playful encounters, such as mimicry, chance, and vertigo. Furthermore, Huizinga failed to distinguish the spontaneous expressions of play from the more game-like forms (i.e., orderly, rule-bound play). Thus, the famous oppositions and complexities of Huizinga's definition are largely failures to separate these terms. A somewhat different tack has been taken by Gruneau (1983). In that author's view, Huizinga overestimates the freedom or voluntarism of play. Instead, "real" play is characterized by all kinds of custom and constraint and external incentive. Other researchers, especially those from social history and anthropology (see, e.g., Blanchard & Cheska, 1985; Cunningham, 1980; Henricks, 1991; Malcolmson, 1973), have documented these concerns as well.

More recent criticisms have focused on the rhetorical and ideological dimensions undergirding *Homo Ludens*. In Duncan's (1988) view, Huizinga's contentions and supporting evidence betray a worldview that is elitist and patriarchal. His celebrated notion of play, it seems, is largely a commentary on the socially competitive exploits of Western, leisure-class males. Reminiscent of the British amateur tradition in sport, Huizinga's ideas extol the virtues and accomplishments of those few people who have the resources to be free and "distinterested"; against these pure players stand the forces of professionalism and mass culture and ordinary existence. This opposition between some idealized level of cultural development and the activities of ordinary people (as well as those in "lower" societies) has also been criticized by both Ehrmann (1968) and Nagel (1998). Lugones (1987) has connected it specifically to imperialism.

As Sutton-Smith (1997, pp. 202–203) has explained, Huizinga's work reflects an idealized, romantic version of human conduct that rarely coincides with public, or even private, life. In this chapter, I not so much dispute this claim as try to show that Huizinga's approach, interpreted in a certain way, remains central to the ongoing study of play. More to the point, I argue that Huizinga's insights can be the basis of a far-reaching conceptualization that unites some of the disparate approaches in the field of play studies.

To accomplish this objective, it will be necessary to review some of the central themes of *Homo Ludens*. As a prelude to that process, I examine certain features of Huizinga's life and intellectual career. In so doing, I attempt to supplement the contemporary views of Huizinga as either an idealistic but misguided uncle or as a villain in aristocrat's garb with reminders of his brilliant contribution and his continued pertinence to modern scholarship.

HUIZINGA'S CAREER AS CONTEXT

Published in 1938, *Homo Ludens* was, as Colie (1964, pp. 613–614) explains, a "most remarkable book, remarkable both for what it did and what it did not do." Written by an eminent Dutch historian, the book was clearly not a work of history. Instead, it was a curious gathering of information from seemingly all times and places to support a thesis about the importance of the play element in the development of human societies. The book features abundant historical examples from the ancient, medieval, and modern worlds in Europe; but these are mixed intentionally with depictions of the Western Pacific's kula ring, the potlatch customs of America's northwest coast, dice playing in the Mahabharata, the public ceremonies of the ancient Chinese, and so forth. Equally impressive is the range of academic disciplines that enter the fray: philology, comparative linguistics, literature, music and art history, sociology, anthropology, and philosophy all occupy conspicuous roles. Moving as it does from topics in law and war to epistemology and poetry and mythopoeism to philosophy and art, *Homo Ludens* is a triumph of scholarship writ large. It is a book that moves the aesthetically inclined to rapture and the intellectually fastidious to despair.

Looking backward from a distance of 60 years, Huizinga's self-styled book is the culmination of a variety of concerns that characterized his life and intellectual career. Born in 1872 to a Mennonite family, Huizinga was truly a spirit from an earlier age. His father was a medical doctor who became a professor at the University of Groningen in Holland; and, with his brother a doctor as well, the family was a model of bourgeois respectability. Young Johan was, by his own account (Huizinga, 1968, pp. 251–253), a dreamer who enjoyed fairy stories and long, brooding walks through the countryside. As he put it (p. 253), such walks put him in a "kind of trance" that "allowed my mind to roam freely outside the confines of daily life in an ethereal state of bliss, akin to nature worship." It was a habit he maintained for a lifetime.

During his early adulthood, Huizinga was much influenced by the "Tachtigers" (literally, "men of the eighties")—a group of young Dutch literati and patrons of the arts. In addition to revolutionizing Dutch poetry and criticism, the group was instrumental in introducing modern painters (including Van Gogh) to a Dutch audience. By nature, Huizinga possessed a poetic sensibility; and his later uses of literary and art historical materials changed the shape of intellectual history.

This sensibility is perhaps expressed best in the work that is generally considered to be his greatest, *The Waning of the Middle Ages*. First published in 1919, the book presents an original thesis that life in the 14th and 15th centuries in France and the Low Countries was not an awakening of the Renaissance but rather a withering of medievalism. In this regard, his contribution challenged the thesis of his intellectual mentor and sometime rival, Jacob Burckhardt, who had seen a more abrupt transformation in Italy during this same period.

Many of the themes in *The Waning of the Middle Ages* foreshadow those of *Homo Ludens*. As Burckhardt had done, Huizinga sought to portray fully the cultural life of his period. Such matters included the conception of society itself, the idea of chivalry, the formalization of love, the understanding of death, and the types of religious expression. Therefore, in Huizinga's hands, cultural history became a description of the ideas, sentiments, and social forms that shaped public life. Furthermore, the general theme of the book—that is, cultural decline or decay—is prevalent in *Homo Ludens* as well. In each book, one gains a sense that there have been golden ages, but these have long since receded from view.

Like Burckhardt, Huizinga believed that culture had a kind of coherence; therefore, each age was characterized by a distinctive style or spirit. Although he (1968, pp. 158–218) was severely critical of the historian Spengler for indulging in grand generalizations, Huizinga himself was wont to characterize whole epochs with a few well-chosen words. This inclination, coupled with a beautiful writing style, produced arguments that are as intoxicating as they are intellectually compelling. As testament to this, consider his opening paragraph from *The Waning of the Middle Ages*:

To the world when it was half a thousand years younger, the outlines of all things seemed more clearly marked than to us. The contrast between suffering and joy, between adversity and happiness, appeared more striking. All experience had yet to the minds of men the directness and absoluteness of the pleasure and pain of child-life. Every event, every action was still embodied in expressive and solemn forms, which raised them to the dignity of a ritual. For it was not merely the great facts of birth, marriage, and death which, by the sacredness of the sacrament, were raised to the rank of mysteries; incidents of less importance, like a journey, a task, a visit, were equally attended by a thousand formalities: benedictions, ceremonies, formulae.

To read the description above is to enter simultaneously the worlds of the artist and the scholar. Huizinga's genius was his ability to set forth the opposing elements of an age (for example, in the Middle Ages between darkness and light, silence and din, cruelty and compassion) in a way that speaks to universal human experience. Like a talented artist, he not only displayed the movement and tension between these bright opposites but also the richer, subtler themes that could be found in the shadows. As Duncan (1988) has argued, this dwelling on oppositions (e.g., between play and ordinariness or play and overseriousness) is central to *Homo Ludens* as well.

Huizinga's general approach to history was articulated quite early in his career—indeed, in his inaugural lecture as Professor of History at Groningen University in 1905. In "The Aesthetic Element in Historical Thought," Huizinga (1968, pp. 219–243) argues that the rational and intuitive modes of interpretation must work together. Representation of the past is not merely reflection, but rather transformation or reconstruction through the use of simplifying images and concepts. The aesthetic sensibility thus abets the more rational one "by conjuring up living pictures" (p. 237) that address our needs for deeper, emotionally resonant knowledge.

As noted above, critics of Huizinga have charged that his historical portraits focus too much on intellectual and even spiritual matters and too little on the grimmer routines of politics and economics. In Huizinga's work, one will not find detailed accounts of political machination or military affairs. More damning in the modern judgment is his failure to describe the profound transformations in land, labor, and capital or the struggles of the masses to better their lives. Against the backdrop of these concerns, Huizinga seems too much the aesthete, "playing with beautiful forms and ideas" (Geyl, 1963, p. 232).

Was Huizinga indifferent or even hostile to the aspirations of ordinary people and to the concerns of everyday existence? Did he live a "charmed life," insulating himself from such matters? As Colie (1964) has argued, Huizinga was by temperament and background ill-suited for the crises and intellectual concerns of his own age. His upbringing as a Mennonite contributed to a profound otherworldliness; stoicism, pacifism, and the rejection of materialistic values were seen as virtues. By such standards, nonconformity or "standing apart" was an appropriate response to the hurly-burly of daily affairs. Throughout his life, such themes found expression in a love for the past—and for fantasy, ritual, and ancient language. These fascinations seem to have affected his social sympathies as well. In his autobiography, Huizinga (1968, p. 246) confesses to "a secret vice, a hankering for patrician origins and names and a certain scorn for my own, all too obviously plebeian descent from Baptist preachers and provincial farmers." Such inclinations meshed easily with a European university system that harbored reproving monk-like tendencies, intellectual austerity, and disdain for all things public.

Huizinga's accusers have claimed that his later public prominence—and the deepening crises in Europe during the 1930s—made such a pristine stance wrong. They claim also that he benefited from the very world he despised. In short, he became less the monk and more the abbot. It does seem true that Huizinga was fortunate in his academic appointments. After a stint of nine years as a high school teacher (a position that owed itself in part to his father's social connections), Huizinga was appointed chair of history at Groningen University.

Remarkable in this appointment were several factors. He was young (32 years old), he was relatively unknown, and he was a comparative philologist rather than a historian. Furthermore, he won the chair against the candidacy of the director of Holland's national archives. The sponsorship of a former professor was clearly key as it was 10 years later when he was appointed Professor of History at the University of Leiden. Ultimately, he became rector at Leiden, where his duties included tutoring history to the young Princess Juliana. In short, by the end of his career, Huizinga was less the nonconformist and more the symbol of official Dutch academic culture.

It should be pointed out that Huizinga was concerned with the character of modern society and that he turned his attentions near the end of his life to the great political events of his time. However, his responses, at least to modern minds, seem oddly shaped or even misdirected. Indeed, to read Huizinga's criticisms of contemporary life is to hear the voice of the Old World (contemplative, formal, traditional, duty-bound, spiritual, hierarchical, etc.) raging against the New.

Huizinga's views of modern life are perhaps most clearly stated in his influential *In the Shadow of Tomorrow*, published in 1936 and quickly translated into nine languages. In formulations reminiscent of Spengler's *Decline of the West*, Huizinga portrays the contemporary dangers to Western civilization as essentially a cultural crisis or, more specifically, a disconnection between morality and reason. By such lights, the "economic dislocation" of the 1930s is "only one aspect of a transformation process of much wider import" (Huizinga, 1936, p. 17). Similarly, the rise of fascism and Stalinism are merely manifestations of a larger issue, the "amoral autonomy of the State" (p. 152). For its part, science has advanced wonderfully but only with the effect that "the foundations of our thinking grow ever more precarious and unstable" (p. 60). And art "has come to the complete abandonment of the principles of observation and thought" (p. 196).

In each case, specific events and dangers are subsumed under general principles. In that sense, the crisis of the 1930s is fundamentally a crisis of moral thinking; the contending ideologies of the times are merely symptoms of the same disease. Despite his fears that Europeans "are living in a demented world" (p. 15) and that they may "be submerged by centuries of barbarism" (p. 16), Huizinga thought he saw a way out. The solution to these ailments was to recommit to the spirit of culture properly defined—that is, to a rebalancing of material and spiritual values, to a "metaphysical" idealism that transcends person and group, and to a considerate relationship with nature, including human nature.

Such moralizing may have soothed the general public, but Huizinga's academic critics (see Geyl, 1963) found these pronouncements to be too unspecified—both as an analysis of the coming catastrophe and as a sociopolitical response to it. Furthermore, Huizinga's failure to "take sides" or even to distinguish between evils was seen as morally irresponsible.

For our purposes, it is important to emphasize the extent of Huizinga's condemnation of the modern world. This theme pervades *Homo Ludens*, and it is also prominent in his writings on America (see Huizinga, 1972). Much like Alexis de Tocqueville 100 years before, Huizinga was drawn to the society that seemed to symbolize the coming changes. To Tocqueville's concerns about the dangers of mediocrity and public opinion, Huizinga's adds more contemporary themes about the mechanization of life and the advancement of social technique. In America people become slaves to the machine and the organization. They are nattered by the radio and cinema. Civilization is buried in an avalanche of crude, fleeting sensations.

These themes of course are not distinctive to Huizinga's thought alone. They are familiar elements in a broader traditionalist critique of society (from Plato on) that emphasizes the importance of social stability and trusts the sensibilities of educated elites. The good society features an ethic of service to self, community, and (more abstractly) culture. Indeed, culture occupies an honored position as a kind of living link between generations, a carefully crafted gift from those who have worked and loved and died. Primary custodianship for this gift is granted to the socially and intellectually prominent, those who have the training, the talent, and, significantly, the freedom for the task. Uniting as it does the cognitive, moral, and aesthetic elements of experience, culture emerges as a kind of art form. Like constellations in the sky, culture fixes the gaze of ordinary people and otherwise guides their journeys. In its loftiest formulations, it rescues them from earthly distraction.

However, Huizinga was too much the historian to believe in the possibility, or even the benefit, of social stasis. While much of his writing seems to be a study in contrasts—between a spiritually enriching past and a deteriorating present—he was, by his own declaration, an optimist (see Huizinga, 1936, Preface). In that sense, *Homo Ludens* articulates a theory of cultural change that addresses the concerns discussed above.

HUIZINGA'S CONCEPT OF PLAY

What Marx is to the study of work so Huizinga is to the study of play. For Marx (see Marx & Engels, 1972, pp. 56–67), work was the process by which people created the boundaries of their world. By the same token, work was a process of self-discovery, a realization of one's true nature through the rendering of material form. For such reasons, the right of people to control their own working conditions and outputs was crucial. Furthermore, the organization of work was perhaps the key factor in the character of societies; other forms and activities (i.e., religion, politics, art, etc.) were "epiphenomenal." Indeed, work was the crucible of history. For Huizinga, play occupies a similar station. Indeed, in the opening passages of his book (1938/1955, Foreword), he installs *homo ludens* ("man the player") as the equivalent of the two more established categories: *homo sapiens* ("man the knower") and *homo faber* ("man the maker"). While Huizinga was of course familiar with (and completely hostile to) Marxism, it would be wrong to interpret his book as a dialogue with the Marxists. However, his work is a kind of holding forth of the idealist tradition against materialism and its consequences. As Gruneau (1983, pp. 23–30) has pointed out, Huizinga's philosophical idealism stands at the center of his interpretation of play. As an intellectual position, idealism typically asserts the primacy of mind and consciousness, or even "spirit," in human affairs. Some varieties of idealist philosophy consider the human mind and the world we live in to be expressions of divine consciousness (which indeed may "play" with the world); others focus on the relative independence and creative possibilities of human consciousness itself. Although Huizinga was a religiously sensitive person, *Homo Ludens* does not rely upon transcendental or religious explanations. Instead, his book is essentially an argument about the importance of protected spaces where the autonomous, creative spirit can flourish.

It is perhaps surprising then that Huizinga sets himself against psychological as well as biological explanations of play (1938/1955, pp. 1–4). However, Huizinga's view of mind or consciousness typically discounts the role of emotions or sense data as a groundwork for thought. Indeed, his idealist sensibilities chafe not only at Freudianism (for its supposed attention to carnal desire) but also at the whole scientific enterprise (both for its preoccupation with the transitory, physical world and for its deterministic inclinations). While Huizinga is rightly famous for his emphasis upon the mirth, tension, and fun that figure centrally in the play experience (see, e.g., p. 2), these concepts are more an explanation of play's appeal than a rationale for its importance.

More than anything else, play is a celebration of the possibilities for human consciousness. As Huizinga puts it (1938/1955, p. 3), "Play only becomes possible, thinkable, and understandable when an influx of *mind* breaks down the absolute determinism of the cosmos." To that degree, Huizinga's book is a profession of faith in human ingenuity. However, this quality of mental creativity is quite different from that articulated by Max Weber as the great "rationalization" process sweeping Western civilization (see Loewith, 1970), for Huizinga, like Weber, distrusted isolated reason or sheer mental calculation. As he goes on to say (p. 3), "The very existence of play continually confirms the supra-logical nature of the human situation." Fundamentally, "play is irrational" (p. 4). Huizinga was too much the aesthete to let reason break away completely from human experience, as he was too much the moralist to allow science and technocracy to pursue their fateful course.

Comprehending Huizinga's contribution then depends on a recognition not only of his idealism but also of his formalism. Like the great German sociologist Simmel, with whose work he was familiar, Huizinga saw human experience essentially as an encounter with form (see Simmel, 1971). These forms are not some abstract, Platonic ideals to which human beings aspire in their inarticulate, groping way. Rather, Huizinga's forms (like Simmel's) are cultural and social creations—that is, patterns of conception and organization that frame human activity. It is through the enactment of these forms that people realize the common enterprise of their humanity. Significantly, Huizinga's concept of mental creation is not *mimesis* (i.e., imitation of some higher, more perfect reality) but *methexis* (i.e., the act of making real or bringing forth in a new way). In that context, Huizinga champions "imagination" in its older sense—as a conversion of reality into images (p. 4).

Although Huizinga's book is ultimately about the modification and even creation of form through play, he was too traditional not to respect the established, sophisticated forms handed down from the past. Without such moorings, society would drift aimlessly; crude, unregulated sensations would reign. However, Huizinga also stands within that rural, conservative tradition that despised the state-enforced order and business-dominated sensibility of the Industrial Age. The world of the "boiler suit" brought with it social gigantism, impersonality, and the separation of morality from power. Systematization and regimentation spread widely. Experience became mechanized.

Huizinga's work remains important because he made a profound response to the question of how order and disorder should be distributed in the good society. His solution was to institutionalize (and otherwise safeguard) protected occasions within which people could indulge their creative capabilities. Such events should not be marginalized or consigned to the category of "festive release" but rather woven tightly into the social fabric. Such an argument, it should be noted, is a 20th-century version of the romantic poet Schiller's view of play, expressed nearly 150 years before (see Schiller, 1795/1965). In his struggle to find a common ground between the extremes of reason and sensuous experience, Schiller postulated the importance of a "play drive," that is, a desire to create and then explore the formal possibilities of life without enduring consequence. By this process, idealism could be realized in material expression, and material reality could be idealized in symbolic form. The principal effect of such cultural exploration was to make societies more self-conscious about their ideas and procedures. By avoiding the real-life extremes of a shrill moral idealism and a sensuous barbarism, the good society could be created.

Although Huizinga shares Schiller's concerns about the dangers of unbounded sensuality and formlessness of all types, Huizinga's book does not emphasize Schiller's themes about the critical importance of art or beauty to social improvement. While Huizinga is receptive to these ideas, the treatment of play in *Homo Ludens* is broader and more focused on the agonistic (i.e., socially competitive) aspects of life. Furthermore, Huizinga is not concerned primarily with the romantic experience of the individual, that is, with the welling up and expression of personal creativity. Instead, his is a much more sociological interpretation of the origins and consequences of play forms.

What, then, is "play"? For Huizinga, play is a "special form of activity" (1938/ 1955, p. 4), "a well-defined quality of action which is different from ordinary life" (p. 4). Huizinga is emphatic that this special form of relationship be seen "as an absolutely primary category of life" (p. 3), that is, that it not be reducible to other forms or purposes. Hence, many of the early pages of *Homo Ludens* are devoted to a search for (and ultimate rejection of) categories that might be used to encompass, oppose, or even explain play. Through such arguments we learn that play is an activity that people share with animals but that this activity is not attributable to physiological patterning (such as drives, instincts, or reflexes). Instead, play is "minded" or "significant." There is always "something 'at play' which transcends the immediate needs of life and imparts meaning to the action" (p. 1). Put differently, play entails a special quality of awareness, a recognition of the contexts within which players (both animal and human) routinely operate.

Because he emphasizes the mental implications of play, Huizinga is keen to dismiss various biological or "functional" explanations then popular in psychology and animal studies. Rejected explanations of play include its purported status as a useful discharge of energy, as a satisfaction of the imitative instinct, as a need for relaxation, as a training of the young, as an exercise in restraint, as a desire to dominate, as an outlet for harmful impulses, as a wish fulfillment, and as a fiction designed to keep up feelings of personal worth. While he admits that such explanations may be pertinent to play, they are not distinctive of play alone. In fact, all scientific explanations, in his view, tend to neglect the "profoundly aesthetic quality" of play (1938/1955, p. 2). For Huizinga, play is an involvement like no other. The roar of the football crowd or the baby's crow of pleasure transcend biology. As he puts it, "in this intensity, this absorption, this power of maddening, lies the very essence, the primordial quality of play" (p. 2).

Does play have an opposite? Huizinga considers a range of possibilities. Of first importance is the relationship of play to "seriousness." Although "nonseriousness" is generally considered to be a trait of play, he argues that ultimately this distinction cannot hold, for play may be conducted with desperate intention. Furthermore, neither "laughter" nor the "comic" have any direct connection to play. As Huizinga explains, "Play lies outside the antithesis of wisdom and folly, and equally outside those of truth and falsehood, good and evil" (p. 6). With much difficulty, he also admits that play has no intrinsic connection to beauty (even though beauty commonly evokes sublime emotions).

Is play opposed to ritual? Although Huizinga struggles with this issue throughout the book, his general conclusion is that play and ritual are fused, at least in the rituals of traditional and archaic societies. Does play oppose work? Surprisingly, he does not consider this issue at length. However, he argues that play is "never imposed by physical necessity" (1938/1955, p. 8) and that it is "never a task" (p. 8). Nevertheless, he immediately undoes this distinction by stating: "Only when play is a recognized cultural function—a rite, a ceremony— is it bound up with notions of obligation and duty."

Duncan (1988) has argued that if there is any abiding opposition in *Homo Ludens* it is the contrast between play and "ordinary" or "real" life. Ordinary existence, as Huizinga sees it, is heavy with obligation, continuity, and material interest. In the modern world these elements become exaggerated by the spirit of utilitarianism and by the growing influence of science and technology. Duncan has identified a "cluster" of these modern traits as rationality, logic, causation, determinism, and materiality. Against this order stands a host of playful, child-like tendencies: simplicity, innocence, absorption, naturalness, intuition, mysticism, and proximity to the sacred. Seen in this way, Huizinga's play world develops ultimately as a bastion for the romantic, poetic sensibility in a bureaucratic age.

Because Huizinga himself despaired of the possibility of an exact definition of play, he created his famous list of the characteristics of play. These elements are as follows:

1. *Play is voluntary.* Play represents an escape from the world of obligation and even from "natural" process. And although children and animals feel impelled to play, they do so on their own terms and at times and places they control. Play can be deferred or suspended by the players; it is not (typically) a duty.

2. *Play is not ordinary or real life.* As noted previously, play is inhabited by feelings of specialness and difference. Players know their activity is "only pretend," but this does not trivialize their efforts. Indeed, during moments of complete absorption or even rapture, the "only" quality of their pretending disappears. Huizinga also connects this quality to the theme of "disinterestedness." By this, he means especially the absence of material consequence. In play, people's ambitions are restricted to the play world itself. Status in the external society is not at stake.

3. *Play is secluded or limited.* In play, people experience eventfulness. That is, they enter a relationship that is played out within its own limits of time and space. For such reasons, play is "ecstatic," that is, players step into a world set apart from ordinary life. With that separation comes a distinctive view of the world left behind.

4. *Play creates order, is order.* As a formalist himself, Huizinga understood that human experience is couched in form. The acceptance of form brings feelings of union and completion; the rebellion against form is associated with separation, tension, and spontaneity. Furthermore, the acceptance of some forms facilitates the bringing of others to consciousness for creative manipulation. Play, then, is a commentary on the alternating experiences of order and disorder. As he (1938/1955, p. 10) puts it, play is characterized by "tension, poise, balance, contrast, variation, solution, resolution." In this regard, a particular issue for Huizinga is the importance of rules. It is crucial that these be observed so that the specific issues of play may be brought into sharpest relief. Finally, commitment to rules signifies a broader commitment to the play world itself.

5. *Play tends to surround itself with secrecy.* A concluding characteristic is the proclivity of players to set themselves away from nonplayers and to adopt distinguishing forms of dress, language, and playing equipment. The theme of disguise is especially important, for masking facilitates both the departure from the old world and the creation of the altered identity that is necessary in the new one. As Huizinga (p. 13) explains, "The disguised or masked individual 'plays' another part, another being. He *is* another being."

At three points in the text, Huizinga (1938/1955) gathers these themes into a summarizing description of play. Because the summaries are different in intriguing ways, I will reproduce them here:

Summing up the formal characteristics of play we might call it a free activity standing quite consciously outside "ordinary" life as being "not serious," but at the same time absorbing the player intensely and utterly. It is an activity connected with no material interest, and no profit can be gained by it. It proceeds within its own proper boundaries of time and space according to fixed rules and in an orderly manner. It promotes the formation of social groupings which tend to surround themselves with secrecy and to stress their difference from the common world by disguise or other means. (p. 13)

. . . play is a voluntary activity or occupation executed within certain fixed limits of time and place, according to rules freely accepted but absolutely binding, having its aim in itself and accompanied by a feeling of tension, joy, and the consciousness that it is "different" from "ordinary life." (p. 28)

It is an activity which proceeds within certain limits of time and space, in a visible order, according to rules freely accepted, and outside the sphere of necessity or material utility. The play mood is one of rapture and enthusiasm, and is sacred or festive with the occasion. A feeling of exaltation and tension accompanies the action, mirth and relaxation follow. (p. 132)

Consistent with his developing argument about the changing role of play in society, Huizinga's summaries shift toward an emphasis on the more public or "visible" forms of play. In that sense, the focus on secrecy in the first definition gives way to the public quality of the festive occasion in the last. Furthermore, play changes slightly from being a "free activity" (set away from ordinary life) to a more rule-bound affair that people "freely accept." Finally, the summaries provide an increasing emphasis on the emotions involved in play, including a recognition of the differences between sacred and festive engagement.

As I have indicated above, it has become fashionable to criticize Huizinga's view of play as overly idealistic or even "metaphysical" (see Gruneau, 1983, p. 30). Real play, the critics tell us, is as tangled and consequence-ridden as the other portions of our lives. They remind us that play events do not survive in pristine isolation. The moments of real life always run over one another; the distinction between play and "routine" existence cannot hold. As I will indicate shortly, I think that such an approach is the wrong way to interpret Huizinga's work.

Furthermore, it should be pointed out that Huizinga himself was aware of the complexity of play and of its connections to other phenomena. Indeed, to carry the arguments in the substantive chapters of the book, Huizinga had to rely on examples from two "higher forms" (1938/1955, p. 13) of play; specifically, its manifestations as *a representation of something* and as *a contest for something*. Play in such guises is colored by worldly concerns and consequences; and it becomes even more compromised as culture "develops" to its current stage. Of course, the extent of Huizinga's understanding of these tensions is debatable. As Stone (1955) later explained, the public representation of something—that is, display—introduces elements that make it quite different from play more purely understood. Likewise, ludic contests, as Caillois (1961) pointed out, are different not only from more spontaneous activities but from other types of playful encounters as well.

Some of the difficulty in determining Huizinga's views on this issue (i.e., on the connection of play to other forms of activity) resides with his style of argument. On the one hand, he is keen to establish play as an "irreducible quality ... which is not, in our opinion, amenable to further analysis" (1938/1955, p. 6). On the other, he wishes to claim a virtual identity of play with other categories of activity that are commonly thought to be more important. Consider, for example, his comments on the relationship between ritual and play:

We would merely be playing with words were we to stretch the play-concept unduly. But all things considered, I do not think we are falling into that error when we characterize ritual as play. The ritual act has all the formal and essential characteristics of play which we enumerated above, particularly insofar as it transports the participants to another world. (p. 18)

However, a page later, this identity has been downgraded to a "substantial similarity" and, by another page, to a comparison that is merely "formally indistinguishable." This approach is replicated by his comparison of the concepts "play" and "contest":

... despite the fact that Greek is not alone in distinguishing between contest and play, I am fervently convinced of their underlying identity.... The *agon* in Greek life, or the contest anywhere else in the world, bears all the formal characteristics of play, and as to its function belongs almost wholly to the sphere of the festival, which is the play-sphere. It is quite impossible to separate the contest as a cultural function from the complex, "play-festival-rite." (p. 31)

With the wind firmly behind him, Huizinga can posit an identity between entire epochs and play. Thus, "the whole of life was play for the Greeks" (p. 30) and "... the whole mental attitude of the Renaissance was one of play" (p. 180).

It is easy to dismiss such claims, and thus the argument as a whole, as enthusiastic overstatement. However, some of these generalizations seem attributable to Huizinga's desire to persuade his readers of the importance of play, and the rest to his intellectual style of setting up and then (almost mystically) closing conceptual oppositions. Huizinga, in my view, was well aware of the unresolved differences between these terms. Indeed, he does not discard these oppositions (i.e., play-ritual, play-seriousness, play-contest, etc.) but rather continues to work with them throughout the book.

I do not claim that Huizinga's understanding of play is "correct" or "complete." After all, it is hardly the function of classic books to end thought. However, like other classics, *Homo Ludens* raises the standard for thought on its topic to a new level and furthermore defines a number of intellectual directions for future generations to follow. More successfully than anyone else, Huizinga brought play into view as a key element in the makeup of societies. Similarly, his attempt to connect play with such related concepts as festival, ritual, myth, contest, game, art, war, poetry, and soon, demand response from later thinkers.

Furthermore, it is my opinion that play scholars would profit more by viewing Huizinga's definition of play less as a statement about play's essence or conceptual purity and more as an "ideal type" in the Weberian sense. For Weber, definitions were devices or lenses to capture a changing world. His famous definition of bureaucracy is an example (see Weber, 1958, pp. 196–244). Basing his model on the German civil service of the early 20th century, Weber enumerated the characteristics of bureaucracy as explicit rules, a strict chain of command, offices controlled by the organization, selection of personnel by merit, clear possibilities for promotion and tenure, and impersonality in relationships. This model remains important, not because it mimics reality (one doubts the German civil service ever completely conformed) but because it gathers issues that are useful in the study of any formal organization. To be sure, real organizations feature informal personal networks, "good old boy" hiring systems, tenured time-servers, and evasions of written procedure. Such messy interventions of real life into theory do not vitiate Weber's definition but rather make social scientists think harder about the *relative* presence/absence of each element in an organization under study. To be specific, which elements exist and why is this so?

In that context, Huizinga calls us to think about the themes of voluntarism, opposition to ordinary life, seclusion, orderliness, and secrecy as these apply to the events he termed "play." In the face of so many criteria, the real world perhaps will provide few moments of pure, "essential" play. However, what will be gained is a sense of the relative "playfulness" of human conduct. And, as Huizinga shows, the resulting framework can be used to evaluate different societies and historical epochs as well.

PLAY AND CULTURE

In the foreword to *Homo Ludens*, Huizinga plainly states his thesis: "that civilization arises and unfolds in and as play." It is notable that this thesis was first developed as a series of lectures given in Zurich, Vienna, and London under the title, "The Play Element of Culture." Each time Huizinga's hosts tried to change the title to "The Play Element in Culture," he resisted. As he explains (Foreword):

. . . each time I protested and clung to the genitive, because it was not my object to define the place of play among all the other manifestations of culture, but rather to ascertain how far culture itself bears the character of play. The aim of the present full-length study is to try to integrate the concept of play into that of culture.

It is a touch of irony then that the translator of the American edition ignores his intentions and substitutes instead the "more euphonious ablative."

Although Huizinga's writing style is remarkable for its elegant circumlocutions and celebrations of paradox, some elements of his thesis are developed in a straightforward way. Play, in his view, is older and more fundamental than culture because animals do it. Furthermore, in Huizinga's view, animal play is formally indistinguishable from the play of humans (both children and adults). As he (1938/1955, p. 47) argues:

. . . all the basic factors of play, both individual and communal, are already present in animal life—to wit, contests, performances, exhibitions, challenges, preenings, struttings, and showings-off, pretenses and binding rules.

For example, animals invite one another to play "by a certain ceremoniousness of attitude and gesture" (p. 1). Animals recognize the limits that must be put on biting and roughhousing; they "pretend to get terribly angry" (p. 1); and they seem to enjoy it all. In short, although many people think of animals as non-rational or even "mechanical" creatures, their ability to suspend or reframe customary behavior patterns in play argues for their signifying capacities. This latter point is especially important for Huizinga, for he is determined to cast off physiological or instinctual explanations of play. For him, the act of playing suggests a new kind of awareness.

Of course, comparing animal "understanding" and behavior guidance to that of humans is a matter of continuing study and debate (see Fagen, 1981); and Huizinga has neither the expertise nor inclination to address the matter further. What is important for our purposes is his view of play (in both humans and animals) as a social creation, that is, as a making-up of action through the display of—and response to—mutually recognized intentions. For Huizinga, play is largely an exercise in social awareness, between the players themselves or even between the players and, as he describes some animal audiences, "an admiring public" (1938/1955, p. 1). In this light, it is interesting that *Homo Ludens* gives almost no attention to the various forms of individual play. As Huizinga sees it, "Solitary play is productive of culture only in a limited degree" (p. 47).

Huizinga's entire argument then is built on an understanding of the "social" as prior to and formative of the "cultural." As he puts it in the opening sentence of Chapter 1, ". . . culture, however, inadequately defined, always presupposes human society." By contrast, one could well imagine a theory of cultural development that emphasizes the explorations and inventions of talented and powerful "individuals." Their resulting contributions would then be disseminated to or implemented by a straining populace. However, this is not Huizinga's theory.

Instead, his theme is the enactment, modification, and even production of ideas in public settings.

Within the social sciences, perhaps the best-known scholar adopting a similar view of cultural origins is French sociologist Emile Durkheim. Like Huizinga, Durkheim was (in some respects) a conservative thinker who recognized the dangers (to both the individual and society) of unregulated personal appetite. Culture, especially in the sense of publicly acknowledged norms, was needed to safeguard social intercourse and to guide personal aspiration. These norms should not be forced upon people but rather developed and then administered in ways that benefit society as a whole.

Although Durkheim was much more concerned with ritual (as the public reaffirmation of social ideals) and Huizinga with play (as the creative rendering of these ideals), their paths cross with Durkheim's concept of "collective ferment" or "effervescence" (see Durkheim, 1972, pp. 228–229). In his discussion of the origins of idealism, Durkheim points to special historical moments and public occasions when people's relationships become closer and more intense. Motivated sometimes by a sense of public crisis, individuals become aware of their need for one another. They separate themselves from social routine and surrender to powerful social forces that are the energy of the group. In words that could have been written by Huizinga, Durkheim explains:

[These forces] necessarily overflow, for the sake of overflowing, as in play without any specific objective, at one time in the form of stupid destructive violence or, at another, of heroic folly. It is a sense of luxurious activity since it is extremely rich. For all these reasons this activity is qualitatively different from the everyday life of the individual, as is the superior to the inferior, the ideal to the real. (p. 228)

As he continues, "It is, in fact, at such moments of collective ferment that are born the great ideals upon which civilization rests."

While Durkheim tended to see such moments as very exceptional departures from routine social order, Huizinga saw them as both more commonplace and more central in the evolution of societies. As noted previously, the empirical chapters of *Homo Ludens* are attempts to document the institutionalization of play activities (and play attitudes) in the cultural life of historic and traditional societies. These chapters include (in order of presentation) law, war, knowing, poetry, mythopoeism, philosophy, and art. The reader who follows Huizinga on his excursions through these areas will surely be impressed by the scope of Huizinga's knowledge and by the comparative and synthesizing qualities of his mind. However, it is not unfair to say that Huizinga's parade of examples, drawn from seemingly all times and places, stand out more as jewels of illustration than as elements in a tightly reasoned description of the process of innovation. For such reasons, it falls to the reader to piece together the elements of Huizinga's account.

In that light, I would argue that Huizinga's explanation exists on two different levels. The first level concerns the general functions of play in (any) society. The second level concerns the changing position of play in the development of "civilization."

The General Functions of Play in Society

As we have seen, Huizinga's book is fundamentally a claim for the importance of play; and his early chapters are devoted to this topic. While admitting that play has consequences for the body and the psyche, he is determined that explanations from these quarters play almost no part in his analysis. Furthermore, his relative disinterest in economic and political matters prevents these issues from emerging as either causes or effects. What is left, then, is a more general focus on the sociocultural consequences of play; and his argument is cast primarily in sociological and anthropological terms. In keeping with that approach, I will attempt to place Huizinga's scattered comments on these matters into a division between social and cultural functions of play.

Before beginning this process, I should note that Huizinga would probably not approve. As stated previously, he was emphatic that play needs neither justification nor statement of purpose. Furthermore, to speak of "functions" typically is to suggest that an activity or event somehow contributes to the stability of broader organizational and cultural patterns. Huizinga's book, it will be remembered, is about the role of play in changing societies, not in stabilizing them. Nevertheless, *Homo Ludens* does offer a great range of comments about the effects of play on public life; thus, some cataloguing of social and cultural consequences seems pertinent.

Social Functions of Play

For Huizinga, play has consequences not only for the ideas/ideals guiding people's lives (i.e., culture) but also for their patterns of organization and interaction (i.e., society). In that latter sense, play both creates and articulates social order. A first social function of play then is the way in which it "promotes the formation of social groupings" (1938/1955, p. 13). Play takes people from various walks of life and places them together in special, often exotic predicaments. Players have a sense of being "apart together," a feeling that is perpetuated by such devices as disguise and secrecy. What might be a fleeting experience of shared identity is made permanent through the organization of play-focused clubs and associations. Play lubricates and expands the range of social interaction; trust and commitment are built. In short, play provides a basis for group identity and personal networking that can be turned to many purposes. The gentlemen's clubs of 18th-century England are an example of this process.

A second function of play is its role in dramatizing the major divisions of society and their relationship to one another. In this regard, Huizinga draws attention to the phratriai system of certain traditional societies (1938/1955, pp. 53–54), a division of the community into social halves existing in a relationship of both mutual antagonism and support. Likewise, he cites the universal social distinction between men and women (p. 54). Festive community events (which in his view are largely synonymous with play) make people act out publicly their commitments to these groups. However, it must be emphasized that the relationships between these groups may not be a simple rivalry. As he explains in another context (p. 47), sometimes play (in the form of dances, pageants, and performances) is not "antithetical" at all. Sometimes it is antithetical but not "agonistic" (as in part-songs, choruses, and minuets); and sometimes it is directly rivalrous or agonistic (as in sporting contests, duels, boasting contests, etc.). The implication of all this is that play seizes vibrant social identities and then allows the holders of these identities to spell out (potential) relationships they can have with one another.

Play also allows individuals and groups to negotiate social status in controlled ways. This is a third social function of play. Of all the many manifestations of play, *Homo Ludens* focuses mostly on the social contest, that is, on closely regulated competitions between people. Indeed, to read Huizinga's book is to imagine the development of human civilization largely as a history of public boasting matches, contests in conspicuous consumption, competitions for cosmogonic knowledge, fights for brides, judicial duels, desperate wagers, parliamentary debates, and so on. Of key importance in such a viewpoint is the fact that the outcomes of playful contests are unknown; although rule-bound, they are otherwise unscripted and tense. Winners and losers emerge through their own efforts. They create their own destiny.

Although Huizinga's initial treatment of play emphasizes the relative disconnection of play from external consequences, his later comments on the contest modify that view. As he (1938/1955, p. 50) puts it:

We play or compete "for" something. The object for which we play and compete is first and foremost victory, but victory is associated with all the various ways in which it can be enjoyed—for instance a triumph celebrated by the group with massed pomps, applause, and ovations. The fruits of victory may be honour, esteem, and prestige. As a rule, however, something more than honour is associated with winning. . . . Every game has its stake. It can be of material or symbolical value, but also ideal. The stake can be a gold cup or a jewel or the king's daughter or a shilling; the life of the player or the welfare of the whole tribe.

And as he comments further, the evidence of superiority on the playing field "tends to confer upon the winner a semblance of superiority in general" (p. 50). This honor or esteem falls not only to the victor but also to the group that he or she represents. Arguably, then, the contest achieves these effects in ways that are both more visible to the public at large and less societally damaging than the internecine struggles of the political and economic orders.

A fourth social function is play's capacity for integration; that is, play brings the community together in refreshing ways. Although Huizinga's central theme is the potential uses of controlled antagonism, he is clearly aware of the community-building implications of play. This theme is displayed most effectively in his discussions (pp. 62–63) of the kula ring, the elaborate circle of gift exchange among the islanders of the Western Pacific. Although this exchange of valued ceremonial objects brings individual honor to the groups who make these perilous ocean journeys, it much more importantly cements the tribes together in an atmosphere of mutual obligation and trust. In the same sense, contests more generally reflect the agreement of differing people (even deadly enemies) to operate together under a framework of shared rules.

Cultural Functions of Play

A related, but analytically distinct, issue is the way in which play transforms or even creates cultural ideas and artifacts. As before, Huizinga's examples of this process come from the two "higher forms" of play—that is, play as contest and play as representation. When combined, the two forms create public dramas of what the world may be. In that light, some of the cultural functions of play are indicated below.

A first function is play's role as both creator and repository of public memory. Play events are often exciting and exotic—and therefore memorable. As Huizinga (1938/1955, p. 14) explains:

But with the end of the play its effect is not lost; rather it continues to shed its radiance on the ordinary world outside, a wholesome influence working security, order, and prosperity for the whole community until the sacred play-season comes round again.

Play is "radiant" not just in the sense that spectacular performances are stored in public consciousness. Play is memory-invoking also in the sense that its very form creates a continual stream of heroes, villains, and fools. The community can compare one past event to another and looks forward to coming events that will be framed in a similar fashion. In that sense, play events commonly represent rhythmic intercessions in the way people think about their lives.

A second cultural function is play's uses in displaying persistent cultural oppositions. The players or teams who stand against one another on the playground are commonly representatives—not only of groups but of ideas, values, and even ways of life. Particularly in the case of debates or other intellectual contests, participants play out the strengths and limitations of their own positions. While Huizinga does not develop the nature of such ideological collisions as fully as he might, this idea is clearly central to his theory of cultural progress. As he (1938/1955, p. 156) explains:

All knowledge—and this naturally includes philosophy—is polemical by nature, and polemics cannot be divorced from agonistics. Epochs in which great treasures of the mind come to light are generally epochs of violent controversy.

In terms of a general conception of play, the special value of these confrontations is again their relative harmlessness. Combatants can play out the implications of ideas without immediately imposing their effects on society. Scholarly dispute is in this sense both playful and "academic."

A third, and final, cultural function is play's manner of reaffirming fundamental societal concerns. The fact that contests are typically "for" a prize or reward is important, not just because of the status gained by the winner but because the prize reaffirms what society holds to be of value. Huizinga develops this theme further (1938/1955, p. 51):

Competition is not only "for" something but also "in" and "with" something. People compete to be the first "in" strength or dexterity, in knowledge or riches, in splendour, liberality, noble descent, or in the number of their progeny. They compete "with" bodily strength or force of arms, with their reason or their fists, contending against one another with extravagant displays, big words, boasting, and finally with cunning and deceit.

In other words, play events typically display one set of socially desired goals and a related set of strategies more or less appropriate for attaining these. As he explains in another passage (p. 65), the nobleman of the European Renaissance "demonstrates his 'virtue' by feats of strength, skill, courage, wit, wisdom, wealth, or liberality." Failing these, he turns to self-promotion and contests of words. Critical here is the degree to which play allows people to negotiate their place through methods framed by the value system of society. For example, some societies permit trickery or even cheating as appropriate responses to difficulty; others hold to different conceptions of "sportsmanship." In a more complicated fashion, societies may permit trickery or cheating in festive events but not in routine affairs—or vice versa. In other words, play tends either to reaffirm basic societal values or to oppose them in (typically) sanctioned ways. In either case, players explore the tensions created by their society's value system (see Roberts & Sutton-Smith, 1962). Public contests are excursions in strength–weakness, masculinity–femininity, fairness–unfairness, and other societally established polarities.

In summary, Huizinga's account of the sociocultural implications of play keys upon his conception of the play sphere as a model of human possibility. Within the boundaries of the playground, people play out the implications of intriguing social identities and cultural commitments. They experience the vicissitudes of success and failure, glory and humiliation, in limited and protected ways. To the degree that play is a spectacle, it becomes a vehicle for public education as well as amusement. To the degree that play is a contest, it highlights the apparent strengths and weaknesses of people, positions, and ideologies. In that sense, play heightens self-consciousness about routine social order.

But how does play lead to new ideas spreading forth into routine affairs? In this regard, the theory must be found wanting. For Huizinga, the artist, it is enough to display the possibilities for existence. Dialogical confrontations may find their way into creative synthesis but the specific process by which this happens is not explained. Furthermore, there is no description of how new ideas supersede old ones or even defeat their contemporary rivals. Indeed, the actual processes of cultural change are typically carried forth by a set of politically and economically interested actors who not only sponsor the innovation but also work to see that it prevails. The various schemes and wrangling of these actors, the dirty work of history, is not addressed here.

Play in the Development of Civilization

As in his other major works, Huizinga contends in *Homo Ludens* that recent history is profoundly different from what has gone before. In particular, play activities have lost their central position as elements in personal experience and as building blocks of society. After completing the empirical demonstrations of his middle chapters, Huizinga (1938/1955) recaps his view of play's role in earlier times as follows:

It has not been difficult to show that a certain play-factor was extremely active all through the cultural process and that it produces many of the fundamental forms of social life. The spirit of playful competition is, as a social impulse, older than culture itself and pervades all cultural life like a veritable ferment. Ritual grew up in sacred play; poetry was born in play and nourished on play; music and dancing were pure play. Wisdom and philosophy found expression in words and forms derived from religious contests. The rules of warfare, the conventions of noble living were built up on play-patterns. We have to conclude, therefore, that civilization is, in its earliest stages played. It does not come *from play* like a babe detaching itself from the womb; it arises *in* and *as* play, and never leaves it. (p. 173)

For Huizinga, this affinity between play and culture is clearly expressed in archaic, especially Greek, civilization and is still found throughout the world in traditional societies. Furthermore, the play sphere continues to be important in Europe through the 18th century. For example, "Medieval life was brimful of play, the joyous and unbuttoned play of the people" (p. 179). Following that, "the whole mental attitude of the Renaissance was one of play" (p. 180). In Huizinga's treatment of the 17th century, a period of sharp religious conflict, he reminds his readers instead of the fanciful extravagance of the Baroque. All this exuberance only prepares the way for the great and culminating century of play, the 18th century. As he (p. 189) puts it, "If ever a style and a Zeitgeist were born in play it was in the middle of the eighteenth century."

The great watershed in the history of play is the 19th century. With industrial society comes the anonymity of city life and the fearful efficiencies of capitalism, scientism, and bureaucracy. Culture becomes a rigid form administered from above. Life is no longer played—or rather play is consigned to a quite altered and marginalized existence. Such conditions have only worsened in the contemporary era.

No serious book, not even a great one, sounds convincing in summary form. Huizinga's accomplishment in *Homo Ludens* is great not because of the adequacy of his theory as a whole but because of the compelling insights he provides regarding earlier societies and our own. These trails of thought become the pathways for modern scholarship.

Huizinga's view of the initial connection between play and culture has been described in the previous pages. Play has primacy (over later creative expressions) because the animal precedes the human; the social, the cultural; the nonrational, the rational; and the child, the adult. What all this signifies is the importance of action—and especially social interaction isolated from its normal consequences—as a springboard to thought. Before poetry, there is the dance.

Huizinga is particularly interested then in the use of play to create and sustain vibrant images of the world. These images are not reproductions of ordinary life as much as envisionments of what ordinary life might be. By inhabiting these newly created shadow worlds, players experience the consequences (in modest, largely harmless ways) of different cultural schemes. In that sense, play provides a touchstone for the possibilities (and dangers) of conception. Furthermore, the enactment of these living images keeps the moral, aesthetic, and cognitive dimensions of life in a kind of creative balance with one another.

Huizinga argues then that earlier societies gave wider scope to such public enactments and imaginings. Indeed, the "play-festival-rite complex," as he calls it, provided a certain rhythm to the year. More importantly, the willingness of premodern societies to merge two apparently contrary forms and attitudes (i.e., ritual and play, sacredness and frivolity) gives their world a vibrancy that ours has lost. As he (1938/1955, p. 25) explains:

Primitive, or let us say, archaic ritual, is thus sacred play, indispensable for the well-being of the community, fecund of cosmic insight and social development but always play in the sense Plato gave to it—an action accomplishing itself outside and above the necessities and seriousness of everyday life.

In this sense, festivals in ancient times were vehicles to the sacred. People were not simply listeners or observers of profound cultural matters; they were participants who called the sacred out of hiding. Again, to quote Huizinga (1938/1955, p. 14):

The sacred performance is more than an actualization in appearance only, a sham reality; it is also more than a symbolical actualization—it is a mystical one. In it something invisible and inactual takes beautiful, actual, holy form. The participants in the rite are convinced the action actualizes and effects a definite beatification, brings about an order of things higher than that in which they customarily live. All the same this "actualization by representation" still retains the formal characteristics of play in every respect.

Together, the festive participants of traditional societies "make a world" that is, in many ways, superior to ordinary life. Far from being a frivolous excursion, that world augments and informs the return of people to their daily affairs.

With this beginning, one might expect Huizinga to organize his book around the various uses of play in the different types of human societies. Instead, he attempts to show how play has been central to the early development of a number of significant cultural forms (i.e., law, war, poetry, art, etc.). Furthermore, he recasts his analysis as a treatment of the agon, or social contest; in so doing he shifts the subject of his book away from a more general consideration of play.

Huizinga's intellectual model, Jacob Burckhardt, had defined the agonal and demonstrated its importance to Greek civilization. However, Burckhardt had argued that this approach to life was distinctive to the Greeks. By contrast, Huizinga was determined to show that the agonistic spirit was a key part of many other early societies as well. As he (1938/1955, p. 101) explains:

In the beginning of civilization rivalry for the first rank was undoubtedly a formative and ennobling factor. Together with a genuine naivete of mind and a lively sense of honour it produces that proud personal courage so essential to a young culture. And not only this: cultural forms will themselves develop in these ever-recurrent sacred contests, in them the structure of society will unfold.

Ritualized contests among equals thus represented a process for distributing social status and displaying ideals in early societies; only later did these societies settle into more centralized and regimented patterns of cultural expression. And as Huizinga's critics have noted, his special interest seems to have been in the use of the contest to develop and stabilize a social elite composed of warriors and noblemen.

This view of play as ritualized contest is best expressed in his chapters on law, war, knowing, and philosophy. With regard to law, Huizinga emphasizes how the court of law remains similar to the tennis court; both are consecrated spots cut off from the ordinary world by costume, rules, and terminology. Both are dominated by an intense desire of each party to gain its cause. As he summarizes:

The judicial contest is always subject to a system of restrictive rules, which quite apart from the limitations of time and place, set the lawsuit firmly and squarely in the domain of orderly, antithetical play. The active association of law and play, particularly in archaic culture, can be seen from three points of view. The lawsuit can be regarded as a game of chance, a contest, or a verbal battle. (1938/1955, p. 78)

Huizinga's general point regarding early legal proceedings is that these forms were dominated not by some overarching, abstract conception of justice but rather by a spirit of partisanship broadly considered. Greek legal disputes, like

Eskimo drumming matches (p. 85), were full of spirited accusations, satire, and slander. Participants not only courted the community but courted the divine. More to the point, participants did not meekly await official or divine judgment; they fought hard for their victories in noisy public settings surrounded by gossip and gambling. For all their changes, modern legal proceedings still retain elements of the public boasting matches that are their basis.

The development of warfare receives similar treatment, though here Huizinga is more intent on exposing the ritualized aspects of the activity rather than its partisanship. In that light, he first establishes that war can only be considered agonistic to the extent that the combatants mutually recognize certain rules of engagement and furthermore regard each other as worthy equals. By such criteria, ambushes, raids, and wholesale extermination are eliminated from the discussion.

As in Huizinga's previous chapter on play and law, the discussion quickly turns to the symbolic (rather than material) consequences of contests in archaic societies. As he (1938/1955, p. 91) puts it:

One wages war in order to obtain a decision of holy validity. The test of the will of the gods is victory or defeat. So that instead of trying out your strength in a contest, or throwing dice, or consulting the oracle, or disputing by fierce words—all of which may equally well serve to elicit the divine decision—you can resort to war.

However, one must observe the agreed-upon formalities to win the favor of either the gods or the wider community of warriors.

Such matters apply as well to the judicial combat or to the single combat (which early societies saw as a worthy substitute for wider war). As Huizinga explains, the purpose of the single combat was not to spare bloodshed by the armies but rather to distill the contest into a more perfect expression of the confrontation with chance, fate, and divine judgment. Such an interpretation is pertinent to the private duel as well. In his words:

Being essentially a play-form, the duel is symbolical; it is the shedding of blood and not the killing that matters. . . . The spot where the duel is fought bears all the marks of a play-ground; the weapons have to be exactly alike as in certain games; there is signal for the start and the finish, and the number of shots is prescribed. When blood flows, honour is vindicated and restored. (1938/1955, p. 95)

What all this signifies is the development of a system of mutual respect among privileged equals. From this formalization of "noble strife" rises ultimately the cult of chivalry and later international law itself (p. 96). Such formalities exist still (though in a markedly reduced way) in the exchanges of prisoners and other civilities between modern enemies.

It is only a short step from physical confrontation to the war of words. As in his chapter on warfare, Huizinga's subsequent treatments of knowing, poetry, and philosophy emphasize the themes of public competition and supplication to the divine. In archaic societies, knowledge represented a kind of magical power, an ability to connect the particular, mundane world with the sacred world that stands above it. As he (1938/1955, p. 105) continues:

> For this reason, there must be competitions in such knowledge at the sacred feasts, because the spoken word has a direct influence on the world order. Competitions in esoteric knowledge are deeply rooted in ritual and form an essential part of it. The questions which the hierophants put to one another in turn or by way of challenges are riddles in the fullest sense of the word, exactly resembling the riddles in a parlour-game but for their sacred import.

Huizinga's focus then is the public exhibitions and competitions of poet-priests who attempted to defy others with cosmogonic riddle-questions. To solve the riddles, one had to have a knowledge of both the riddling ritual itself and an elaborate set of symbols that excluded all but sages from participation. Sheer logic could not master the riddles, for many were enigmas that defied logic; instead, success came (or appeared to come) as a result of sudden inspiration.

These feats of religious mystification, in Huizinga's view, stand behind the development of both poetry and philosophy. For poetry in archaic societies was not yet restricted to aesthetic contemplation. Instead, as he (1938/1955, p. 120) argues:

> All antique poetry is at one and the same time ritual, entertainment, artistry, riddle-making, doctrine, persuasion, sorcery, soothsaying, prophecy, and competition.

More generally, then, poetry was part of the play-festival-rite complex described in earlier pages. Poets were often conjurers who played on the ambiguous and contradictory meanings of life in ways that amazed or even stupefied their audiences. However, they too were limited by a system of play rules that fixed the range of ideas and the symbols to be used.

The movement from such forms of knowledge-making to what we think of as philosophy was slow and incomplete. Indeed, mythic thinking—as the creation of image-laden, even personified stories of the origin and operation of the world—remains important today. Although myth provided a kind of canopy for human affairs, it also opposed everyday life through its depictions of extraordinary characters and events. Furthermore, myth was commonly supralogical; ordinary, conscious thinking could not enter this superior domain or break its spell. Thus, the archaic poet was sometimes "the possessed, the God-smitten, the raving one" (1938/1955, p. 120).

Philosophy, in the sense of more strictly rational or logical contemplation, is a famous contribution of the Greeks. However, before philosophy became wedded to writing, it was still a matter of oratorical display and public bombast. In this regard, Huizinga's discussion focuses on the sophists, those "professional windbags" who went about the countryside challenging all comers to displays of intellectual skill. This oral tradition continued with the dialogues of Socrates and Plato, though by that latter thinker the arguments had taken a more polished, literary turn. Ultimately, then, the history of philosophy becomes a search for increasingly logical, abstract, universally applicable conceptions of the world. What started out as public bantering and raving ends as a surrender to formal rationality.

Finally, Huizinga turns his attention to the connection between play and art. Again, he sees the origin of this form in the play-festival-rite complex of archaic times. Within the chapter itself, his special interest is the development of music, which was formerly linked in a kind of "indissoluble union" with poetry. As he (1938/1955, p. 158) continues:

All true ritual is sung, danced, and played. We moderns have lost the sense for ritual and sacred play. But nothing helps us to regain that sense so much as musical sensibility. In music we feel ritual.

For Huizinga, music remains the key example of artistic play because it is performed (and therefore continually alive), because it is nonlogical in its appeal, and because it immerses people in the rhythmical and tension-confronting themes so pertinent to play.

Many of these elements are shared by "music's twin sister," dance. However, dance, because it is connected to material form (i.e., to the human body), is more compromised in its playfulness. Even less playful are the "plastic arts" (e.g., sculpture and painting). Again, to use Huizinga's (p. 166) words:

The case is quite different with the plastic arts. The very fact of their being bound to matter and to the limitations of form inherent in it, is enough to forbid them absolutely free play and deny them that flight into ethereal spaces open to music and poetry. In this respect dancing is in an anomalous position. It is musical and plastic at once: musical since rhythm and movement are its chief elements, plastic because inevitably bound to matter.

Sculpture and other types of visual art are thus trapped in their own form. Although the process of their creation may be playful, the completed works themselves sit there "dumb and immobile"; there is no "public *action* within which the work of plastic art comes to life" (p. 166).

Although Huizinga feels that the play spirit lives on in modern music and poetry, he mourns the more general withdrawal of art from the public festival. Indeed, he even sees dancing in pairs as a symptom of cultural decline. Much superior, in his view, is the "atmosphere of common rejoicing" where art joins religion in pursuit of the sublime.

With such an auspicious beginning, why has play declined in our modern age? In Huizinga's view, the play spirit was destroyed largely by the great forces of the 19th century: materialist philosophy, individualism, science and technology, and even public education. Previously play had figured prominently in that long-standing world of village communities, ruled at some level by aristocratic elites. As working people recreated at their seasonal festivals, so aristocrats recreated as part of a finely wrought lifestyle. Huizinga, it seems clear, was drawn to an older, even Greek view, in which the ideal life involved freedom from menial duties. In recognition of that freedom and in deference to a sacred realm that overwhelmed mundane existence, life was to be held lightly—to be played. However, the idleness of the privileged few was not merely escape; it was also (at its best) a basis for public responsibility and personal refinement. In Huizinga's view, then, the behavior of elites in their play-circles was more than simple diversion; it was an articulation and coordination of significant cultural standards.

The 19th century, on the other hand, was awash with middle-class morality and "portentous seriousness." As Huizinga (1938/1955, p. 192) declares:

... the great currents of its thought, however looked at, were all inimical to the play-factor in social life. Neither liberalism nor socialism offered it any nourishment. Experimental and analytical science, philosophy, reformism, Church and State, economics were all pursued in deadly earnest in the 19th century.

Even art and literature, once pursued with a "fine careless rapture," enter a long period of sobriety. Work rather than leisure becomes the idol of the age. The "shameful misconception of Marxism"—that economic forces direct the course of history—becomes common currency. Dull, unimaginative dress replaces the fanciful costumes of earlier days.

Others may point out that celebration, festivity, and high spirits are still prominent features of the modern age. However, Huizinga argues that what we experience is different than the play of earlier times. For example, some aspects of our celebrations, such as the Santa Claus customs, are now "ready-mades" (1938/1955, p. 24). That is, they are handed down to a mass public as firmly established, commercial concoctions. In that sense, the difference between archaic and modern play parallels that between myth and mythology. Myth is an evocative, mysterious form that draws life from its adherents; mythology is instead a fetish of literalism, a set of stories that merely accentuates our distance from the sacred and the past.

Huizinga is critical of modern festivity in other ways as well. The use of massive spectacle and pageantry by the emerging powers in Europe is a particularly malignant form of the play impulse. Festivals on those occasions are "false play," that is, play turned to the social and political purposes of the state (1938/1955, p. 205). Play, in his view, is an expressive rather than instrumental activity; it must not be used to cover up (or make palatable) the ambitions of the powerful. In that context, Huizinga also objects to the "insatiable thirst for trivial recreation and crude sensationalism" (p. 205) and the desire to extend the principles of club life to entire nations. This "rah-rah" spirit he terms "puerilism," a combination of the adolescent and the barbaric. He (p. 205) continues:

Of these habits that of gregariousness is perhaps the strongest and most alarming. It results in puerilism of the lowest order: yells or other signs of greeting, the wearing of badges and sundry items of political haberdashery, walking in marching order or at a special pace and the whole rigmarole of collective voodoo and mumbo-jumbo.

A transformation of perhaps even more importance has been the isolation and development of play activities under the terms of formal organizations. The development of modern sport is an instructive example of this change. Modern sports have been given over to systematization and regimentation. Sporting clubs have evolved into organized leagues; rules have proliferated; records have become an obsession; professionalism abounds. However, such increased seriousness belies the fact that sports are culturally "sterile." Cut loose from the festivals that were once their base, sporting events have become a reality *sui generis* (i.e., of its own type).

This sporting model has also been taken over by modern business, politics, and art. In each case, the competitive theme is highly pronounced. However, like sport, they become developed as isolated institutional forms following their own creeds and directions. So guided, they drift off on their own course, away from the broader moral commitments that must frame our lives. Indeed, Huizinga brings his essay to a close by reminding his readers of the limitations of play itself. Play lies outside the realm of ethics; it is a setting but not a set of moral directions. As he (1938/1955, p. 213) concludes:

In itself it is neither good nor bad. But if we have to decide whether an action to which our will impels us is a serious duty or is licit as play, our moral conscience will at once provide the touchstone. As soon as truth and justice, compassion and forgiveness have part in our resolve to act, our anxious question loses all meaning. One drop of pity is enough to lift our doing beyond intellectual distinctions. Springing as it does from a belief in justice and divine grace, conscience, which is moral awareness, will always whelm the question that eludes and deludes us to the end, in a lasting silence.

People more firmly planted in the Industrial Age will likely disagree with Huizinga's diagnosis and response to our contemporary ills. Conscience alone cannot save us—if indeed we need saving at all. Nor can we hold the world lightly and playfully as Plato did. For such reasons, Huizinga's true contribution to modern thought lies more in the questions he asks than in the answers he provides. In this regard, no question remains more fundamental (and largely unresolved) than the very nature of play, including its differences from other categories of human activity. Huizinga's work continues to challenge play scholars to establish the relationship of that elusive phenomenon to ritual, work, love, and festive communion. Is play essentially a dance with freedom or is it partnered equally by obligation? Does it live only in the moment or does it stretch across our lives? When is play truly itself and when does it drift, almost imperceptibly, into something else?

Even within the terms of Huizinga's own solution to this question, issues arise. As noted above, to comprehend Huizinga's model as an ideal type is to ask questions about such matters as voluntarism, disconnection from ordinary life, seclusion, orderliness, and secrecy. Under what conditions do these themes become manifest? To what extent are they willful, almost spontaneous creations of individual players, and when are they institutionalized by established groups and individuals? Truly, play is a distinctive and socially intricate construction of reality, but who creates it and why?

Finally, Huizinga's claims for the social and cultural importance of play beget continuing questions for social and historical analyses. Do play events have more or less universal consequences for society or do these functions vary cross-culturally? Within the historical development of any one society, do distinctive functions become more or less prominent? For his part, Huizinga struggled to understand why play seems to have lost its spark from earlier ages. Regardless of one's feelings about Huizinga's analysis, understanding the transformation of public expression—that is, how people proclaim the possibilities for their lives together—remains one of the great challenges for modern scholarship. We in the West celebrate private consciousness and the experience of the playful individual. However, Huizinga's work reminds us of the other side of play as well, that is, its connections to the social and cultural forms that sustain us. It is this more panoramic view that we gain from the heights of Huizinga's shoulders.

REFERENCES

Blanchard, K., & Cheska, A. (1985). *The anthropology of sport.* Boston: Bergin and Garvey.

Caillois, R. (1961). *Man, play, and games.* New York: Free Press.

Colie, R. (1964). Johan Huizinga and the task of cultural history. *American Historical Review, 69*(3), 607–630.

Cunningham, H. (1980). *Leisure in the industrial revolution 1780–1880.* New York: St. Martin's Press.

Duncan, M. (1988). Play discourse and the rhetorical turn: A semiological analysis of *Homo Ludens. Play and Culture, 1,* 28–42.

Dunning, E. (Ed). (1972). *Sport: Readings from a sociological perspective.* Toronto: University of Toronto Press.

Durkheim, E. (1972). *Selected writings* (A. Giddens, Ed.). Cambridge: Cambridge University Press.

Ehrmann, J. (1968). *Homo Ludens* revisited. *Yale French Studies, 41,* 31–57.

Fagen, R. (1981). *Animal play behavior.* New York: Oxford University Press.

Figler, S., & Whitaker, G. (1991). *Sport and play in American life.* Dubuque, IA: William C. Brown.

Geyl, P. (1963). Huizinga as accuser of his age. *History and Theory, 2,* 231–262.

Gruneau, R. (1983). *Class, sports, and social development*. Amherst: University of Massachusetts Press.

Hart, M. (Ed.). (1972). *Sport in the socio-cultural process*. Dubuque, IA: William C. Brown.

Henricks, T. (1991). *Disputed pleasures: Sport and society in preindustrial England*. Westport, CT: Greenwood Press.

Huizinga, J. (1936). *In the shadow of tomorrow*. New York: Norton.

Huizinga, J. (1954). *The waning of the middle ages*. Garden City, NY: Doubleday Anchor. (Original work published 1919)

Huizinga, J. (1955). *Homo Ludens: A study of the play-element in culture*. Boston: Beacon Press. (Original work published 1938)

Huizinga, J. (1968). *Dutch civilization in the seventeenth centuries and other essays*. New York: Frederick Ungar.

Huizinga, J. (1972). *America: A Dutch historian's vision, from afar and near* (H. H. Rowen, Trans.). New York: Harper Torchbooks.

Levy, J. (1978). *Play behavior*. New York: Wiley.

Loewith, K. (1970). Weber's interpretation of the bourgeois-capitalistic world in terms of the guiding principle of rationalization. In D. Wrong (Ed.), *Max Weber* (pp. 101–122). Englewood Cliffs, NJ: Prentice-Hall.

Lugones, M. (1987). Playfulness, world-traveling, and loving perception. *Hypatia, 2* (2), 3–19.

Malcolmson, R. (1973). *Popular recreations in english society: 1700–1850*. Cambridge: Cambridge University.

Marx, K., & Engels, F. (1972). *The Marx-Engels reader* (R. C. Tucker, Ed.). New York: Norton.

Morgan, W., & Meier, K. (Eds.) (1995). *Philosophic inquiry in sport* (2nd ed.). Champaign, IL: Human Kinetics.

Nagel, M. (1998). Play in culture and the jargon of primordiality: A critique of *Homo Ludens. Play and Culture Studies, 1*, 19–30.

Roberts, J., & Sutton-Smith, B. (1962). Child training and game involvement. *Ethnology, 1*(2), 166–185.

Roszak, T. (1972). Forbidden games. In M. Hart (Ed.), *Sport in the socio-cultural process*. Dubuque, IA: William C. Brown.

Schiller, J. (1965). *On the aesthetic education of man*. New York: Frederick Unger. (Original work published 1795)

Simmel, G. (1971). *On individuality and social forms* (D. Levine, Ed.). Chicago: University of Chicago Press.

Stone, G. (1955). American sports—Play and display. *Chicago Review, 9*, 83–100.

Sutton-Smith, B. (1997). *The ambiguity of play*. Cambridge, MA: Harvard University Press.

Weber, M. (1958). *From Max Weber: Essays in sociology* (H. H. Gerth & C. Wright Mills, Ed. & Trans.). New York: Oxford University Press.

3

Cultural Constraints on Children's Play

David F. Lancy

For at least 40 years the literature on children's play has been colored by the view that play is "good for children." Indeed, there are organizations that specifically promote the notion that play is a universal "right" of children.[1] Societies that limit children's play are to be sanctioned. My position in this chapter is different. From the point of view of inclusive fitness, children should probably *not* be allowed to play at all (Fagen, 1977). Children engaged in vigorous play will attract the attention of predators and, being distracted, are less vigilant and aware of potential threats. Lion cubs, for example, remain quiescent in tall grass while their mother is hunting and become active and playful only when she is there to protect them. Playing, children use precious energy (Rubin, Flowers, & Gross, 1986) and increase their risk of accident and injury (Fagen, 1993). Energetic games of tag, rough-and-tumble play, and mock battles all threaten people and property. Equally dysfunctional, playing children are not contributing to subsistence; in effect they are parasites. So rather than considering strategies to increase, channel, or promote children's play, let us instead consider the many constraints that exist to curb it.

Bogin (1998) persuasively argues that childhood is a stage in mammalian development unique to humans. As compared to the other apes, humans have much higher fertility, which Bogin attributes to the crèche-like character of childhood. Its purpose is to provide a kind of holding pattern in which the child can be weaned, freeing the mother to bear another child, though the child is still somewhat dependent on others. Human children require relatively little care and feeding—as contrasted with the young of, say, chimps. However, children are quite vulnerable and parents are in danger of losing their investment. The ethnographic literature is replete with parents (e.g., Japanese [Hendry, 1986]) using scare tactics to curb children's behavior.

The Kpelle, in common with numerous other societies, expect that children younger than eight will play "on the mother ground," that is, they will play in open areas in the village or on the rice farm adjacent to areas where adults congregate as they work or take their ease in gossip. Playing on the mother ground affords adults the opportunity to supervise children with minimal effort (Lancy, 1996). Parents intervene rarely but will curtail children's play when: the child hasn't completed a chore; the child's play threatens to injure a younger sibling and children's play is so active and exuberant that it threatens injury to persons or to property. Parents must balance their concern for the child's welfare with the desire to be rid of child-care duties. Promoting children's autonomy begins to look like "neglect" in some cases (Hewlett, 1991) although, in a careful review of the ethnographic literature on childhood, I found only one case—the Marquesas Islands—where adults seem downright blasé about the potential for self-injury in play (e.g., Martini, 1994). Aside from the potential for crippling or fatal injury, parents have other reasons to curb play.

I know of no society where children do not play at all, but there is wide variation in time budgeted for play. Hadza children exhibit typical patterns of play—make-believe, singing, dancing, and games. But this Tanzanian hunting and gathering society also expects children as young as age 3 to begin foraging independent of their mothers. By age 5, they gather about half their own caloric needs (especially baobab and tamarind fruits, berries). By age 10 boys are proficient hunters, girls proficient gatherers, and they're economically self-sufficient[2] (Jeliffe et al., 1962). When adults are in camp, children are assigned many chores and errands, including fetching firewood and water, caring for younger siblings, and driving snakes away. Adults, not surprisingly, are largely intolerant of children's play and show little inclination to "indulge" their children (Blurton-Jones, 1993). The Hadza represent an extreme along a continuum of time available for play in the individual's lifetime, with our society representing the opposite pole.

Research on the Hadza also provides an antidote to studies of !Kung childrearing, which indicated a prolonged period of free play and a warmly indulgent attitude on the part of adults (Blurton-Jones, 1993). On the other hand, Draper and Cashdan (1988) showed that as the !Kung were forced to become sedentary agriculturists, their approach to child-rearing changed. There was less parent–child interaction, more sibling caretaking, and children were expected to make an economic contribution to the household from an early age. This is consistent with research on Mayan children from an agricultural community. In one study (Kramer & Boone, 1999), children as young as age 13 (girls, 15 for boys) were producing more than they consumed. And the family enjoyed the fruits of children's surplus output for at least six years before the children married and started families of their own.

Playtime is, therefore, typically limited by the expectation that, from a certain age, children will contribute to subsistence (Munroe, Munroe, & Shimmin, 1984). Rogoff and colleagues (1975) conducted a comparative analysis using Human Relations Area Files data. Using a sample of 50 societies, they found evidence that the majority provide a transition during the child's fifth to seventh years in which they are assigned certain responsibilities such as the care of livestock and younger siblings, and the gathering of materials. They are ready to begin learning from their elders and are expected to reduce the time spent in play. Hence, the ethnographic record shows that, for most subsistence-based societies, tribes, chiefdoms, and such, children's play is gradually replaced by work beginning at age 5 or even earlier in some cases (Gaskins, 1990).

Our own society, therefore, presents an extreme contrast to the Hadza. As individuals are excused from making a living until later and later in their lives, play fills the vacuum, or at least there is a corresponding tolerance for heavy involvement in play at later and later ages. I would stick my neck out here and argue that adult responsibility in our society has become so drastically delayed that individuals "never grow up." I return to this idea in my conclusion.

The play–work dichotomy maps on to a male–female dichotomy. For example, Bloch and Adler (1994) found, in a Senegalese village, that girls were more likely than boys to engage in "play work," girls transitioned from play to work earlier than boys, and girls were more likely than boys to be called away from play to work. This disparity seems to hold true in most societies, according to Whiting and Edwards (1988; see also Munroe et al., 1984). I am not aware of any carefully conducted study of playtime budgets in our own society, but I see no reason not to extrapolate from studies of child-minding and household chore allocation (Hochschild, 1989) in the United States, which show a similarity disparity—women work, men play.

The prevailing wisdom in our society seems to be that gender differences in play are primarily, or even exclusively, influenced by the culture and especially parents, through such things as toy selection (see, e.g., Garvey, 1991). I do not think so. I believe that gender-specific patterns of play are influenced as much by genes as culture. Twenty years ago, I conducted a small-scale experiment with my own daughters, Nadia and Sonia. They spent infancy and toddlerhood in Papua, New Guinea, isolated from television; their mother worked and domestic duties were performed by our houseboy. I had shipped to PNG a rich collection of "boy toys"—Fisher-Price dumptrucks, graders, and the like; wooden cars and mechanical pull-toys; a large sandbox for them to play in; a jungle gym to climb over, slide down, and swing on. And, most importantly, there were no dolls in the house. It was a safe, secure environment indoors and out, and they had the run of the place. Weather was not an issue. The only time they played with the construction toys was when I was there to play with them; otherwise they never went near the materials. Instead, they took to raiding the dirty clothes hamper to "dress up," and when we relented and admitted a few dolls into the house, they were enormously popular, as were most of the feminine-oriented play things that started to arrive as presents over the years. While gender clearly constrains play, careful comparative analysis *within species* has yet to be done.

In traditional, non-Western societies, parents emphatically do *not* actively shape their children's play (Göncü, Mistry, & Moisier, 1999), and toy-making by adults is fairly rare. Nevertheless, children reliably gravitate toward "gender-appropriate" play. Among the Kpelle (Lancy, 1996), I cannot think of a single occasion when I observed a parent directing a child's play in a positive sense and only a few occasions when I saw them curtailing children's play. Playing on the mother ground makes it easy for adults to supervise children,[3] and equally important, children, observing the nearby adults, gain access to prime script material for their make-believe play. Adults, when asked, gave their hearty approval of make-believe play and, indeed, as is widely reported in the literature, parents believe that the primary means for children to acquire the skills of adults is through observation, imitation, and trial and error—not, in other words, through adult instruction.

Make-believe, or at least the imitation of one's elders, seems to be the bedrock upon which all play is built. Fantasy play, in which the characters are taken from legend (cowboys and Indians, Romans and Carthaginians) is merely a more elaborate version of "playing house." In one memorable scene from my Kpelle study, three toddlers, using found objects, were pretending to hull rice with a mortar and pestle—an adult activity they have witnessed every day of their lives. Games with rules also seem to be rooted in fantasy; thus, while playing "hop-scotch," children recite a litany of conquest—each square is a "town." And it is in make-believe that children—with no guidance from adults—unerringly home in on gender-specific roles. However, societies vary in the scripts they make available for children to take up in make-believe. In a U.S. study of make-believe play in upper-middle-class and lower-class neighborhoods, there were large differences in the amount and richness of children's make-believe scripts—especially of make-believe work, which closely corresponded to the number of people employed and the range of occupations in the two communities (Lancy, 1982). The findings of Smilansky's (1968) and other studies of the paucity of make-believe play in poor migrant communities also come to mind. Despite the heart-warming rhetoric we dish out in our teacher-training classes, children do *not* have unlimited imagination; their make-believe and, by extension, other play forms are constrained by the roles, scripts, and props of the culture they live in. In fact, in Ashley Maynard's (1999) recently completed study in a Mayan village in Chiapas, she observed older siblings guiding and teaching younger children during make-believe, focusing their attention on washing, caring for babies, and cooking.

Children imitating their elders—especially at work—is looked on with indulgence,[4] and when adults fashion toys for children, they are, invariably, miniature tools—knives, bow and arrows, hoes, canoes (Hewlett, 1991; Hogbin, 1970). Dolls can be seen as tools when the emphasis is on learning how to carry and hold an infant as opposed to learning to dress up and primp one's Barbie doll.[5] Similarly, most child-produced toys are miniature tools, cooking utensils, miniature houses, and the like. The primary difference is that adults take considerable care in fashioning toy or scaled down versions of adult equipment, whereas children, as often as not, grab whatever is at hand and let their imagination do the rest. Put differently, if a child's skill level is such that he or she can fashion accurate replicas of tools, chances are they are apprentice toolmakers in their own right—no longer playing with toys. On the other hand, play that appears to be unrelated to adult work or is otherwise unfamiliar is probably discouraged, if not forbidden outright by adults. Children's play, in societies without formal schooling (e.g., all but a handful), is the curriculum that prepares them for adulthood and is looked upon with the same conservative eye we focus on "academic standards" and the "canon."

A quite subtle influence that culture exerts on play, while noted by some anthropologists (Burridge, 1957), was called to the world's attention initially by a social psychologist. I am referring to Millard Madsen's (e.g., Madsen & Lancy, 1981) studies of cooperation and competition among children. In study after study, Madsen showed that U.S. children inevitably treated as competitive a novel game while children from village-based societies treated the same game as requiring a cooperative approach. That is, in our society, we might say that the "default option" for play is competition—including competition for toys as scarce resources—whereas in non-Western societies, the default option is cooperation.

I discovered another way children's play is constrained in less complex, smaller-scale societies. We were testing one of Brian Sutton-Smith's (1976) theories about the relationship between cultural complexity and the complexity of games in the play-form inventory. We found, in a sample of seven societies in Papua New Guinea, that most of Sutton-Smith's more complex game types were absent. The reason turned out to be that in these very small hamlets where children were to forego play for work at an early age, play groups were, inevitably, small and of mixed age/gender. The only available games were those that could be played effectively by children as young as 4. Hence, only the most rudimentary—tag, target-shooting—games were played (Lancy, 1984).

A final and quite obvious limitation on children's play is their physical and emotional health. Children who are malnourished, ill, or physically abused suffer a sharp drop in play. And from a purely statistical point of view, these privations affect an enormous number of the world's children at any given time (Worthman, 1993). According to Edgerton's (1992) analysis, at least some of this privation is brought on by well-established, almost hallowed customs that are patently maladaptive for child health and well-being.

To sum up matters, culture constrains children's play by:

- Imposing limits on where and how vigorously children may play in the interests of *safety*—an interest that must be balanced against the need for children to become self-sufficient at an early age.
- Imposing chores earlier for girls than boys—leading to the expectation of economic self-sufficiency.
- Ensuring that play is appropriate to the child's sex.
- Providing a finite set of scripts—from contemporary adult activity and from myth and legend—which children may draw on in play.
- Promoting an ethos of cooperation, at least where children are concerned.
- The sheer physical size of the community influences the composition of the play group. Game inventories, in particular, are likely to be richer and more complex, where play groups of same age/gender are the norm.
- Failing to provide a "benign environment" (Lancy, 1980), the society limits children's play time.

All of which suggests that the *benefits* of play to children must be extensive and profound in order to overcome these pervasive attempts at restraint.

NOTES

1. The International Association for the Children's Right to Play was formed in Denmark in 1961. An American branch was instituted in 1973.

2. A survey found little evidence of malnutrition or chronic illness among Hadza children (Jeliffe et al., 1962).

3. Sutton-Smith (1994) cites safety concerns in an increasingly urbanized environment as accounting for the movement *indoors* of modern childhood play.

4. Nor are children discouraged from *observing* adults at work, providing they are not shirking on their chores. In fact, non-Western societies create a very favorable climate for children to serve as passive observers—television did not give birth to the first couch potatoes.

5. I was fascinated to learn (Wiedemann, 1989) that daughters of the Roman aristocracy *did* play with Barbie-like dolls—to prepare themselves as decorative accessories to their husbands. As high-ranking wives they were relieved of virtually all child-care responsibilities, hence had no need to acquire *those* skills.

REFERENCES

Bloch, M. N., & Adler, S. M. (1994). African children's play and the emergence of the sexual division of labor. In J. L. Roopnarine, J. E. Johnson, & F. H. Hooper (Eds.), *Children's play in diverse cultures* (pp. 148–178). Albany: SUNY Press.

Blurton-Jones, N. (1993). The lives of hunter–gatherer children: Effects of parental behavior and parental reproduction strategy. In M. E. Pereira & L. A. Fairbanks (Eds.), *Juvenile primates* (pp. 405–426). Oxford: Oxford University Press.

Bogin, B. (1998). Evolutionary and biological aspects of childhood. In C. Panter-Brick (Ed.), *Biosocial perspectives on children* (pp. 10–44). Cambridge: Cambridge University Press.

Burridge, K. O. (1957). A Tangu game. *Man 57*, 88–89.

Draper, P., & Cashdan, E. (1988). Technological change and child behavior among the !Kung. *Ethnology, 27*, 339–365.

Edgerton, R. B. (1992). *Sick societies*. New York: Free Press.

Fagen, R. (1977). Selection for optimal age-dependent schedules of play behavior. *American Naturalist, 111*, 395–414.

Fagen, R. (1993). Primate juveniles and primate play. In M. E. Pereira & L. A. Fairbanks (Eds.), *Juvenile primates* (pp. 182–196). Oxford: Oxford University Press.

Garvey, C. (1991). *Play* (2nd ed.). Boston: Harvard University Press.

Gaskins, S. (1990). *Exploratory play and development in Mayan infants*. Unpublished doctoral dissertation, University of Chicago.

Göncü, A, Mistry, J., & Moisier, C. (1999, November). *Cultural variation in the play of toddlers*. Paper presented at the annual meeting of the American Anthropological Association, Chicago.

Hendry, J. (1986). *Becoming Japanese*. Manchester, UK: Manchester University Press.

Hewlett, B. (1991). *Intimate fathers*. Ann Arbor: University of Michigan Press.

Hochschild, A. (1989). *The second shift: Working parents and the revolution at home*. New York: Viking.

Hogbin, I. I. (1970). A New Guinea childhood. In J. Middleton (Ed.), *From child to adult* (pp. 134–162). Garden City, NY: Natural History Press.

Jeliffe, D.B., Woodburn, J., Bennett, F.J., & Jeliffe, E.F.P. (1962). The children of Hadza hunters. *Tropical Pediatrics, 60*(2), 907–913.

Kramer, K., & Boone, J. (1999, February). *Foragers and farmers: Children's work and maternal tradeoffs*. Paper presented at the annual meeting of the Society for Cross-Cultural Research, Santa Fe, NM.

Lancy, D. F. (1980). Play in species adaptation. In B. J. Siegel (Ed.), *Annual Review of anthropology, IX* (pp. 471–495). Palo Alto, CA: Annual Reviews Inc.

Lancy, D. F. (1982). Socio-dramatic play and the acquisition of occupational roles. *Review Journal of Philosophy and Social Science, 7*, 285–295.

Lancy, D.F. (1984). Play in anthropological perspective. In P. K. Smith (Ed.), *Play in animals and humans* (pp. 295–304). London: Basil Blackwell.

Lancy, D. F. (1996). *Playing on the mother ground: Cultural routines for children's development*. New York: Guilford Press.

Madsen, M. C., & Lancy, D. F. (1981). Cooperative and competitive behavior: Experiments related to ethnic identity and urbanization in Papua New Guinea. *Journal of Cross-Cultural Psychology, 12*, 389–408.

Martini, M. (1994). Peer interactions in Polynesia: A view from the Marquesas. In J. L. Roopnarine, J. E. Johnson, & F. H. Hooper (Eds.), *Children's play in diverse cultures* (pp. 73–103). Albany: SUNY Press.

Maynard, A. (1999, November). *The social organization and development of teaching in Zinacantec Maya sibling play*. Paper presented at the annual meeting of the American Anthropological Association, Chicago.

Munroe, R. H., Munroe, R.L., & Shimmin, H.S. (1984). Children's work in four cultures: Determinants and consequences. *American Anthropologist, 86*, 369–379.

Rogoff, B. et al. (1975). Age of assignment of roles and responsibilities to children. *Human Development, 18*, 353–369.

Rogoff, B. (1990). *Apprenticeship in thinking: Cognitive development in social context.* New York: Oxford University Press.

Rubin, J., Flowers, N. M., & Gross, D.R. (1986). The adaptive dimensions of leisure. *American Ethnologist, 13*, 524–536.

Smilansky, S. (1968). *The effects of sociodramatic play on disadvantaged preschool children.* New York: Wiley.

Sutton-Smith, B. (1976) A structural grammar of games and sports. *International Review of Sport Sociology, 2*, 117–137.

Sutton-Smith, B. (1994). Does play prepare the future? In J.H. Goldstein (Ed.), *Toys, play and child development* (pp. 130–146). Cambridge: Cambridge University Press.

van Gennep, A. (1960). *Rites of passage.* London: Routledge, Kegan Paul. (Original work published 1906)

Whiting, B. B., & Edwards, C. P. (1988). *Children of different worlds.* Cambridge, MA: Harvard University Press.

Wiedemann, T. (1989). *Adults and children in the Roman empire.* New Haven, CT: Yale University Press.

Worthman, C.M. (1993). Biocultural interactions in human development. In M. E. Pereira & L. A. Fairbanks (Eds.), *Juvenile primates* (pp. 359–366). New York: Oxford University Press.

Part II

Role of Age, Gender, and Ethnicity in Play

4

Play in Same-Age and Multiage Grouping Arrangements

James F. Christie, Sandra J. Stone, and
Rebecca Deutscher

The multiage classroom is becoming a popular organizational strategy in the current school restructuring movement. Multiage advocates claim that in mixed-age groups, younger children benefit from collaborative learning with older children (Goodlad & Anderson, 1987; Katz, Evangelou, & Hartman, 1990). Vygotsky (1978) envisions what he calls a "zone of proximal development." This zone is the distance between the actual development of the child and the level of potential development that can be reached with help from adults or more capable peers. In a multiage classroom, opportunities should arise for older peers to provide this "zone" for younger classmates, helping the younger ones learn skills and concepts in all areas of the curriculum.

A growing body of research indicates that mixed-age settings create opportunities for older children to help younger children move beyond their current level of cognitive functioning (see Roopnarine & Clawson, 2000). For example, Shatz and Gelman (1973) found that 4-year-olds used shorter, simpler speech when talking to 2-year-olds than when conversing with same-age peers. Mc-Closkey (1996) found that, in mixed-age dyads, elementary-grade girls were more "instructive" in the speech that they used with younger peers. In addition, children were more likely to use tutorial speech in mixed-age dyads than in same-age dyads.

In an earlier study, we found evidence that supports this connection between mixed-age grouping and peer scaffolding (Christie & Stone, 1999). We examined the collaborative literacy activity that occurred in one teacher's print-enriched sociodramatic play center in two situations: (a) when she taught a multiage (K-2) class, and (b) a year later, when she taught a same-age kindergarten group in the same classroom. Our findings showed that more literacy activity, peer scaffolding, and other forms of collaboration occurred in the play center under the multiage grouping arrangement than in the same-age classroom. Multiage grouping appeared to interface well with the print-enriched play center strategy, creating a dynamic social context in which older, "expert" peers helped younger children engage in play-related literacy activities.

The older peers in a multiage classroom may have also had an effect on the younger children's play behavior. Several studies have reported that younger children engage in more mature modes of play in mixed-age rather than same-age settings (Brownell, 1990; Mounts & Roopnarine, 1987; Rothstein-Fisch & Howes, 1988; Urberg & Kaplan, 1986). For example, Mounts and Roopnarine (1987) found that 3-year-olds were more likely to engage in constructive play in mixed-age classrooms, whereas they showed a preference for the less mature manipulative play mode in same-age groupings.

The relationship between mixed-age grouping and dramatic play, another mature mode of play, is less clear. Roopnarine and colleagues (1992) reported that dramatic play was more prevalent in same-age rather than mixed-age classrooms. While this finding indicates that mixed-age grouping does not increase levels of participation in dramatic play, the possibility still exists that this form of grouping may have positive effects on structural characteristics of children's dramatic play, such as narrative structure and choice of theme.

As children mature, their dramatic play becomes more sustained and integrated (Fenson, 1984), and the narrative structure of the stories they enact also changes. Researchers have reported that the length and complexity of children's play narrative increases with age, evolving from a series of loosely connected events at age 3 to elaborate, multiepisode stories at age 6 or 7 (Botvin & Sutton-Smith, 1977; Eckler & Weininger, 1989; Fein, 1975, 1995). The themes children enact in their play also change with age (Garvey, 1977; Rubin, Fein, & Vandenberg, 1983). Initially, children adopt highly familiar roles, such as family members, and act out very routine types of domestic activity, such as preparing dinner or going shopping. As they mature, children begin taking on less familiar roles, such as occupations (e.g., firefighter) and fictional characters (e.g., Batman).

These developmental trends in the structure of play raise the possibility that, in a multiage classroom, older children may help younger classmates act out higher-level narrative stories during sociodramatic play. The older children might also encourage the younger children to choose more mature occupational and fantasy themes for their play and to engage in lengthier play episodes. On the other hand, it is also possible that multiage grouping could have a negative impact on these aspects of younger children's sociodramatic play. Research has shown that sociodramatic play tends to decline after age 6, being replaced with game and nonplay activities (Rubin et al., 1983). The older children in a multiage class might prefer to engage in activities such as reading for pleasure or practicing the alphabet while in the play center, discouraging younger children from acting out narrative stories via dramatic play.

The purpose of the present study was to examine structural characteristics of the play that occurred in a dramatic play center during the multiage and same-age grouping arrangements. We reanalyzed the transcripts from our earlier study, examining the narrative complexity, theme, and duration of the play episodes that occurred in the two grouping arrangements.

METHOD

Setting

During both years of the study, the classroom was organized around activity centers (reading, writing, play, blocks, art, science, math, etc.). The centers offered open-ended, process-oriented experiences, rather than narrowly defined, skill-related practice.

In both grouping arrangements, the children did not have their own desks or assigned seating. Whole-group instruction was conducted on a large carpeted area of the floor, whereas small-group instruction occurred during "center time." When the teacher met with small groups at the horseshoe-shaped table, the rest of the class worked at centers. At the beginning of this 45- to 60-minute period, the children chose which centers they wanted to use, how much time they would spend there, and with whom they would work and play. The only constraint on their freedom of choice was a "hook and name tag" system used to control the number of children who used each center.

The play center, which was the focus of this study, was partially partitioned off from the rest of the classroom with bookshelves, a chart stand, and furniture. The center was stocked with miniature furniture and appliances (refrigerator, stove, crib, table and chairs), household items (phone, dishes, cookware, etc.), and dolls. The play center also contained a variety of children's books on open-faced bookshelves and on a "book rail" mounted on the wall at the children's eye level. Other literacy items included environmental print (empty food containers and store coupons), newspapers, and writing materials (markers, pens, pencils, and paper). The play center had four hooks, so four children could hang up their name tags and play in the center at one time. When a child left and removed his or her tag, another child could use the center.

The play center was equipped identically during both years of the study, with one exception. Without the knowledge of the researchers, a doctor kit was added by the teacher during the second year. This prop was available for the kindergarten class but not for the multiage group.

Subjects

The multiage class contained 10 kindergartners (5 female, 5 male), 7 first graders (3 female, 4 male), and 10 second graders (7 female, 3 male). The kindergarten class contained 22 students (12 female, 10 male). The children in both classes were from low-income families and represented diverse ethnic backgrounds, including African American, Anglo, Hispanic, Pacific Islander, Indian, and Native American. Approximately 80 percent of the subjects received free or reduced-price lunches.

Data Collection

During the first year of data collection, 15 hours of free play were videotaped in the play center of the multiage class. During the second year, 15 hours of play were videotaped in the same play center while it was being used by children in the same-age kindergarten. In both years, the videotaping occurred over a four-week period during April and May. The camera was positioned so that it covered most of the area in the play center. The teacher turned on the video camera at the beginning of "center time" and turned it off at the completion of the period. She went about her normal routine, providing small-group instruction at a horseshoe-shaped table some distance from the play center. Occasionally, the teacher adjusted the camera angle if it appeared that significant activity was occurring off-camera. The directional microphone on the camera and favorable room acoustics enabled most speech in the play center to be clearly recorded. The teacher intervened in the play only if there was a significant disruption (which was a rare occurrence).

Data Analysis

A detailed transcript was made of the action and dialogue that occurred in the play center during each session. This yielded a total of 477 typed pages of transcript for the multiage classroom and 577 pages for the same-age kindergarten.

In our earlier study, we used qualitative and quantitative methods to analyze the data to determine the collaborative literacy behaviors that occurred in the play center under the two grouping arrangements (Christie & Stone, 1999). In the present study, these same transcripts were reanalyzed to determine the structural nature of the play that occurred in the multiage and kindergarten classes.

The play structure analysis involved three phases. First, sociodramatic play frames were identified and labeled. A play frame started when two or more children adopted roles or began to act out a series of events connected to a theme. The frame ended when group play connected to the theme ceased. Themes arising in the middle of a play frame were treated as embedded themes and indicated with brackets. Two researchers identified the play frames independently and then compared their codings. When their codings did not agree, they met with a third investigator who helped to reach consensus. Forty-three play frames were identified in the multiage transcript, and 38 were found in the same-age kindergarten transcript.

Second, the narrative complexity of each play frame was coded, using categories adapted from Fein (1995) and Botvin and Sutton-Smith (1977). Table 4.1 illustrates the six categories, which ranged from simple Thematic Event Sequences (Level 1) to complex Problem/Attempt/Resolution Cycles (Level 6). Simultaneously, the theme of each narrative was coded using the following three categories: (a) Domestic—themes connected with everyday family life, such as home activities (cleaning, cooking, eating), events (moving, vacations, shopping), and pets; (b) Occupational—themes connected with a profession (running a restaurant, selling merchandise, law enforcement); and (c) Fantasy—themes derived from TV, movies, stories, or children's imaginations (Batman, fairy tales, ghosts).

Prior to coding the data, two researchers were trained on the coding system. They then coded the narrative level and theme of the play frames on the first multiage tape together, reaching consensus on disagreements. In order to establish interrater reliability, each researcher coded the narrative level of the play frames on the first kindergarten tape independently. They agreed on 23 out of the 24 coding decisions on that tape (96 percent agreement). The researchers then proceeded to code the rest of the sets of tapes in a counterbalanced order to control for any changes in coding across time. Each tape was coded independently by the researchers, and then the codings were compared. In cases of disagreement, the video was viewed again and consensus was reached.

Finally, the tapes were viewed again by the two researchers in order to determine the duration in minutes of each play frame. This was done independently, with each researcher timing the play frames in half of the kindergarten tapes and half of the multiage tapes.

RESULTS

Because we were interested in comparing the play experiences of kindergartners in the two grouping arrangements, our analyses of the multiage data were restricted to the play frames in which kindergartners were present. Kindergartners were present in 36 out of the 43 play frames in the multiage class (see Table 4.2). Seventy-five percent of play frames in which the kindergartners participated also contained first graders, and 88 percent involved second graders. Thus, many opportunities existed for older students to assist the kindergartners in their play activities.

Table 4.3 displays the narrative complexity levels of the play frames enacted by the kindergartners in the kindergarten and multiage classes. Examination of this table reveals that narrative complexity of the stories enacted by the two groups of children was quite similar, except at Levels 5 and 6. Figure 4.1 pres-

Table 4.1
Levels of Narrative Complexity in Play

_____

Prestory Narratives

Level 1   Thematic Event Sequences

               Multiple events are connected by a theme, but
               there is no problem to solve.

               Example: Family members feed a baby and then
               give the baby a bath.

Incomplete Story Narratives

Level 2   Problem/No Attempt

               A problem is created but no attempt is made to solve it. (The problem
               must be agreed upon by at least 2 players.)

               Example: Family members prepare to feed a baby and discover they are
               out of food. They give the baby a bath.

Level 3   Problem/No Attempt/Resolution

               A problem is created and resolved, but the attempt leading to resolution is
               omitted.

               Example: Family members prepare to feed a baby and discover that they
               are out of food. Food is suddenly discovered and the baby is fed.

Level 4   Problem/Attempt/No Resolution

               A problem is created, one or more attempts are made to resolve it, but no
               resolution occurs.

               Example: Family members prepare to feed a baby and discover they are
               out of food. They decide to make a trip to the store. The play setting is
               transformed into a store and several items are purchased. However, the
               items are not taken back home and fed to the baby.

Complete Story Narratives

Level 5   Problem/Attempt/Resolution

               A problem is created and one or more attempts are
               made to resolve it, and resolution occurs.

               Example: Family members prepare to feed the baby and discover they are
               out of food. They make a pretend trip to the store, purchase several items,
               and return home and feed the baby.

Level 6   Problem/Attempt/Resolution Cycle

               Two or more Level 5 stories are chained together.

               Example: Family members prepare to feed a baby and discover they are
               out of food. They make a pretend trip to the store, purchase several items,
               and return home and feed the baby. Then, the family attempts to bathe the
               baby, but a burglar kidnaps the baby. The family searches and finds the
               baby.

Table 4.2
Composition of Play Groups in the Multiage Classroom

Grades represented	Number of play frames
K only	1
K, Grade 1	4
K, Grade 2	8
K, Grade 1, Grade 2	23
Grade 1 only	0
Grade 2 only	3
Grades 1 and 2	4

ents the 95-percent confidence intervals for the two groups' narrative complexity scores. This figure reveals that the only level at which the confidence intervals of two groups' scores do not overlap is Level 6. Thus, we can safely infer that kindergartners in the multiage class engaged in more Level 6 narratives than did their counterparts in the kindergarten class. For all other levels, it is not likely that significant differences existed between the two groups' scores.

As illustrated in Table 4.4, substantial differences were found in play themes enacted by the two groups. The kindergarten group's stories were almost equally divided between domestic and occupational themes, whereas more than 90 percent of the multiage group's stories centered on domestic themes. Fantasy themes were rare in both groups. Figure 4.2 illustrates that the 95-percent confidence intervals for the two groups' scores for domestic and occupational themes do not overlap. Thus, we can safely say that the children in the kindergarten class engaged in more occupational play themes, whereas the multiage class kindergartners engaged in more domestic play themes.

The kindergarten play frames had a mean duration of 19.4 minutes, compared with a mean length of 22.4 minutes for the frames in which kindergartners were involved in the multiage class. A t test revealed that these means were not statistically significant ($t = 1.523$, $p = .13$).

Table 4.3
Narrative Complexity Levels of the Play Frames Enacted by Kindergartners in
the Two Grouping Arrangements

Level	Kindergarten class	Multiage class
1	51.0%	51.4%
2	9.8%	14.3%
3	2.0%	5.7%
4	17.6%	14.3%
5	19.6%	2.9%
6	0.0%	11.4%

DISCUSSION

This study examined the structural characteristics of play that occurred in a
dramatic play center under two grouping arrangements: a kindergarten classroom
with same-age students and a multiage classroom with kindergarten, first-, and
second-grade students. A prior analysis of activity in the play center revealed
that kindergartners in the multiage classroom engaged in more collaborative
literacy activity than their counterparts in the same-age kindergarten (Christie
& Stone, 1999). In accordance with Vygotsky's (1932/1978) zone of proximal
development, the youngest students in the multiage class appeared to benefit
from interacting with the older primary-grade peers.

The findings of the present study show that the benefits of the "zone" on the
dramatic play of the kindergartners in the multiage class are less clear. Our
results show that the narrative complexity of the play of multiage group kindergartners was very similar to that of the children in the same-age kindergarten
class. As in Roopnarine and colleagues' (1992) earlier study, there was little
evidence to suggest that multiage grouping promotes dramatic play. The only
possible benefit was that the kindergartners in the multiage group engaged in
more Level 6 Problem/Attempt/Resolution Cycle narratives, in which two or
more complete Level 5 narratives are chained together. Because this advanced
form of narrative structure typically does not emerge until children are 6 or 7

Figure 4.1
Narrative complexity confidence intervals.

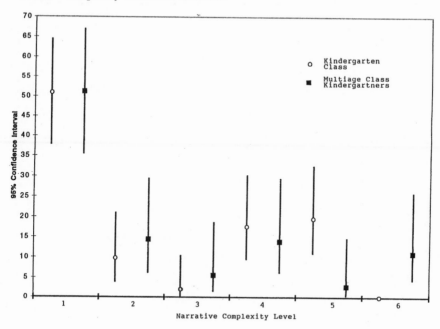

Table 4.4
Themes of the Play Frames Enacted by Kindergartners in the Two Grouping Arrangements

Theme	Kindergarten class	Multiage class
Domestic	49.2%	90.9%
Occupational	44.3%	6.1%
Fantasy	6.6%	3.0%

Figure 4.2
Play theme confidence intervals.

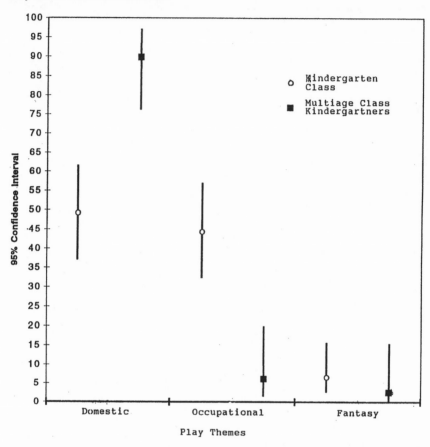

years old (Botvin & Sutton-Smith, 1977), its presence in the multiage group kindergartners' play may indicate some scaffolding by older students. However, the complexity of the great majority of the multiage group kindergartners' play was similar to that of the children in the kindergarten class. In addition, the duration of the play episodes acted out by the two groups was similar. The stories of the multiage group kindergartners were slightly longer, but this difference was not statistically significant.

The major difference in the play of the two groups involved theme. The same-age kindergarten group engaged in more diverse and mature occupational play themes, whereas the play in the multiage class was primarily restricted to domestic themes involving everyday household activities. This is not what we had predicted. Given that developmental sequence in play theme proceeds from domestic to occupational (Garvey, 1977; Rubin et al., 1983), we had expected that the kindergartners in the multiage class would engage in more occupational themes due to modeling and scaffolding by older students.

The same-age kindergarten group's preference for occupational themes may simply reflect the powerful influence of play materials. Most of this group's occupational themes involved doctors and medical activities. This preoccupation with the medical profession appeared to be related to children's discovery of a doctor kit in the center. The doctor kit was not in the play center when the multiage group used it, so it is possible that this one prop was responsible for the difference in theme preference of the two groups.

Materials were also likely behind the multiage group's preference for domestic themes. The play center was set up as a housekeeping area, and when the multiage group used this center, all of the props fit this theme. In addition, a previous study had revealed that the older children in the multiage class spent a considerable amount of time using the literacy materials in the play center (Christie & Stone, 1999; Stone & Christie, 1996). The fact that all of these literacy materials—cookbooks, children's books, empty food containers with environmental print, newspapers, and so on—were at least tangentially related to household life may have added an additional impetus for domestic play themes.

From a play development perspective, the domestic themes enacted by these children were less mature than the occupational themes acted out by the same-age kindergarten group. From an academic perspective, however, the literacy-related domestic themes enacted by the kindergartners in the multiage class may be viewed as more beneficial than the doctor play preferred by the same-age kindergarten class. The kindergartners in the multiage class engaged in a variety of meaningful reading and writing activities connected with their play (Stone & Christie, 1996).

It would have been interesting to observe what might have happened if the doctor kit had also been available in the multiage classroom. Perhaps the kit would have shifted this group's focus toward occupational themes. On the other hand, the pull of literacy materials, which were related to home life, might have maintained the dominance of domestic themes. Perhaps it would require both the doctor kit and theme-related literacy materials (e.g., prescription pads, patient folders, an appointment book, etc.) to get the literacy-oriented first and second graders to shift toward medically related play themes.

If future research confirms this possibility, it would imply that teachers who use print-enriched play centers should employ a rotating theme center strategy (Woodard, 1984), particularly in multiage classrooms. In this strategy, socio-dramatic play centers are changed every two or three weeks to resemble different settings, such as a store, restaurant, veterinarian's office, or auto repair center. Theme-related literacy materials are included for each theme. This strategy should encourage children of all ages to engage in diverse occupational play themes and greatly expand the range of possible play-related literacy activities.

Play is deemed as vitally important to the growth of the whole child by many experts (see Johnson, Christie, & Yawkey, 1999). The National Association for the Education of Young Children and the Association for Childhood Education International have both taken a strong position on play, recognizing its essential role in all aspects of children's development (see, e.g., Bredekamp & Copple, 1997). With multiage education on the forefront of school change, it would be difficult for early childhood educators to embrace this concept if mixed-age grouping had a negative impact on younger children's sociodramatic play. This study confirms that the quality of play of the youngest children in mixed-age settings was not compromised. In addition, the quality of play for all children (5 through 7 years old) appeared to be maintained and, in some respects, enhanced.

REFERENCES

Botvin, G., & Sutton-Smith, B. (1977). The development of structural complexity in children's fantasy narratives. *Developmental Psychology, 13*(4), 377–388.

Bredekamp S., & Copple, C. (1997). *Developmentally appropriate practice in early childhood programs* (Rev. ed.). Washington, DC: National Association for the Education of Young Children.

Brownell, C. (1990). Peer social skills in toddlers: Competencies and constraints illustrated by same-age and mixed-age interaction. *Child Development, 61*, 838–848.

Christie, J., & Stone, S. (1999). Collaborative literacy activity in same-age and multi-age groupings. *Journal of Literacy Research, 31*, 109–131.

Eckler, J., & Weininger, O. (1989). Structural parallels between pretend play and narratives. *Developmental Psychology, 25*, 736–743.

Fein, G. (1975). A transformational analysis of pretending. *Developmental Psychology, 11*, 291–296.

Fein, G. (1995). Toys and stories. In A. Pellegrini (Ed.), *The future of play theory: A multidisciplinary inquiry into the contributions of Brian Sutton-Smith* (pp. 151–164). Albany: SUNY Press.

Fenson, L. (1984). Developmental trends for action and speech in pretend play. In I. Bretherton (Ed.), *Symbolic play: The development of social understanding* (pp. 249–270). Orlando, FL: Academic Press.

Garvey, C. (1977). *Play.* Cambridge, MA: Harvard University Press.

Goodlad, J., & Anderson, R. (1987). *The non-graded elementary school* (Rev. ed.). New York: Teachers College Press.

Johnson, J., Christie, J., & Yawkey, T. (1999). *Play and early childhood development* (2nd ed.). New York: Allyn-Bacon/Longman.

Katz, L., Evangelou, D., & Hartman, J. (1990). *The case for mixed-age grouping in early education.* Washington, DC: National Association for the Education of Young Children.

McCloskey, L. (1996). Gender and the expression of status in children's mixed-age conversations. *Journal of Applied Developmental Psychology, 17*, 117–133.

Mounts, N., & Roopnarine, J. (1987). Social-cognitive play patterns in same-age and mixed-age preschool classrooms. *American Educational Research Journal, 24*, 463–476.

Roopnarine, J., Ahmeduzzaman, M., Donnely, S., Gill, P., Mennis, A., Arky, L., Mc-Laughlin, M., Dingler, K., & Talukder, E. (1992). Social and cognitive play behaviors and playmate preferences in same-age and mixed-age classrooms. *American Educational Research Journal, 28,* 757–776.

Roopnarine, J., & Clawson, M. (2000). Mixed-age classrooms for young children. In J. Roopnarine & J. Johnson (Eds.), *Approaches to early childhood education* (3rd ed., pp. 221–237). Upper Saddle River, NJ: Merrill/Prentice-Hall.

Rothstein-Fisch, C., & Howes, C. (1988). Toddler peer interaction in mixed-age groups. *Journal of Applied Developmental Psychology, 20,* 828–832.

Rubin, K. H., Fein, G. G., & Vandenberg, B. (1983). Play. In P. H. Mussen (Ed.), *Handbook of child psychology: Vol. 4. Socialization, personality, and social development* (4th ed., pp. 693–774). New York: Wiley.

Shatz, M., & Gelman, R. (1973). The development of communication skills: Modifications in the speech of young children as a function of listener. *Monographs of the Society for Research in Child Development, 38*(5, Serial No. 152).

Stone, S., & Christie, J. (1996). Collaborative literacy learning during sociodramatic play in a multiage (K-2) primary classroom. *Journal of Research in Childhood Education, 10,* 123–133.

Urberg, K., & Kaplan, M. (1986). Effects of classroom age composition on the play and social behavior of preschool children. *Journal of Applied Developmental Psychology, 7,* 403–415.

Vygotsky, L. S. (1978). *Mind in society: The development of psychological processes.* Cambridge, MA: Harvard University Press. (Original work published 1932)

Woodard, C. Y. (1984). Guidelines for facilitating sociodramatic play. *Childhood Education, 60,* 172–177.

5

Block Play Complexity in Same-Sex Dyads of Preschool Children

Dorothy Justus Sluss

The premise that girls and boys play differently is not new (Erikson, 1951; Maccoby, 1988; Mounts & Roopnarine, 1987; Pitcher & Schultz, 1983). Gender has long been one of the best predictors of play (Christie & Johnson, 1987). Though studies of sex-linked behaviors have escalated during the past two decades, findings continue to be inconsistent and controversial (Ausch, 1994; Black, 1989; Eaton & Enns, 1986; Howes & Farver, 1987). For this reason, this study was designed to investigate the complexity of block play among same-sex dyads of unfamiliar 4-year-old girls and boys.

Differences in the way girls and boys play with blocks were first reported by Erik Erikson (1951). He found that pubescent girls and boys build different kinds of structures during block play; boys tended to build towers while girls focused more on enclosures. Erikson's explanation of gender differences in terms of psychoanalytic theory enveloped his study in controversy.

Goodfader (1982) also found evidence that girls and boys use blocks in different ways. By examining spatial relationships in terms of degree of towerness, enclosures, variety of use, and number of blocks, she noted that girls build smaller structures while boys build larger structures. Additional findings of sex-related differences during block play were reported by Dyanne Tracy (1987). Tracy examined the relationship between block play and spatial relationships and found a positive correlation between boys' block play and spatial relationships. Boys displayed more skills in both block play and spatial relationships than girls. Overall, these studies indicate that girls and boys play with blocks in different ways.

The basis for these differences may be related to the amount of time girls and boys spend playing with blocks. Rubin (1977) found that boys play with blocks more frequently than girls. Beeson and Williams (1979) also found that boys spend more time in block areas than girls. More recent reports by the Froebel Blockplay Research Group (Gura, 1992) also noted a difference in the availability and frequency of block play among girls and boys. They found that boys frequently took over the block area and that the "dominating group had the effect of pushing [the girls] to the periphery with few blocks for their use. This lack of space and lack of materials constrained development of block play for children not in the dominant group" (p. 18). It appears that, the amount of time children spend playing with blocks affects their skill level. If boys tend to spend more time in block play, they may indeed be more skilled than girls who choose to spend less time in block play.

If this is the case, then it would be logical to surmise that boys are in a far better position than girls to accrue developmental benefits through block play. Several studies, however, have reported findings that refute this premise. For example, Budd, Clance, and Simerly (1985) used the same blocks, props, and age group that Erikson used and found no differences in the play of pubescent boys and girls.

Studies of young children too have reported no differences in the way pre-school girls and boys play. In his study, Rogers (1985) used a laboratory setting to ensure that girls had equal access to blocks throughout the year. Two girls and two boys were in groups that rotated in and out of centers on a regular basis throughout the year. Rogers found that girls played as frequently and in ways that were just as complex as those used by boys. He noted that the frequency of play may have contributed to the results. That is, in a controlled setting that encouraged girls to use blocks as frequently as boys, they both displayed the same skill level.

A recent content analysis completed by Conrad (1995) also failed to find evidence of sex-related differences during play. Conrad looked at 14 studies of gender differences during play and concluded that sufficient evidence did not exist to support the view that girls and boys play in different ways. Since Conrad neglected to include the context of the studies, the validity of the content analysis is limited and, therefore, questionable. Given the contradictory nature of the existing literature, we need to examine not only differences among girls and boys during play, but also the intricacies and complexities of their play. Block play appears uniquely suitable for observing differing levels of play complexity among girls and boys. During block play, children have the opportunity to develop creative problem-solving skills and refine innovative ways of thinking

(Tegano, Lookabaugh, May, & Burdette, 1991). To fully understand the activities that occur during block play, it is necessary to examine block play as a multifaceted entity. Looking only at the spatial relationships that occur during block play provides a unidimensional view. The current study was designed to ensure that block play is viewed as multidimensional by defining block play complexity as a composite of play level, block play, and communication. It was hypothesized that when girls and boys play together in same-sex dyads, block play complexity among unfamiliar 4-year-old boys will be more complex than block play among unfamiliar 4-year-old girls.

METHOD

Subjects

Participants were selected from the population of 4-year-olds in child-care settings in a small town surrounding a major research university. Six centers serving a population of middle- and upper-class families agreed to participate in the study. One hundred and fifty 4-year-old children were originally selected for this study. Parent(s) or guardian(s) of 100 children agreed to allow their children to participate. From this group, 48 children (24 girls) were selected to participate in the study. Selection for a group was based on the child's sex and unfamiliarity with the play partner. An equal number of boys and girls were selected to ensure the same number of pairs in each group. Unfamiliarity controlled for the possibility of bringing established play patterns to the play session. All of the children in the study attended private child-care centers that served middle- and upper-class families. Ethnicity and culture reflected the general population of the town and mirrored the global constituency of the research university (i.e., Russian, Indian, Asian, African, European, etc.). The mean age of the participants was 4 years 7 months.

Procedure

Observational Method

Forty-eight children (24 dyads) were observed in a laboratory setting that resembled an early childhood classroom. Only one dyad was observed during each play session. Play sessions were composed of two segments. The first part of the session focused on play and generally lasted about 30 minutes. The session began when both children arrived. They were invited to play with blocks in the play room and were told by the adult, "I have some blocks in this room. You may come inside and play. There will be someone else playing in the room also. I will be in the room and watch you while you play. Your parent(s) will wait outside the room while you play. Do you want to play?" Children were familiarized with the room, with each other, and were aware that they could leave at any time prior to beginning the play session. The amount of time required to familiarize the children with the play varied based on the child's comfort level but usually ranged from 10 to 15 minutes. The play itself lasted about 15 minutes. Ceiling cameras were used to record the entire session. When the children completed their constructions, photographs of the constructions were made.

The second part of the session occurred when the adult asked the children to talk about their experiences. Only one child at a time was recorded so that neither child could influence the other child's comments. The children were encouraged to decide who would be first to speak on the microphone and who would be first to begin clean-up. The adult asked the children individually, "Please tell me about your play." Children were given the opportunity to hold the microphone and conversations were recorded on tape.

Data Collection and Coding

All data were collected on videotapes, audiotapes, and photographs. Each observer examined the videotapes, pictures, and audiotapes. Block play complexity was evaluated by coding for play level, block play, and communication on separate passes.

(1) *Play level.* The child's play level was assessed using the Play Observation Scale (POS) developed by Rubin (1989). The POS was designed to rate the frequency of play behaviors that reflect social and cognitive domains of play. Selection of this instrument was based on the frequency of use in past studies (Pellegrini & Boyd, 1993). Time-frame sampling was used to record the play behaviors. The play behaviors of the target child were observed for a period of 10 seconds, after which the dominant behavior was recorded during a 5-second interval. This resulted in 6 recorded observations per minute or a total of 60 per 10-minute session.

The child's play level was operationalized into 12 levels by Rubin (1989) and included two levels of nonplay, that is, unoccupied and onlooker. Play categories included nonplay behaviors, solitary-functional, solitary-constructive, solitary-dramatic, parallel-functional, parallel-constructive, parallel-dramatic, associative-functional, associative-constructive, associative-dramatic, cooperative-constructive, cooperative-dramatic, and cooperative-games. A score was obtained by multiplying the frequency of occurrence by a predetermined weight. For example, beginning with onlooker behavior, the behavior was weighted in terms of complexity with onlooker rating a 1 and cooperative games rating a 6. This number representing the complexity of the play was multiplied by the frequency score. When children engaged in a variety of play for different amounts of time, the type of play was multiplied by the duration and these were totaled. Very few children engaged in one type of play throughout the session.

(2) *Block play.* Coding was based on previously reported measures used in a study conducted by Reifel and Greenfield (1982). Block play complexity was viewed as a composite of both spatial relationships and symbolism. Spatial relationships were operationalized as in Reifel and Greenfield's study. Hierarchical integration was composed of five levels, which differentiated the interconnectedness of the blocks. These included: (a) Level 0: No true integration; (b) Level 1: At least one block is used to tie together or span other blocks; (c) Level 1a: Simple integrations; arches or bridges on the same plane, and simple enclosures; (d) Level 1b: Complexity increases; arches or bridges may be on two nonparallel planes; and (e) Level 2: At least two arches or bridges are joined together by one other block. Scores were obtained by ranking the levels hierarchically to reflect the complexity.

Dimensionality reflected geometric planes and was actualized in four levels: (a) Level 0: No dimensions; one block or geometric point; (b) Level 1: One dimension; linear patterns that are either vertical or horizonal; (c) Level 2: Two dimensions; observed when at least three blocks are placed so that two lines or one plane exists; bidirectional use of blocks; (d) Level 3: Three dimensions; occurs when blocks are placed together to form at least one plane plus one line that is actually two planes.

Symbolism, defined as occurring when a child "acts independently of what he/she sees" (Vygotsky, 1932/1978, p. 96), was operationalized as a measure of the child's action during constructive play. After the play episodes, each child was interviewed separately. Their descriptions of their activities with blocks were coded for symbolism. Three different levels were differentiated: presymbolism, first-level symbolism, and second-level symbolism. In Level 0, presymbolism, the block was used as a block. The child carries or stacks the blocks. No symbolism is observed whatsoever; the blocks are used only as blocks. The child might say, "I just stacked the blocks" when quizzed about intentionality. In Level 1, a reproduction of reality begins. The child uses the block to reproduce a table in the room, a house, or a school bus. The child might say, "It's a house or my table at home," and there is some reflection of the object's shape. Pretense is occurring but it is closely aligned to reality. The child's perspective begins to change in Level 2. Level 2 occurs when the object is transformed completely. The child builds a space shuttle, a pirate ship, or a candy machine. These shapes may or may not resemble real life objects. For example, one child built a rather simple structure on the floor. In terms of structural complexity, the building only rated a 3. The child had simply laid one block after another, and at first glance, it looked as though blocks were just laid side by side. When the child explained his structure, he indicated that it was a dinosaur. This child's representational level was the highest, Level 2.

(3) *Communication*. Communication was coded by examining both the videotapes and transcripts of the audiotapes. Communication was operationalized in seven levels, as in Farver (1992). The seven categories were rated hierarchically: paralinguistic cues 1, description of action 2, repetition 3, semantic tying 4, calls for attention 5, directive 6, tags 7. A child who used two paralinguistic cues (1) during a 15-minute period would receive a score of 2 (the frequency, 2, was then multiplied by the category, 1. The theoretical range of the scores were 0 to 31, with zero considered a low score and 31 considered a high score. The scores for each child were combined with the play partner's score to form a mean score for the dyad. Even though there was no validation information available, interrater reliability was 90 percent.

Reliability

Research assistants were trained prior to coding the data and kappa levels were established for play level ($k = .92$), block play (subscales: hierarchical integration $k = .90$, dimensionality $k = .90$, and symbolism $k = .90$), and communication $k = .90$. (Cohen's kappa is an agreement statistic that controls for chance agreements [see Cohen, 1960].) Agreement was assessed at regular intervals throughout the study to guard against observer drift.

Materials

Blocks similar to those used in typical preschool classrooms—that is, wooden hollow and unit blocks—were used for this study. The use of hollow and unit blocks in research was pioneered in the early part of this century (Guanella, 1934). Blocks used for this study were sanded smooth and stained with a clear varnish. The dimensions of the hollow blocks were 24" $\times$ 12" $\times$ 6". The size of the standard unit lightweight block was 5 1/2" $\times$ 2 3/4" $\times$ 1 3/8". There were 365 blocks in 32 different categories that included rectangles, squares, cones, triangles, and arches. A Polaroid camera, a tape recorder, and videotaping equipment were also used to collect data.

RESULTS

Differences in processes used by girls and boys were analyzed by examining mean scores of dyad play in terms of the dependent variables: play level, block play, and communication. A look at the data suggests differences between girls and boys in the areas of play level, block play, and communication, with the greatest differences in the area of block play and the smallest differences occurring in play level (see Figures 5.1–5.3).

In order to know if observed differences were greater than would be expected due to chance, mean scores were analyzed (see Table 5.1). In the analyses, block play complexity was examined in terms of the dependent variables—play level (PL), block play (BP), and communication (C). A between-factors multivariate analysis of variance (MANOVA) design was used to analyze the data. Prior to

Figure 5.1
Play level.

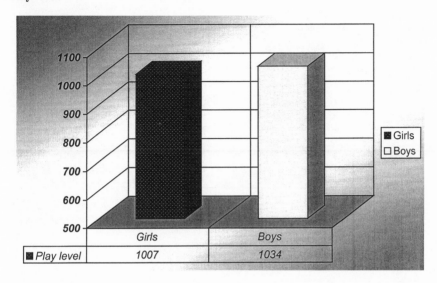

Figure 5.2
Block play complexity.

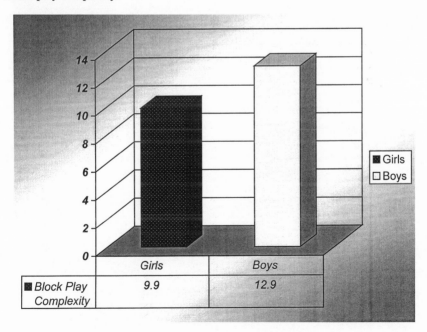

Figure 5.3
Communication.

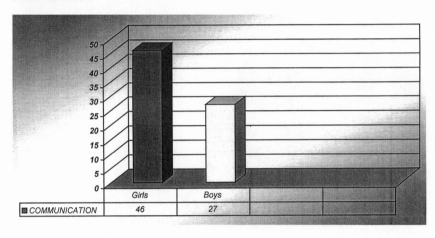

Table 5.1
Means and Standard Deviations of Play Behaviors for Girls and Boys

	M	*S*
Play level		
Girls	1007	66
Boys	1034	66
Block play complexity		
Girls	9.921	.92
Boys	12.91	.92
Communication		
Girls	46	6.07
Boys	27.75	6.07

Table 5.2
Multivariate Analysis of Variance for the Effects of Sex

Source	df	F	p
Sex	3,20	8.58	.0008 **

* $p < .05$ ** $p < .01$

Table 5.3
Univariate Analysis of Variance for the Effects of Sex on Play Level, Block Play Complexity, and Communication

Source	df	F	p
Play level	1,22	1.09	.17
Blocks	1,22	5.26	.03*
Comm.	1,22	4.51	.04*

* $p < .05$ ** $p < .01$

the analyses, the assumptions of, MANOVA, that is, homogeneity, normality, and independence of data collection—were satisfied. All analyses were conducted at an alpha level of .05.

Block Play Complexity among Boys and Girls

An overall MANOVA for gender indicated significant differences in the way boys and girls play with blocks, $F (3,20) = 8.58$, $p < .0008$ (see Table 5.2).

To further understand the source of variance, an ANOVA was conducted on each of the dependent variables (play level, block play, and communication). The manner in which girls and boys played with blocks was significantly different, $F (1,22) = 5.26$, $p < .03$. In addition, there was a significant difference in the communication that occurred in the dyads of girls and boys, $F (1,22) = 4.51$, $p < .04$. However, there was no significant difference in level of play between boys and girls, $F (1,22) = 1.09$, $p < .17$ (see Table 5.3). Thus, variations among girls and boys resulted from differences in how they played with blocks and talked to each other, not their play level.

DISCUSSION AND CONCLUSIONS

Based on these results, we must conclude that differences exist in the way girls and boys play with same-sex peers during block play. That is, when play level, block play, and communication were considered together, differences in the way girls and boys play with each other were statistically significant. These results support earlier studies that reported differences in the way girls and boys play with blocks (Erikson, 1951; Goodfader, 1982; Gura, 1992). To further understand the findings of the study, play level, block play, and communication are examined separately.

Play Level

Girls and boys in this study displayed similar play levels during play with same-sex peers. This finding provides support for those of other studies that have been completed in this area (Ausch, 1994; Honig & Lim, 1993). One concern is that these results may have been influenced by the setting. Group play was impossible since there were only two children and games with rules were virtually impossible. This was a limiting factor in interpreting the children's play level.

Girls

Girls spent more time engaged in conversations before beginning to use blocks. Though different, their interactions with each other were not unlike those of boys. Even when their goal was different, they interacted with each other to accomplish their goal in ways that resembled those demonstrated by the boys in this study.

Boys

Most of the boys initiated solitary block play on an individual basis but then involved the other partner by the end of the session. In many of the sessions, boys would appear to build their structures separately, then they would intersect their blocks with the other person's blocks. In several instances, the integration of blocks did not occur but an integration of stories or themes did.

Block Play

Differences were found in the way girls and boys played with blocks. Boys used more complex techniques during block building. This supports and extends past findings by Beeson and Williams (1979), Erikson (1951), and Rubin (1977). An interesting aspect of this study is that these results may reflect the amount of block play that the children engaged in prior to engaging in the play session. Although all centers had similar block play areas, the previous use of these materials by the children was not controlled for. Given that familiarity with materials affects block play, this may have influenced the findings (Rogers, 1985; Rubin, 1977). Future studies may need to consider this factor.

Girls

The girls who entered the classroom setting were given the same directions as the boys. Girls, in general, did not go straight to the block area. They engaged in conversations about clothes, shoes, earrings, and hair bows. After initial conversations, they moved to the block area. Initial entry rituals may have affected the complexity of their block structures. This is an area that warrants further investigation as well.

Symbolism also affected the complexity scores of girls in the same way as boys. One unusual episode may provide an example of how symbolism influenced the block play scores of girls. After their initial conversations were completed, the pair began building structures on the table. They carried the blocks from the shelves to the table. After two trips, the adult indicated that they were not restricted to table play and could use the blocks anywhere. They ignored the statement (which was given only to clarify options), and continued to build on the table. They commented on how great it was that no blocks were on the floor. Even when the table was full, they built structures on the chairs and then on other tables. They talked throughout the process of the superiority of their block play because they were not on the floor. When questioned about the block structures, they both indicated separately that they were just building with blocks. Their conversations reflect this view. One comment captured on video, "Look at how well these big blocks fit." Certainly, these were blocks and only blocks to these two girls. Differences in block play may have resulted as much from pretense as from spatial relationships.

Boys

When boys entered the room, they were invited to play with the blocks. Most of the boys in this study went straight to the blocks and immediately started playing with the blocks. This continued throughout the session. Their enthusiasm for block play may have contributed to the complexity of their structures. Boys in this study received higher raw scores on block play than girls. When Erikson studied block play, he looked only at spatial relationships (e.g., towerness or enclosures). In this study, symbolism was included as a component of block play. This may help explain the higher scores that boys received in all areas of block play. Though it was anticipated that their block structures would be complex, the symbolism in their stories was unexpected. For example, one dyad built a structure on the floor that appeared to be very simple from a spatial relationship perspective. When each boy discussed his construction later, each individually told amazing stories about "the dinosaur in Jurassic Park." One dyad engaged in pulling blocks out of the shelves and walking on the blocks for the entire play session. When questioned, they both told wonderful stories about their magical kingdom. Including symbolism as well as dimensionality and hierarchical integration enhanced our knowledge of the child's ability to use blocks to represent the world.

Undoubtedly, including these three dimensions provided a more accurate profile of the action and thought that occurred during block play.

Communication

Differences were also found in the way boys and girls communicated with same-sex playmates. Girls used more frequent and complex conversation. Again, this was not unexpected. Past studies of communication patterns have found differences in the way girls and boys talk to each other (Jones & Glen, 1991).

Girls

Girls used more frequent, complex communication patterns during block play. This started when they entered and, for most pairs, continued throughout the session. One representative sample involves two girls who built one house but had two very different goals. One child started placing the blocks in the form of an enclosure so that they could act out Little Red Riding Hood. The other child followed the lead during the block-building part. When the initiator wanted the other child to pretend to be the Mommy, that child said she was a "real" mommy and had to go to work. The conversation that ensued was both complex and at some points loud. At the end, the initiator tried to convince the second child to do both stories but she refused and never entered the story script. Quite a few communicative strategies were used as these two negotiated the direction of the play script. This scenario illustrates the uniqueness of their communicative strategies reflected in their scores.

Boys

Overall, the communication strategies used by boys were different from those used by girls. Most of the boys did not engage in initial conversations but, rather, made a beeline for the blocks and continued to build throughout the session. Their communication strategies were infrequent. For example, two boys who came in together started removing all 365 blocks from the shelves. One boy suggested that they should find out if this was acceptable. When permission was assured, they continued until every block was pulled from the shelves and placed in a pile on the floor. Upon the removal of the last block from the shelf, the initiator said, "I'll be the king and you follow me." The other child replied, "I won't. I'm the king." At that point, the initiator followed the other child as they walked over to the blocks. They pointed to each block and named countries, "Japan," "Africa." Since they spoke very few words during the 30-minute session, their communication scores were low. In contrast, their block play complexity scores were very high due to the level of symbolism. If their shared intentions had been factored in, these children would have also scored very high on communication. Examining these data in terms of intersubjectivity may add additional insight into their play.

CONCLUSION

Overall, these findings are in line with those of prior studies (Erikson, 1951; Goodfader, 1987; Tracy, 1987). Specific differences were found in the way boys and girls play with blocks when social/cognitive play behaviors, block play, and communication were considered as a single entity. Additional analyses indicated that (1) boys and girls engaged in social interactions that were similar when only solitary or associative play are considered; (2) boys engaged in more complex block play than girls during play in same-sex dyads; and (3) girls used more complex and frequent communication strategies during play in same-sex dyads.

These findings acknowledge the reality of sex-related play behaviors of young children in child-care settings. Playing with unfamiliar peers ensured that differences between centers were not the focus of the study. Children from six different centers displayed the same kinds of sex-related differences during play. Still, boys had a definitive interest in playing with blocks and this resulted in more complex block structures. If complex building with blocks is related to problem solving and other mathematical skills, then a concerted effort must be made to either interest girls in block play or ensure that these skills are enhanced in other ways that are more interesting to young girls.

Further, sex-related strengths were evident as indicated in the previous example. Girls were more adept in communication than boys. If language and literacy skills are related to language usage and development, then it is imperative that boys are encouraged to engage in dialogue or that we find other ways to involve them in language development activities that are interesting to them. For example, the two young boys who did not talk clearly used communication strategies that were nonverbal. In fact, these may be akin to games with rules because they certainly had unspoken rules in place. How can we extend their communication strategies to include a variety of techniques?

Finally, the question of the value of this laboratory study must be considered. Recently, scholars have begun to focus on the value of naturalistic observations for fully understanding social interactions during play (Göncü, 1999). Although naturalistic observations offer valuable insight into children's play this study is worthwhile because it establishes the existence of sex-related differences in the way girls and boys play with same-sex peers during block play. Additional studies conducted in naturalistic settings can increase our understanding of sex-related differences in block play.

REFERENCES

Ausch, L. (1994). Gender comparisons of young children's social interaction in cooperative play activity. *Sex Roles, 31*(3/4), 225–239.

Beeson, B.S., & Williams, R.A. (1979). *A study of sex stereotyping in child-selected play activities of pre-school children.* Muncie, IN: Ball State University. (ERIC Document Reproduction Service No. ED 186102).

Black, B. (1989). Interactive pretense: Social and symbolic skills in preschool play groups. *Merrill-Palmer Quarterly, 35*, 370–397.

Budd, D.E., Clance, P.R., & Simerly, D.E. (1985). Spatial configurations: Erikson re-examined. *Sex Roles, 12*(5/6), 571–577.

Christie, J., & Johnson, P. (1987). Reconceptualizing constructive play: A review of the empirical literature. *Merrill-Palmer Quarterly, 33*(4), 439–452.

Cohen, J. (1960). A coefficient of agreement for nominal scales. *Educational and Psychological Measurement, 20*, 37–46.

Conrad, A. (1995). *Content analysis of block play literature.* (ERIC Reproduction Document Service, No. ED 382 357).

Eaton, W. O., & Enns, L.R. (1986). Sex differences in human motor activity level. *Psychological Bulletin, 100*, 19–28.

Erikson, E. (1951). Sex differences in the play configurations of pre-adolescents. *American Journal of Orthopsychiatry, 21*, 247–256.

Farver, J. A. (1992). Communicating shared meaning in social pretend play. *Early Childhood Research Quarterly, 7*, 501–516.

Göncü, A. (1999). *Children's engagement in the world: Sociocultural perspectives.* Cambridge, UK: Cambridge University Press.

Goodfader, R.A. (1982). Sex differences in the play constructions of pre-school children. *Smith College Studies in Social Work, 52*(2), 129–144.

Guanella, F.M. (1934). Block building activities of young children. *Archives of Psychology, 174*, 1–92.

Gura, P. (1992). *Exploring learning: Young children and block play.* London: Paul Chapman.

Honig, A., & Lim, S.E. (1993, August). *Singapore preschoolers' play in relation to social class, sex, and setting.* Paper presented at the 101st annual conference of the American Psychological Association, Toronto, Ontario, Canada.

Howes, C., & Farver, J. (1987). Social pretend play in 2-year-olds: Effects of age of partner. *Early Childhood Research Quarterly, 2*, 305–314.

Jones, A., & Glen, S. M. (1991). Gender differences in pretend play in a primary school group. *Early Child Development and Care, 77*, 127–135.

Maccoby, E.E. (1988). Gender as a social category. *Developmental Psychology, 24*, 755–765.

Mounts, N., & Roopnarine, J. (1987). Social-cognitive play patterns in same-age and mixed-age preschool classrooms. *American Educational Research Journal, 24*(3), 463–476.

Pellegrini, A. D., & Boyd, B. (1993). The role of play in early childhood development and education: Issues in definition and function. In B. Spodek (Ed.), *Handbook of research on the education of young children* (pp. 337–351). New York: Macmillan.

Pitcher, A., & Schultz, D. (1983). *Boys and girls at play.* New York: Praeger.

Reifel, S., & Greenfield, P. (1982). Structural development in symbolic medium: The representational use of block constructions. In G. Forman (Ed.), *Action and thought: From sensorimotor schemes to symbolic operations* (pp. 203–233). New York: Academic Press.

Rogers, D. L. (1985). Relationships of block play and the social development of young children. *Early Child Development and Care, 20*, 245–261.

Rubin, K. H. (1977). The social and cognitive value of preschool toys and activities. *Canadian Journal of Behavioral Science, 9*, 382–385.

Rubin, K. H. (1989). *The Play Observation Scale*. Waterloo, Ontario, Canada: University of Waterloo.

Tegano, D., Lookabaugh, S., May, G., & Burdette, M. (1991). Constructive play and problem solving: The role of structure and time in the classroom. *Early Child Development and Care, 68*, 27–35.

Tracy, D. M. (1987). Toys, spatial ability, and science and mathematics achievement: Are they related? *Sex Roles, 17*(3/4), 115–142.

Vygotsky, L. S. (1978). *Mind in society: The development of higher psychological processes*. Cambridge, MA: Harvard University Press. (Original work published 1932)

6

Play of Language-Minority Children in an Early Childhood Setting

Mellisa A. Clawson

The play of young children has received a significant amount of attention in recent years and is considered by many to be an integral part of development. Play is a component of various theoretical frameworks and has been linked to several developmental domains. Piaget, for example, incorporated play in his cognitive developmental theory, suggesting that play behaviors reflect changes in intelligence and progress from individual to social (Nicolopoulou, 1993). Research supports Piaget's notion that children's play becomes more social with development (Howes & Matheson, 1992), and measures of children's play (see Howes, 1980; Parten, 1932) also reflect this progression. Solitary play, in which a child plays apart from peers and typically is focused on his/her own activity, is located at the lower end of the play spectrum. At the in-between levels, children engage in varying degrees of attending to and participating in peers' activities. The highest levels of play are characterized by social interaction and pretense.

Play often is used as an index of children's social competence. Successful play requires certain social skills, such as peer entry, monitoring others' responses, and reading verbal and nonverbal cues (Creasey, Jarvis, & Berk, 1998). Children who display these skills tend to be regarded by teachers and peers as more socially competent (Connolly & Doyle, 1984). Play not only reflects social competence but also promotes it. Play with peers can provide a safe context for children to develop conflict-management skills, intimacy, and role taking (Creasey et al., 1998). Social pretend play in particular may have implications for children's developing social competence. Compared to nonpretend social activities, social pretend play is characterized by more positive affect, longer duration of play, higher levels of social interaction, greater compliance with other children's directives, and increased reciprocity (Connolly, Doyle, & Reznick, 1988).

Play is also related to language development. Linguistic skills, such as verbally recruiting play partners, joining a group appropriately, understanding the responses of other children, and enacting play themes, are required for play with others (Creasey et al., 1998). Social pretend play involves verbal communication in order to negotiate roles, transform objects and locations, and enact pretend scenarios (Garvey & Kramer, 1989). It is also likely that play interactions with peers are a means for enhancing language. That is, children's talk during play is a salient source of language input, given its contextualized and repetitive qualities (Logan, 1991).

Given the relations between language and play, it is possible that language-minority children are at a disadvantage in terms of having complex play interactions with peers. Children for whom English is a second language (ESL) exist in what Roopnarine and Johnson (1994) refer to as a "culturally discontinuous context"; that is, these children live in families disenfranchised from the dominant society. ESL children may have little exposure to English prior to entering an early childhood or elementary school setting, and for many, the school environment provides no support in their primary language, although they are expected to perform as well as peers who are fluent English speakers (Cox & Boyd-Batstone, 1997).

Much of the research on language-minority children focuses on strategies for facilitating English language and literacy skills in elementary school. Some methods shown to be successful include provision of texts, reading and writing activities, read-at-home projects, interaction with teachers, and collaborative projects with peers (Han & Ernst-Slavit, 1999). Early childhood settings also can serve as environments for ESL children to learn English. The early childhood classroom allows the language-minority child to come into contact with English-speaking peers who can provide linguistic input that is representative of English as it is spoken by young children (Fillmore, 1991). Rodriguez, Diaz, Duran, and Espinosa (1995) found that ESL children enrolled in a bilingual preschool gained proficiency in English at a faster rate than children who stayed home during the day. The preschool program incorporated a cognitively oriented curriculum in which many opportunities for interactions with adults and peers were provided throughout the day.

In many early childhood environments, however, language-minority children may have fewer and less complex interactions with their English-speaking peers. Interviews with teachers in multicultural nursery schools yielded reports that ESL children did not interact or play with their European, English-speaking peers (Ogilvy, Boath, Cheyne, Jahoda, & Schaffer, 1990). Teachers also mentioned ESL children's preference for same-language peers. In one school where there was a large kinship group of Pakistani children, a teacher stated, "They don't need an English speaker; they just talk to each other" (p. 5).

The teachers' conclusions are congruent with empirical observations of ESL children. In a study of children of Mexican American migrant farm workers attending Head Start, Logan (1991) found that language-minority children actively pursued solitary play and resisted play overtures from their English-speaking peers. Social pretend play took place within rather than between the two language groups. Moreover, attempts by English speakers to initiate or join in pretend play were nearly always met with rejection. ESL children overtly refused access to the interaction, ignored, or moved away from English-speaking peers.

Similarly, Wall and Pickert (1982) found that ESL children showed lower levels of group play and higher levels of solitary and parallel play compared to their English-speaking peers. After a period of six months, however, ESL children functioned at similar play levels. Furthermore, complexity of ESL children's language was positively related to play level. That is, as ESL children's language became more complex, their play became more socially oriented.

Hadley and Schuele (1995) observed children's verbal interactions during free play over a period of four semesters. During the first semester of enrollment, ESL children interacted only with adults in the classroom. They directed no initiations to their peers and avoided play interactions with them. Although the rate of ESL children's verbal initiations and interactions with English-speaking peers increased over the four-semester period, it was not until the fourth semester that ESL children began to approximate the initial rates (i.e., first semester of enrollment) for English-speaking children's peer interactions.

Whereas the previous studies suggest that ESL children avoid play with their English-speaking peers, some evidence suggests that the latter group limits its interactions with the former. Tabors (1987, as cited in Tabors & Snow, 1994), for example, found that English-speaking preschoolers chose to play with linguistically similar peers until language-minority classmates could communicate in English.

Taken together, the results of the studies described above suggest that the play of language-minority children is segregated from that of their English-speaking peers. The ESL child who is the only speaker of his/her language in a classroom may be especially likely to engage in solitary play. It may be that the "language barrier" precludes complex play with English-speaking children. If several ESL children who speak the same language are in a classroom together, then opportunities for more complex play may be more frequent. Whether it is language-minority children who avoid contact with English-speaking peers or vice versa, the lack of interaction between the two groups limits social and language-learning opportunities. That is, second language learning children have to wait to develop friendships with English-speaking children and become involved in social activities, such as pretend play, that require a common language (Tabors, 1987, as cited in Tabors & Snow, 1994).

The present study is a qualitative approach to the play experiences of language-minority children attending a university-based laboratory preschool. Four questions were of interest. First, in what types of play do ESL children engage? Next, how do ESL children play with peers within and between language groups? Third, how does the social play of ESL children with English-speaking peers change over time? Lastly, what do teachers do to facilitate the play interactions of children between language groups?

METHOD

Fieldwork was conducted over a three-month period in one classroom at a university-based laboratory school. This particular classroom served children ranging in age from 37 to 48 months ($M = 43$ months) at the time of enrollment into the program. Eight English-speaking (3 female) and 6 ESL children (2 female) were enrolled. Of the latter group, 4 spoke Arabic (1 female), 1 spoke Korean (female), and 1 spoke Malay. Two of the boys who spoke Arabic were siblings, as were two of the English-speaking boys. Although no formal assessments were conducted of children's language, the lead teacher reported that all ESL children entered the lab school with very low English proficiency.

As in similar early childhood programs, the laboratory school has a threefold mission: (1) it serves as a site for student training in child development and early childhood education; (2) it provides a setting for research and inquiry in child development and early childhood education; and (3) it is a model program for local, state, and national early childhood communities (McBride, 1996). Lead teachers are graduate students enrolled in child development, and several undergraduate students complete their teaching requirements at the lab school each semester. The school serves primarily children of faculty, staff, and students affiliated with the university. In the classroom under investigation, the supervising teacher was Latina and spoke both English and Spanish fluently. The three student teachers all were European-American females completing a course requirement. Most children attended the lab school four half-days per week, although four were present for only two days per week.

The classroom was arranged with different learning centers, including reading, block, computer, home living, and art areas. A large rug was located in the center of the classroom and served as a setting for large group activities. An area for sociodramatic play was designated, and materials included in this setting rotated every few weeks depending on the theme. During the observational period, themes included "grocery store," in which a toy cash register and food-related items were available for play, and "camping," in which a colorful tent and a sleeping bag were available. The room was decorated with children's art and printed posters depicting children from different cultural groups. Also available for children's use were culturally diverse books and dolls.

I attended the classroom twice per week over a three-month period. Most observations were conducted through a one-way mirrored observation booth, although on six occasions, I was located inside the classroom due to problems with the sound system. As an observer, I did not participate in the class, assist with caregiving, or serve a disciplinary or advisory role. When children asked me about my presence, I stated that I was there to learn about how children played. Observations were conducted during the 60- to 90-minute free-play period, in which children were allowed to play in any of the activity areas and select their own playmates. Children could begin free play upon their arrival to the lab school.

I observed each ESL child for 30 minutes on at least four different visits. Because the focus of the study was play with peers, often an observation of one particular child provided data concerning other children as well. Field notes were written and audio-recorded, and later transcribed. Observations began three weeks into the fall semester, which marked the beginning of enrollment for children at the lab school, and continued until the end of the same semester.

RESULTS AND DISCUSSION

Over the course of observation, language-minority children demonstrated a variety of types of play, and there were marked individual differences in the frequencies with which children engaged in play types. Play interactions were largely segregated by language during the first month of observation, and ESL children who were the only speakers of their language in the class tended to engage in less social play than their English-speaking peers. However, by the middle of the second month of observation, more interactions between language groups were occurring. Additionally, teachers became more active in facilitating interactions. Individual differences in ESL children's contacts with their English-speaking peers were evident throughout the observational period.

Types of Play Demonstrated by Language-Minority Children

Transcripts were examined in order to identify different types of play exhibited by language-minority children. The categories of play were derived from the Revised Peer Play Scale (Howes & Matheson, 1992) and include: solitary, in which the child does not play or interact near or with peers; parallel, which occurs when the child plays near and engages in the same activity as peers but does not acknowledge them; parallel aware, in which a child is engaged in the same activity and exchanges a smile or eye contact with peer(s); simple social, occurring when children engage in the same type of activity and direct social bids to each other; complementary-reciprocal, which involves children engaging in play with role reversals; and social pretend play, occurring in pretend play when children enact complementary roles. These categories of play are consid-

Table 6.1
Frequencies of Types of Play for ESL Children

| | ESL Children's Identifiers, Native Language, and Gender | | | | | |
| | "M" | "R" | "A" | "H" | "L" | "T" |
	Arabic/m	Arabic/m	Arabic/m	Arabic/f	Korean/f	Malay/m
Type of Play						
Solitary	1	2	2	5	4	9
	(4%)	(7%)	(7%)	(28%)	(21%)	(56%)
Parallel	2	2	3	2	5	4
	(8%)	(7%)	(11%)	(11%)	(26%)	(25%)
Parallel Aware	4	5	4	4	5	3
	(16%)	(19%)	(14%)	(22%)	(26%)	(19%)
Simple Social	5	7	6	3	4	0
	(20%)	(26%)	(21%)	(17%)	(21%)	
Complementary-	8	7	8	2	1	0
reciprocal	(32%)	(26%)	(29%)	(11%)	(5%)	
Social Pretend	5	4	5	2	0	0
	(20%)	(15%)	(18%)	(11%)		

ered mutually exclusive and lie on a continuum from least to most interactive and competent.

The frequencies and proportions of the types of play demonstrated by each ESL child are provided in Table 6.1. These data indicate marked individual differences in children's involvement with each type of play. The first three children, "M," "R," and "A," all of whom were male and spoke Arabic, demonstrated all six play levels. Much of their play occurred at the level of parallel aware or higher, which according to Howes (1997) is interactive peer play.

Furthermore, nearly half of their play was complementary-reciprocal or social pretend, which are considered the most competent and complex forms of play with peers (Howes, 1997). As will be discussed in the following section, the play of "M," "R," and "A" most often was with each other. It is likely that their common language and familiarity with each other contributed to their advanced play behaviors.

"H," the only female who spoke Arabic, also demonstrated all six play levels, although lower levels of complex play than the male speakers of her language. The remaining ESL children, "L" and "T," both the only speakers of their language in the classroom, appeared to have relatively more limited and less interactive play repertoires. ESL children, particularly when they are the only speakers of their language in a classroom, are more likely to engage in less interactive types of play for various reasons. They may be interested and willing to play with others, but are unable to do so because the language demands are too great (Heath & Chin, 1985). Solitary play also may result from the resistance of language-minority children to approaches by English-speaking peers; that is, the ESL child may wish to remain alone and therefore chooses activities that avoid involvement with others (Logan, 1991). Less interactive types of play, such as solitary, parallel, and parallel aware, allow children greater control of their involvement with others (Logan, 1991). A sense of control over one's social environment may be especially important for language-minority children whose cultural beliefs, values, and cultures may differ in significant ways from other children and adults in the classroom. It is likely that the early childhood environment introduces the ESL child to situations that question or disregard the knowledge they have used in the past to interpret experiences and guide their behavior (Grant, 1995). A child might respond to the discrepancy by limiting his/her interactive behavior with peers. A final consideration is that there may be cultural differences in the value for and engagement in certain types of play (Roopnarine, Lasker, Sacks, & Stores, 1998). For example, if pretend play is not encouraged within the child's family and culture, it is not likely that it will be demonstrated in the early childhood setting.

Caution should be used in interpreting these data for several reasons. First, the Howes and Matheson (1992) measure was not actually implemented; rather, their classification scheme has been used to identify the types of play evident from the qualitative transcripts. Additionally, the frequencies are the sum total of each type of play over the three-month observation period. As such, they do not reflect changes over time in each child's play (although such changes may exist, as demonstrated by qualitative data to be presented in a later section). Lastly, because of my own unfamiliarity with the native languages of the ESL children, I found it necessary at times to classify children's play based on their nonverbal behaviors. This may have resulted in underestimating the occurrence of social pretend play, particularly if I did not understand any language pertaining to roles, themes, or pretense.

Segregation by Language Group

The three boys who spoke Arabic played in close proximity to each other and engaged in social pretend play throughout the semester. During one early observation:

All three boys are standing at the water table and conversing in Arabic. Their conversation seems related to their play with dinosaur figures. The theme of their play involves dinosaurs growling, chasing, and splashing one another. They make the dinosaurs "talk" using motions. It appears that one of the boys is giving directives to his peers about the play. He continues to speak Arabic but no longer moves his dinosaurs. After his comment, the three boys resume the same play.

Some evidence suggests that ESL children prefer to play using their native language (Klee, 1988). This preference may manifest itself in selecting linguistically similar playmates. When other speakers of their language are available, children can more easily engage in the complex interactions required for social pretend play. It may be more challenging and less rewarding to play with linguistically different peers. During the same observation:

"K" (who speaks English), approaches the water table. He stands at the table and watches the three boys play. None of the three look at him, and their conversation continues in Arabic. After several minutes, one boy points to a far corner of the room and makes a comment. All three boys then run to another learning center.

The boys who spoke Arabic may have moved away in order to control their social involvement. That is, children avoid play with those peers whose behaviors do not contribute to the communal construction of shared activities (Logan, 1991). The boys may have assumed "K" could not fully participate in their pretense, and rather than accommodate him in their play, they chose to relocate.

Compared to the boys described above, the other three language-minority children engaged in less complex play. Interestingly, the one female who spoke Arabic, "H," never approached her same-language male peers, and they never approached her to play. Previous research suggests that preschool-age children are more likely to interact with same-sex peers rather than opposite sex peers (Goldman, 1981). Despite sharing a first language, the gender difference may have been an obstacle to playing together. Early in the semester, nearly all of "H's" play was solitary or with one of the classroom teachers. She typically sat on the rug in the center of the room until a teacher guided her to an activity. For example:

"H" has been sitting on the rug for several minutes. One of the student teachers approaches her and says, "Let's go read a book together." "H" follows the teacher to the reading corner, and together they look at a picture book. Twice during the story, "H" points to a picture and says a word in Arabic. She appears to be naming the object in the picture, and the student teacher repeats what "H" has said. The student teacher is called to another area of the room. "H" remains in the reading corner alone and begins stacking books from smallest to largest.

"H" demonstrated a preference for interacting with adults, and if a teacher was not available, "H" would engage in solitary play rather than approach a peer. She also occasionally spoke in her native language, directing a few words to a teacher, as in the above observation, or using private speech during her own activities. It is common for ESL children to use their home languages even in second-language situations (Tabors & Snow, 1994). Because the teachers were receptive to her use of Arabic, "H" may have felt more comfortable interacting with them than with her peers. It also may have been easier for "H" to understand the English conversations that teachers had with her. Adults adjust the complexity of their speech with children by considering the child's level of comprehension and using words and sentences in social contexts (Snow, 1989). In contrast, conversations between children, even within the same language, are challenging due to differences in background, knowledge about a particular topic, and less developed communication skills (Hadley & Schuele, 1995).

The other two language-minority children self-selected activities that could be pursued alone, such as puzzles, painting, or the computer. They differed, however, in terms of their interest in peers. "L," who was the only speaker of Korean in the classroom, frequently observed the play of other children, while "T," the only child who spoke Malay, preferred to play alone at the computer.

"M" and "R" (both English-speaking females) join "L" at the art table. "L" watches them create a picture and listens to them talk and laugh as they draw. She does not make any overtures to participate, nor do the girls extend an invitation to her.

As he has done on most days, "T" spends most of his time playing a game on the computer. Toward the end of the free-play period, "C" (an English-speaking male) approaches him and says, "I want to play, too." "T" does not respond, so "C" uses his body to push "T" out of the chair. "T" uses his hands to push the other child, who then calls for a teacher.

In the first observation, "L" was engaged in her own art activity, but she also was keenly aware of the interaction occurring between her peers. Tabors (1987, as cited in Tabors & Snow, 1994) refers to this behavior as "spectating," which is the active observation by ESL children when they are in proximity to English speakers and focusing on the language being used. While it seems passive in that no verbal interaction between the language-minority child and others occurs, spectating is a useful strategy for learning English as well as for becoming familiar with peers. It may have been especially effective early in the semester when "L" was still adjusting to a new language and social environment. "T's" strategy was quite different; he chose an activity that offered little opportunity for peer interaction. When approached by an English-speaking peer, "T" may not have understood what was said. However, his nonresponse could have been interpreted as social rejection. Young children do not necessarily understand that their ESL peers may not comprehend words said in English (Tabors & Snow, 1994), and may therefore view a nonresponse negatively. On the other hand, "T" may have purposefully ignored the other child as a means of controlling his own social involvement (Logan, 1991). That is, he wished to play alone.

Increases in Play between Language Groups

As the semester progressed, play interactions increased across language groups. The three boys who spoke Arabic, who at first were a very closed group, became more open to their English-speaking peers, joining them in play activities. The boys often played a chase game, during which they continued speaking in Arabic, presumably about the roles of who was to chase and who was to be chased. On one occasion:

The chase game has become louder and less role-specific after several minutes. It appears that one of the boys is pretending to be a "monster," adjusting his posture and voice accordingly. "K" and "C" (both English-speaking males) are attempting to join the game—"K" by becoming a "monster" himself and "C" by positioning himself to be chased. Both are accepted by the original three boys.

The English-speaking children were included by the ESL boys without verbal negotiation or teacher intervention, and at times, the play evolved to where all the children involved would use English to say each other's names or give simple instructions (e.g., "Hide here!"). It appears, then, that over time members of both language groups may become relatively more open to play with the other. The English speakers may have been inclined to play due to the increased English proficiency on the part of the ESL children (Tabors, 1987, as cited in Tabors & Snow, 1994). On the other hand, the "monster" play may have served as a social magnet (Strandell, 1997). That is, this type of play, being loud and active, attracted the English-speaking children.

At other times the boys who spoke Arabic required a prompt from a teacher before opening their play to others.

The boys are using measuring cups to transfer styrofoam peanuts between two buckets. They talk to each other in Arabic, although whether they are discussing a pretend scenario or giving directives is unclear. "R" (an English-speaking female) observes them for about a minute, then asks, "Can I do it?" The boys ignore her. The lead teacher intervenes, first by giving "R" a measuring cup, then by reminding the boys of the rule, "We take turns." The teacher supervises by identifying whose turn it is, and "R," the teacher, and the three boys take turns transferring the peanuts.

A difference existed between the "monster" and peanut activities in terms of the boys' receptiveness to the involvement of English-speaking peers in their play.

The language requirements of each type of play may be different. While "monster" involves the complex play features of pretense and complementary roles, the theme is readily identifiable. Moreover, children can negotiate the play features by altering paralinguistic features or nonverbal signals rather than using language per se (i.e., when a child begins growling, he is indicating that he has assumed the role of the monster). Play with the peanuts, however, may have been part of a theme that was not clear to outsiders or that was relatively more elaborate (e.g., cooking, restaurant, or mealtime), thereby requiring explicit discussion of roles (Garvey & Kramer, 1989). Because the verbal requirement could not be met when the teacher and "R" joined the activity, the play with peanuts lost the social pretend qualities it had when only the Arabic-speaking boys were involved.

Over time the play of "L" (the only child who spoke Korean) was characterized by more complex interactions with English-speaking peers. She demonstrated an interest in peers early in the semester, as evidenced by high levels of parallel play. Some evidence suggests that parallel play predicts future engagement in social play (Bakeman & Brownlee, 1980). In the case of "L," by the third month of observation, she was making social overtures to peers and engaging in simple social play, characterized by low-level interactions, such as giving and receiving of objects and smiling (Howes & Matheson, 1992). On one occasion:

"K" (an English-speaking boy) is building a road using small blocks. "L," who also is in the block center, notices his activity and begins handing him blocks to use in his construction. He accepts her offers, and the road becomes quite long. After the road is built, "K" repeatedly rolls a toy car on it. As the car rolls, he and "L" look at each other and laugh. No language is used throughout the interaction.

The block play described above did not have the qualities of social pretend play, although this may have been due to the nature of the activity. Some activities involve props that have clear uses (e.g., dishes), so verbal negotiation is not a prerequisite for pretense. In contrast, engaging in pretend play with blocks would require language in order to establish a common meaning (French, Lucariello, Seidman, & Nelson, 1985). The language difference between the two children, therefore, may have precluded more sophisticated play.

Teacher Facilitation

As the semester progressed, teachers more frequently facilitated interactions between language-minority and English-speaking children and used various strategies in order to do so. During an interaction with "H," who continued to display a preference for adults throughout the semester, a student teacher tried to heighten interest in other children:

"H" and "M" are sitting at the art table with one of the student teachers. The teacher remarks to "H," "Do you see the pretty picture that 'M' is painting?" "H" looks at "M's" picture, then returns to her own painting.

Comments such as this were useful insofar as encouraging "H" to look at other children, but they did not facilitate her interactions with others. When teachers proactively arranged play situations and/or recruited playmates, it was more effective:

"L" approaches a group (student teacher with three English-speaking children) seated on the floor playing a board game. "L" stands for several seconds on the periphery and watches the game. The student teacher says, "L would like to play with us. Where can she sit?" Two of the children make space for "L" on the floor.

The lead teacher and "R" (English-speaking female) are in the home living area. The teacher calls "H," who is seated alone on the rug, to "come help us make dinner." "H" joins the activity, and she and "R" pretend to cook and serve a meal.

The first observation demonstrates how a teacher can negotiate peer entry for an ESL child. The teacher interpreted "L's" hovering near the game as a request to join. In this case, the teacher was the voice for the request of this child (Urzua, 1989). Moreover, her statement may have served as a model for "L" to use in future peer entry situations. In the second scenario, the teacher recognized that if "H" were to play with other children, a theme would have to be identified. This strategy socializes both sides (the ESL and the English-speaking child) into appropriate behavior (Urzua, 1989). That is, both children adjust their behavior to fit the theme. The teacher continued to guide the children's play by asking them questions such as "Are you making rice?" and giving directives such as "Let's eat what 'R' made." Her comments further established the theme, and "H" was able to participate and enjoy the activity, even after the teacher left the home living area. It should be noted that the theme of the play was one that did not require advanced language skills. The children had similar knowledge of the roles and activities appropriate to the kitchen setting. Once the theme was established, the physical setting and props "afforded meanings" that corresponded to the knowledge that both children possessed (French et al., 1985).

Teachers often were involved as "T" (the only child who spoke Malay) became more interested in his peers. "T's" interest was particularly aroused when peers' play was loud and active.

"T" leaves his usual spot at the computer when he notices the activity of three boys (Arabic-speaking) in the tent. He does not watch the ongoing play of the boys, but instead runs over to the tent, jumps on the outside of it, and causes it to topple. The lead teacher pulls "T" off the tent and tells him to "Say you're sorry" to the other boys. "T" does not speak, but rather pulls away from her and runs back to the computer.

As the semester progressed, many of T's interactions with other children were like the one described above. His behavior often was disruptive of other children's activities and typically resulted in teacher intervention. However, during no observation did "T" use language—either Malay or English—with teachers or peers. Tabors and Snow (1994) suggest that many ESL children, when faced with a social situation in which their home language is not useful for communication, enter a period in which they do not talk at all. They will, however, find alternative ways of communicating with those around them. Nonverbal tactics, such as crying out, whimpering, gesturing, or otherwise attracting the attention of an adult, are common, particularly during the child's first few months in a new setting (Tabors, 1987, as cited in Tabors & Snow, 1994).

A transition occurred over time in teachers' responses to "T's" aggressive behavior with peers. Below are two observations, the first occurring in the third week of the semester, and the second occurring in the eighth week. In both, "T" arrives in the classroom and hurries to the computer, only to find another child already there. He uses physical strategies, such as trying to sit in the same chair as the other child and placing his hands on the keyboard, to gain access to the computer.

"M" (English-speaking female) ignores his efforts. "T" cries out, while continuing to use his physical strategies to acquire the computer. A student teacher says to him, "We have to share the computer, 'T.' " He doesn't respond, and continues his efforts. The teacher then says, " 'M,' let's let 'T' use the computer now. Why don't you come play blocks with me?"

"K" (English-speaking male) says, "No, it's my turn." "T" continues to push "K" out of the chair, and "K" retaliates by hitting. "T" immediately hits back, and "K" begins to cry. "T" also cries. The student teacher asks each child to tell her what happened. "K" says, "He hit me." "T" does not speak. The teacher then tells "T" to go sit by himself until he can tell her what happened.

Initially, teachers responded to "T" by suggesting prosocial solutions. If, as in the first scenario, he did not comply, the teacher altered the social situation by removing the offending peer. Over time, however, it appeared that teachers viewed "T" as the "problem." In the second scenario, "T" was presented with the impossible task of explaining what had happened. The transition in teachers' behaviors toward "T" may have been due to their expectations for an increase in his social and language abilities after two months in the classroom. Alternatively, they may have grown frustrated with "T's" nonverbal and often aggressive interactions. Teachers may react to the difficulty in communicating with ESL children by using higher levels of control and lower levels of responsiveness (Ogilvy, Boath, Cheyne, Jahoda, & Schaffer, 1992). However, children's language and social development is enhanced when teachers engage in interactions that are warm and meaningful (Clawson, 1996; McCartney, 1984). Neither of the above interventions was particularly effective. Rather, teachers should guide children in peer relationships and do so in ways other than mediating disagreements, using directive strategies, or solving the problem for them (Creasey et al., 1998).

CONCLUSIONS AND IMPLICATIONS

The results of this study suggest that language differences initially serve as barriers to social pretend play between language-minority and English-speaking children. Language-minority children were not deficient in terms of their play abilities. In fact, several of the children who had same-language peers in the classroom engaged in high levels of complex play. It is more likely that ESL children, particularly when they are the only speakers of their language in a classroom, do not have the English proficiency to join in or entice the play of their English-speaking peers. However, over time and with appropriate teacher intervention, language-minority children can and do engage in increasingly complex play with others.

Multiple speakers of a language in a classroom may seek each other out for play, thereby building a friendship, which itself facilitates more sophisticated play (Howes, Droege, & Matheson, 1994). In the current study, the three boys who spoke Arabic established a relationship in the classroom early, and their play was complex throughout the semester. For the children who do not have same-language peers (or in the case of "H," who was the only female speaker of Arabic), it may take longer for play with peers to occur. One question concerns whether children in the latter group are at any social risk due to their lower levels of interaction. Rubin and Coplan (1998) argue that a lack of peer interaction does not necessarily promote maladjustment. As in the Hadley and Schuele (1995) study, ESL children without language partners experienced high levels of interaction from teachers, which is known to promote children's language and social development (Clawson, 1996; McCartney, 1984). It also should be recognized that some children simply may be relatively more object- than people-oriented. Such children typically enjoy engaging in exploratory or constructive activity while playing alone (Rubin & Coplan, 1998). They excel in activities such as completing puzzles, creating artwork, reading, or, in the case of "T," working on the computer, although they do not perform as well in social tasks (Coplan, 1995; Coplan & Rubin, 1993). A preference for objects over people appears to be an individual difference that is manifested in solitary play. In contrast, some language-minority children, particularly "H" and "L," seemed quite interested in the activities of their English-speaking peers. They may have had a desire to play but were reticent to join the other children. Reticence may have been due to their limited English proficiency. It also should be noted, however, that in some cultures, children are encouraged to behave in ways that Westerners might consider reticent (Rubin & Coplan, 1998).

After two months into the semester, both groups of children appeared to be more receptive to play with the other. This was possibly due to increased English proficiency on the part of the ESL children, but unlikely, as they used very little English during the three months of observation. Many of the ESL children's play interactions with English-speaking peers simply did not require the use of language. Parallel, simple social, and even some types of social pretend play can be conducted without a common language. Despite the low levels of English produced, it is likely that the language-minority children learned English during their play encounters, as these provided access to fluent English-speaking models other than the teacher (Handscombe, 1989).

This study also highlights the importance of teachers' efforts to facilitate play interactions between ESL and English-speaking children. In early childhood settings free play often is used as an opportunity for children to engage in peer interactions without adult intervention. At the beginning of the semester, this was indeed the case. However, the results of this study suggest that free play may serve as a context in which linguistically different children choose to play separately from one another. Although segregated play meets the needs of these children for exercising control over their interactions (Logan, 1991), it does not promote the acquisition of English or higher levels of interaction between children. Therefore, it may be necessary for early childhood teachers to use "social engineering" strategies to facilitate play between the peer groups (Hirschler, 1991, as cited in Tabors & Snow, 1994). In the present study, teachers invited ESL children to join ongoing play situations. This strategy is useful in that the ESL child does not have to negotiate entry herself, and once in proximity to other children, she can hear the language being used and perhaps engage in the play interaction (Tabors, 1987, as cited in Tabors & Snow, 1994). Teachers also can encourage social pretend play by arranging small, integrated groups with toys that elicit pretense (Connolly et al., 1988).

A final but important issue concerns culture. The child's language reflects his culture, and culture influences the child's ideas about how to behave in educational settings and how to express oneself during play (Garcia, 1991). Whereas the teacher can play a critical role in facilitating the play encounters of ESL children with English-speaking peers, he/she must be mindful of cultural influences on play. The play of language-minority children may reflect aspects of the culture with which peers and teachers are unacquainted (Roopnarine & Johnson, 1994). For instance, some children may be uncomfortable with expressing their feelings during play (Alvarado, 1996). Additionally, some cultures value visual and experiential rather than verbal modes of learning. Children from these groups may prefer to learn through observation and practice, rather than through adults' verbal instructions or participation (Fillmore, 1991). Teachers also should be cautious about intervening in behavior they see as shy or passive because these qualities are encouraged in some cultures (Rubin & Coplan, 1998).

Children's play with peers is influenced by many factors, including the immediate setting, adults' and children's conceptualizations of play, and cultural beliefs relative to the meaning of play (Roopnarine & Johnson, 1994). The play of ESL children is a particularly complex phenomenon, as a language barrier may prevent them from certain types of play with English-speaking peers. However, given time in the early childhood environment and given appropriate opportunities for interaction, language-minority and English-speaking children can successfully engage in complex play with each other.

REFERENCES

Alvarado, C. (1996). Working with children whose home language is other than English: The teacher's role. *Child Care Information Exchange, 107,* 48–50.

Bakeman, R., & Brownlee, J. (1980). The strategic use of parallel play: A sequential analysis. *Child Development, 51,* 873–878.

Clawson, M. A. (1996, April). *Contributions of regulatable quality and teacher-child interaction to children's attachment security with day care teachers.* Paper presented at the biennial meeting of the Society for Research in Children Development, Washington D.C.

Connolly, J., & Doyle, A. (1984). Relation of social fantasy play to social competence in preschoolers. *Developmental Psychology, 20,* 797–806.

Connolly, J., Doyle, A., & Reznick, E. (1988). Social pretend play and social interaction in preschoolers. *Journal of Applied Developmental Psychology, 9,* 301–314.

Coplan, R. J. (1995). *Assessing multiple forms of nonsocial behaviors in a familiar setting: The development and validation of the Preschool Play Behavior Scale.* Poster presented at the Biennial Meeting for the Society for Research in Child Development, Indianapolis, IN.

Coplan, R. J., & Rubin, K. H. (1993). *Multiple forms of social withdrawal in young children: Reticence and solitary-passive behaviors.* Paper presented at the Biennial Meeting of the International Society for the Study of Behavioral Development, Recife, Brazil.

Cox, C., & Boyd-Batstone, P. (1997). *Crossroads: Literature and language in culturally and linguistically diverse classrooms.* Upper Saddle River, NJ: Merrill.

Creasey, G. L., Jarvis, P. A., & Berk, L. E. (1998). Play and social competence. In O. N. Saracho & B. Spodek (Eds.), *Multiple perspective on play in early childhood education* (pp. 116–143). Albany: State University of New York Press.

Fillmore, L. W. (1991). Language and cultural issues in the early education of language minority children. In S. L. Kagan (Ed.), *The care and education of America's young children: Obstacles and opportunities* (pp. 30–49). Chicago: University of Chicago Press.

French, L. A., Lucariello, J., Seidman, S., & Nelson, K. (1985). The influence of discourse content and context on preschoolers' use of language. In L. Galda & A. D. Pellegrini (Eds.), *Play, language, and stories: The development of children's literate behavior* (pp. 1–28). Norwood, NJ: Ablex.

Garcia, E. E. (1991). Caring for infants in a bilingual child care setting. *The Journal of Educational Issues of Language Minority Students, 9,* 1–10.

Garvey, C., & Kramer, T. L. (1989). The language of social pretend play. *Developmental Review, 9,* 364–382.

Goldman, J. (1981). The social participation of preschool children in same-age versus mixed-age groupings. *Child Development, 52,* 644–650.

Grant, R. (1995). Meeting the needs of young second language learners. In E. E. Garcia

& B. McLaughlin (Eds.), *Meeting the challenge of linguistic and cultural diversity in early childhood education* (pp. 1–17). New York: Teachers College Press.

Hadley, P. A., & Schuele, C. M. (1995). Come buddy, help, help me! Verbal interactions with peers in a preschool language intervention classroom. In M. L. Rice & K. A. Wilcox (Eds.), *Building a language-focused curriculum for the preschool classroom. Volume I: A foundation for lifelong communication* (pp. 105–125). Baltimore: Brookes.

Han, J. W., & Ernst-Slavit, G. (1999). Come join the literacy club: One Chinese ESL child's literacy experience in a first grade classroom. *Journal of Research in Childhood Education, 13*, 144–154.

Handscombe, J. (1989). A quality program for learners of English as a second language. In P. Rigg & V. G. Allen (Eds.), *When they don't all speak English* (pp. 1–14). Urbana, IL: National Council of Teachers of English.

Heath, S. B., & Chin, H. (1985). Narrative play in second language learning. In L. Galda & A. D. Pellegrini (Eds.), *Play, language, and stories* (pp. 147–166). Norwood, NJ: Ablex.

Hirschler, J. (1991). *Preschool children's help to second language learners.* Unpublished doctoral dissertation, Harvard University, Boston.

Howes, C. (1980). Peer play scale as an index of complexity of peer interaction. *Developmental Psychology, 6*, 371–372.

Howes, C. (1997). Teacher sensitivity, children's attachment and play with peers. *Early Education and Development, 8*, 41–49.

Howes, C., Droege, K., & Matheson, C. C. (1994). Play and communicative processes within long- and short-term friendship dyads. *Journal of Social and Personal Relationships, 11*, 401–410.

Howes, C., & Matheson, C. C. (1992). Sequences in the development of competent play with peers: Social and social pretend play. *Developmental Psychology, 28*, 961–974.

Klee, C. (1988). A discourse analysis of interactions of Spanish-English bilingual children. In R. Benya & K. E. Muller (Eds.), *Children and language: Research, practice, and rationale for the early grades* (pp. 142–154). New York: The American Forum.

Logan, T. F. (1991). Controlling involvement: A naturalistic study of peer interaction in a bilingual, bicultural preschool. *NABE Journal, 14*, 145–166.

McBride, B. (1996). University-based child development laboratory programs: Emerging issues and challenges. *Early Childhood Education Journal, 24*, 17–21.

McCartney, K. (1984). Effect of quality of day care environment on children's language development. *Developmental Psychology, 20*, 224–260.

Nicolopoulou, A. (1993). Play, cognitive development, and the social world: Piaget, Vygotsky, and beyond. *Human Development, 36*, 1–23.

Ogilvy, C. M., Boath, E. H., Cheyne, W. M., Jahoda, G., & Schaffer, H. R. (1990). Staff attitudes and perceptions in multicultural nursery schools. *Early Child Development and Care, 64*, 1–13.

Ogilvy, C. M., Boath, E. H., Cheyne, W. M., Jahoda, G., & Schaffer, H. R. (1992). Staff-child interaction styles in multi-ethnic nursery schools. *British Journal of Developmental Psychology, 10*, 85–97.

Parten, M. B. (1932). Social participation among preschool children. *Journal of Abnormal Psychology, 27*, 243–269.

Rodriguez, J. L., Diaz, R. M., Duran, D., & Espinosa, L. (1995). The impact of bilingual preschool education on the language development of Spanish speaking children. *Early Childhood Research Quarterly, 10*, 475–490.

Roopnarine, J. L., & Johnson, J. E. (1994). The need to look at play in diverse cultural settings. In J. L. Roopnarine, J. E. Johnson, & F. H. Hooper (Eds.), *Children's play in diverse cultures* (pp. 1–8). Albany: State University of New York Press.

Roopnarine, J. L., Lasker, J., Sacks, M., & Stores, M. (1998). The cultural contexts of children's play. In O. N. Saracho & B. Spodek (Eds.), *Multiple perspectives on play in early childhood education* (pp. 194–219). Albany: State University of New York Press.

Rubin, K. H., & Coplan, R. J. (1998). Social and nonsocial play in childhood: An individual differences perspective. In O. N. Saracho & B. Spodek (Eds.), *Multiple perspective on play in early childhood education* (pp. 144–170). Albany: State University of New York Press.

Snow, C. (1989). Understanding social interaction and language acquisition: Sentences are not enough. In M. H. Bornstein & J. S. Bruner (Eds.), *Interaction in human development*. Hillsdale, NJ: Erlbaum.

Strandell, H. (1997). Doing reality with play: Play as a resource in organizing everyday life in daycare centers. *Childhood, 4*, 445–464.

Tabors, P. O. (1987). *The development of communicative competence by second language learners in a nursery school classroom: An ethnolinguistic study*. Unpublished doctoral dissertation, Harvard University, Boston.

Tabors, P. O., & Snow, C. E. (1994). English as a second language in preschool programs. In F. Genesee (Ed.), *Educating second language children: The whole child, the whole curriculum, the whole community* (pp. 103–126). Cambridge: Cambridge University Press.

Urzua, C. (1989). I grow for a living. In P. Rigg & V. G. Allen (Eds.), *When they don't all speak English* (pp. 15–38). Urbana, IL: National Council of Teachers of English.

Wall, S. M., & Pickert, S. M. (1982). Language and play of preschool children learning English as a second language and native English speakers. *Psychological Reports, 50*, 119–124.

7

Developmental Aspects of Play-Partner Selection in Young Rhesus Monkeys

Peggy O'Neill-Wagner, Rosemary Bolig, and
Cristofer S. Price

INTRODUCTION

Social play in young nonhuman primates is thought to be a primary means for practicing the social roles that will be assumed later in adulthood (Poirier, Bellisari, & Haines, 1978). This active form of social interaction provides opportunities for young monkeys to become involved with individuals outside of their immediate families and thereby contributes to the development of new social relationships (Cheney, 1978). Social play behaviors are also considered as predictive of adult dominance rank and of gender roles for various primate species (Biben, 1989). But at what age might the adult dominance and gender roles of nonhuman primates be reflected through the social play behavior of their young?

Perhaps using a developmental approach to examine the early formation of social play partnerships for monkeys would offer insights into related processes underlying the troop social structure. For example, if young monkeys in a matrilineal society begin to demonstrate distinct maternal-rank-related social choices in their selection of playmates, when might we expect such choices to appear? By the time rhesus monkeys reach adolescence in a matrilineal social organization, the females remain with their natal troops to raise offspring (Pusey & Packer, 1987), but the natal males are likely to be expelled or will disperse voluntarily (Colvin, 1983; Moore & Ali, 1984). Though males from the highest-ranking matriline may be allowed to remain somewhat longer than their low-ranking counterparts, the final outcome for them is typically the same. If early social play behavior is a predictor of this social destiny, then at what stage of early development might play behavior begin to accurately reflect these future divergences for females and males?

Behavior studies of young macaques and baboons relating to these questions suggest that factors influencing play partner selection may include the demographics of the primate population (Cheney, 1978; Walters, 1986). Likewise, kinship has been shown to have an impact (Baldwin, 1986; Bernstein, 1988, Cheney, 1978; MacKenzie, McGrew, & Chamove, 1985; Owens, 1975). Other findings are more specific about the role of dominance rank as it relates to play (Caine & Mitchell, 1979; Cheney, 1978; French, 1981; Gard & Meier, 1977; Tartabini & Dienske, 1979). The age and gender of the players have also gotten significant attention in the analyses of play partner selection (Altmann, 1962; Baldwin, 1986; Bekoff, 1978; Cheney, 1978; Lee, 1983; Owens, 1975; Rhine & Hendy-Neely, 1978; Symons, 1978). These are the primary factors thought to contribute to the formation of play partnerships in heterogeneous groups of primates.

Yet many studies investigating social play focus on singular factors and do not consider the interdependence of multiple factors influencing the formation of these partnerships. For example, in a study of rhesus monkeys located on Cayo Santiago Island in Puerto Rico, Symons (1978) reported preference for play partners by age and sex class but did not identify any kinship effects. Papers describing play partner selection in young baboons by Cheney (1978) and Owens (1975) have been more comprehensive by providing evidence for sibling preferences as well as the impact of age and gender. Even the number and the age of siblings have been shown to influence play partnership formation and the play experiences of young monkeys (Baldwin, 1986; Rhine & Hendy-Neely, 1978). For rhesus monkeys, however, age has been considered the primary predictor of social play partnerships, and gender the second most influential factor (Altmann, 1962; Bekoff, 1978).

Some factors may actually hinder the formation of play partnerships. First, demographic factors may restrict the opportunity for expression of play partner choice(s) in a number of ways. In the case of very small subject groups, there may not be the full range of potential play partners for youngsters as are available in larger troops (Walters, 1986). Next, the influence of a monkey's social rank through the maternal line has also been shown to play a significant role in the development of social play partnerships. Plus, according to Tartabini, Genta, and Bertacchini (1980), rhesus mothers of higher social rank are generally more likely than those of lower rank to permit their infants to engage in play.

In this study of rhesus monkeys, three factors—age, gender, and family—were investigated in a developmental context to determine their separate and interactive influence on rhesus monkey play-partner selection. We initially focus on the formation of play partnerships during the first year, when infants are most dependent upon the mother for guidance and security. Then, the three subsequent juvenile years are explored to determine if play partnership changes occur as the monkeys grow more independent. Thus, by examining the play interactions of immature monkeys over a period of four years, we attempt to gain an understanding of the developmental course for social relationships involving play among young rhesus monkeys. Valuable insights might also be gained about underlying social mechanisms that serve to maintain the matrilineal social structure.

METHODS

Subjects

The subjects of this study were infant and juvenile members of a troop of rhesus monkeys observed over a four-year period. All subjects were mother-reared and familiar with each other from birth. They were all members of one of the three matrilines composing the study troop. Because dominance status closely parallels matriline in the immature monkeys, the maternal rank of each youngster was considered as its social rank. The total number of subjects ranged from 8 in the first year to 12 in the fourth year. The age and gender for subjects is shown in Table 7.1. During the course of the study, the troop population grew from 19 to 25 animals.

Research Area

The site was a protected and provisioned 5-acre outdoor field environment (see Figure 7.1) with two housing units composed of two corncribs (5.03 m. in diameter, with 3.04 m. mesh sides and a conical roof 2.44 m. high) and two adjacent barns (2.89 m. × 3.35 m. × 2.51 m. and 3.50 m. × 2.89 m. × 2.74 m.).

Data Collection

A five-minute continuous focal animal scoring was utilized to collect behavioral data. The order of observation for subjects was randomized. During the five-minute observation period, each new occurrence of social play behavior by the focal animal was recorded along with the identity of the play partner. Social play was identified as chase play and/or rough-and-tumble wrestling play involving two or more animals.

All observations were made between the hours of 8:30 AM and 12:30 PM. There were a total of 219 five-minute observation sessions per subject. Five observers collected data over the four-year period. During years one and two there were 34 observation sessions per subject. In years three and four the number of observation sessions increased to 89 and 62, respectively. Reliability

Table 7.1
Age, Gender, and Matriline of Subjects

	High Rank Matriline	Mid Rank Matriline	Low Rank Matriline
Infants			
Females	Pearl	Muffin	Bardot
	Denise		Lilly
Males	Trout	Schlim	Billy
	Orbit		Turbo
	Willow		Kaos
One-Years			
Females	Kiwi	Muffin	Bardot
	Pearl		Lilly
Males	Tanker	Schlim	Taurus
	Trout		Billy
	Orbit		
Two-Years			
Females	Kiwi	Muffin	Linda
	Pearl		
Males	Hershey	Schlim	Evan
	Tanker		Billy
	Trout		Taurus
Three-Years			
Females	Pearl	Muffin	Linda
Males	Hershey		Evan
	Tanker		Billy
			Taurus

(Pearson product-moment correlation) between observers for observed frequencies of social play behavior was established at above .90.

ANALYSES

The means selected to best analyze this data may be summarized as a point estimate from a standardized ratio including preference for same-age, same-

Figure 7.1

gender, and same-matriline, with all three factors allowed to interact. The test assumption was that social play is distributed equally among all possible partners. This test was used to determine whether subjects play with partners of their own family, gender, or age, more than would be expected from the proportion of animals represented by each of these groups. An "expected" number was calculated to serve as the standard for occurrence of social play in each of the within-family (matriline), within-gender, and within-age groups. A deviation from the standard would then imply that the play-partner selection deviated from a chance occurrence. A ratio was calculated from the total number of observed social play scores relative to the expected number of social play scores. This ratio is referred to as a *point-estimate* of the standardized play ratio. A 95 percent confidence interval was constructed for each point-estimate. If the point-estimate was 1.0 or the confidence interval included 1.0, the subject was considered to play approximately equal to expected values. Otherwise, a significant preference was implied.

For this analysis, a set of specified players was identified for each subject. These analyses were limited to specified players (subject group) so that expected value calculations would not include the older animals that played infrequently.

RESULTS

The results of the matriline test indicate that a majority of infants, especially female infants, played more within-matriline than expected (see Figure 7.2). All 1-year-olds played with same-matriline partners more than would be expected from the proportion of same-matriline partners available, although for two of the subjects (one male and one female), significance was not demonstrated. All 2-year-old female subjects showed significant same-matriline preference. By contrast, only half of the 2-year-old males had significant same-matriline preference. Two out of the three males in this age group with significant same-matriline preference were from the high-ranking matriline and the third was from the lowest-ranking matriline. These findings continued through age 3. By the time the female subjects reached 3 years of age, however, social play rarely occurred. This was not the case for males; they continued to engage in frequent rough-and-tumble play bouts. In no case did any subject play within-matriline significantly less than expected.

Choice of same-age partners for social play was most evident in the infants. All 12 infants played more within-age than expected (see Figure 7.3). For 10 of the 12 subjects this result was significant. There was greater variability in results for juvenile subjects. Twelve of the 25 juvenile subjects tended to play with same-age partners less than expected, while the remaining 13 subjects played more with same-age partners than expected. This split cannot be explained by social rank of the 1- and 2-year-olds, but the 3-year-old males showed a distinct split for same-age selection patterns relative to their matriline social ranking. Low-ranking males in the 3-year-old juvenile group showed more than expected same-age play, whereas both males from the high-ranking matriline showed less than expected same-age play. Findings were significant for two of the low-ranking males and one of the high-ranking males.

Point-estimate tests indicate that for infants there was no clear-cut gender preference for play partners (Figure 7.4). Only 3 of 12 infants showed a significant same-gender preference. These three infants (one male and two females) belonged to each of the three matrilines. Same-gender preference was more

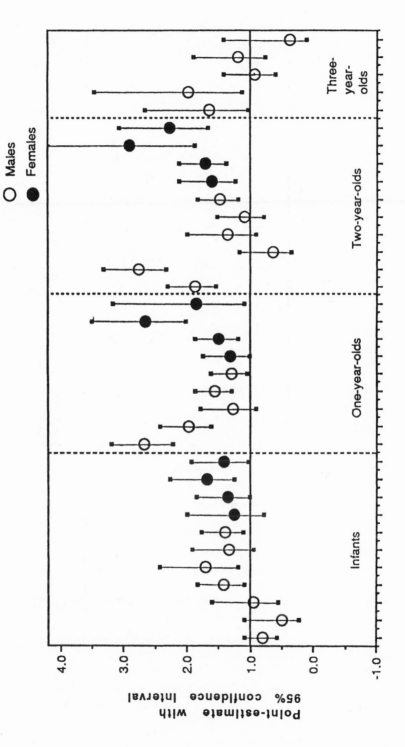

Figure 7.2
Within-matriline play.

Figure 7.3
Within-age play.

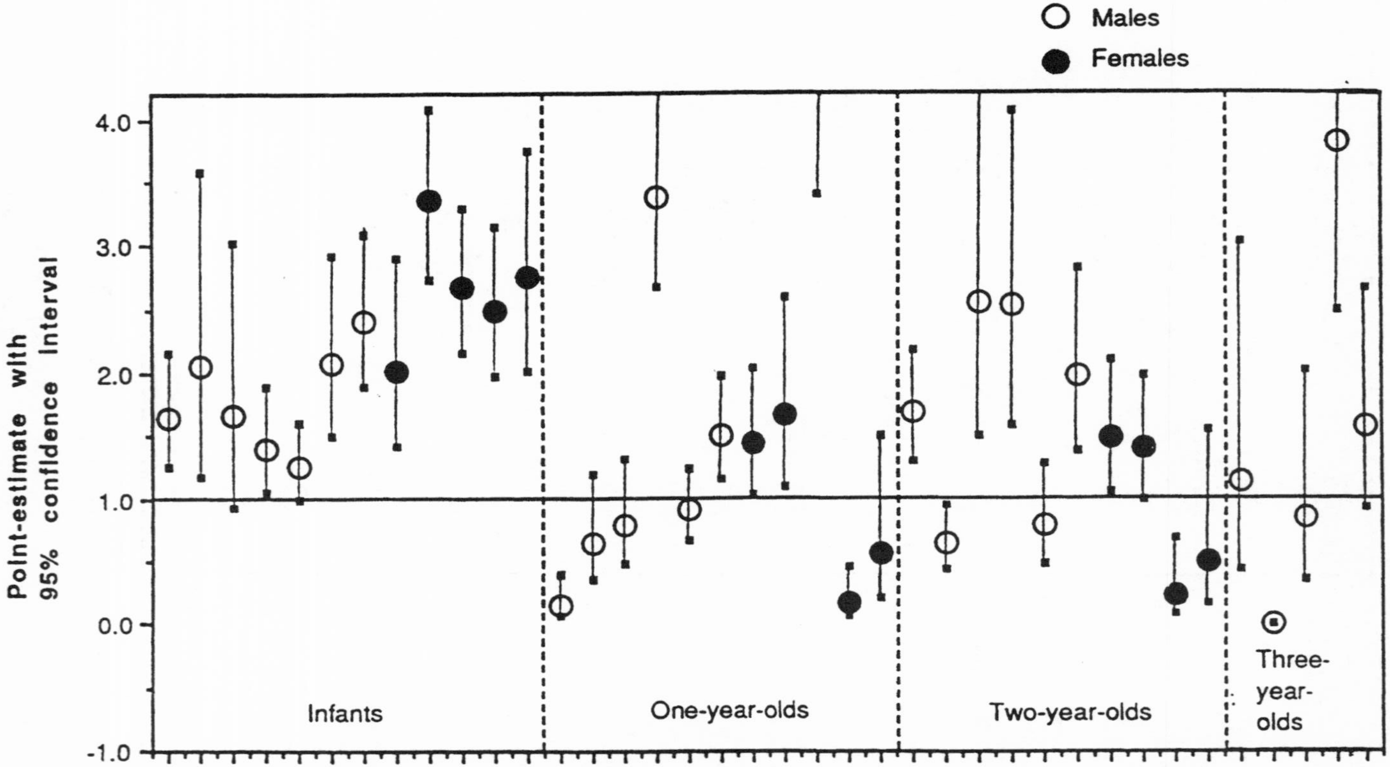

118

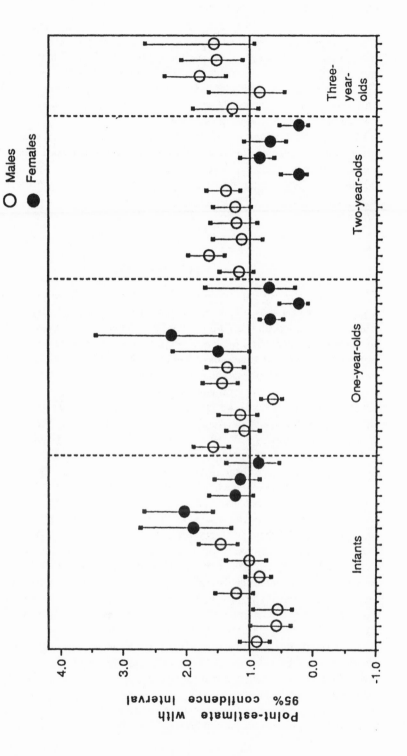

Figure 7.4
Within-gender play.

119

evident in juvenile males than in juvenile females. Juvenile males in most cases played more with other males than with females. For 7 of 17 male subjects, this finding was significant. The outcomes for 1-year-old females, by contrast, were variable. But, as 2-year-olds, female subjects tended to play more than expected with male partners. For half of them, represented by two high-ranking and two low-ranking subjects, the result was significant.

When overall findings shown in Figures 7.2, 7.3, and 7.4 are analyzed for interactions, the choice for same-matriline partners superseded the choice for same-age partners for all subject groups except infants and 3-year-old males, although a majority of the infant's play partners came from their birth cohorts. Same-gender play partner selection only superseded same-age choice for 1-year-old males.

DISCUSSION

The results show a complex interaction between the three factors selected. Like the rhesus monkey infants on Cayo Santiago described by Symons (1978), infants in this troop played more with other infants than with juveniles, regardless of their gender. Perhaps preference for same-age partners is robust for infants across large and small study populations because age-mates have similar strength, weight, and skills. Thus, the infant's social play is most likely to lead to a mutually rewarding exchange when directed to other infants (Baldwin, 1986). Infants are likely to be more vulnerable and fragile, making the play of older and larger animals too rough and vigorous. In addition, the infant's withdrawal or protection by its mother frequently terminates rough play.

Although age was the primary predictor of play partnerships for infants, the same did not hold true for the juveniles. Choosing within-matriline partners was clearly the primary choice factor for juveniles. For both genders, preference for same-matriline social play was most evident. For 1- and 2-year-olds it superseded both age and gender choices. In the present study and in Cheney (1978) and Owens (1975), these interactions were controlled for by examining whether individuals chose play with kin over nonkin when potential partners were matched on age and sex. As young monkeys mature and their play gets rougher, perhaps there is increased disciplinary intervention by protective mothers in favor of their own offspring. According to Quiatt (1967), play combined with interventions by mothers may serve to perpetuate maternal dominance rank by allowing high-ranking youngsters to emerge as winners. He referred to this as "supportive advantage" during the play bout. While the animal with the higher-ranking mother benefits from the "exclusive environment," it is likely that the lower-dominance animals are learning to submit or to escape. Selecting within-matriline play partners may increase the odds for lower-ranking 1- and 2-year-olds to dominate in play, by eliminating the protective and often painful interventions by outside matriline mothers.

Whether the result of a direct or indirect choice, it is between 1 and 2 years of age that the hierarchical expression of social rank becomes evident in the social play partnerships of young rhesus monkeys.

Even though same-age choice superseded same-matriline choice for infant play, clearly kinship was already a highly influential factor for infants as well.

As infants, males and females typically interact in social play. For infants, there were no clear within-gender effects, probably due to overriding same-age and same-matriline preferences. However, the pattern shifts to males playing predominately with other males by the time they reach 2 years of age. Females at this stage, by contrast, play less than expected with other females as they engage in play with younger siblings of both genders. Findings from other studies for same-gender preference by juvenile females are conflicting (Cheney, 1978; Symons, 1978). Symons (1978) found that 1- and 2-year-old females played more than expected with other females; the findings in this study do not concur with his results. Instead, they are similar to those of Cheney (1978), who reported that juvenile females often played more with males. One explanation for this mix in results is that kinship and age primarily determine juvenile female partner choice, and not gender: If a female's most desirably aged play partners are kin, she will always exhibit same-gender preference if they are females, but exhibit the opposite if they are males.

Changes in gender-related patterns and age-related patterns for choice of play partners after infancy interact to reflect the future social divergences for males and females. By age 3 females are no longer reliable candidates as same-age play partners for males. Thus, finding suitable same-age partners is increasingly difficult for 3-year-old males. As a result, within-gender play predominates for males of this age. But the higher-ranking 3-year-old males are still playing with younger animals.

By contrast, the males from the low-ranking matriline are playing more than expected with same-age males.

Now facing adolescence, these males may soon be in conflict with each other and with other conspecifics as they experience the breeding season and/or their own expulsion from the natal troop. One strategy, to reduce risks of serious injury during this life-threatening transition, is to build and strengthen peer social alliances through social play. Preparation via intensive physical wrestling bouts in play would also be an effective way to enhance their fighting skills while avoiding serious injury.

So, at a time when juvenile females are becoming less playful and more maternal, juvenile males are showing continued high rates of social play and testing their strength and mobility against peers.

Perhaps females become less available and/or less desirable by age 3 as play partners because around 3 years of age they become potential breeding partners for the adult males. It is possible that the dominant troop males are more watchful of these females as they mature and may break up or subtly discourage female play contact with 3-year-old males at this stage. If this were the case, young males would seek safety by playing with females within their own matriline. Likewise, they may reduce the chance for within-matriline disciplinary intervention of the adult females by selecting same-size age-mates. In addition, as social play declines in 3-year-old females, they are typically increasing their orientation toward infant siblings. Females practice their mothering techniques at this time. They will be having infants themselves within a year or two.

Not all 3-year-old males exhibited higher than expected rates of rough-and-tumble with peers. One male, the eldest son of the dominant troop female, engaged in significantly less than expected within-age play. His unique play profile was significantly within-matriline, with kin youngsters of both genders. In contrast to the other males this may appear inappropriate. However, his strategy may have contributed to his future social success. Like the young females, he strengthened social alliances with males and females of varied ages within his own matriline. At the same time, a 3-year-old male from the low-ranking matriline engaged in significantly more play than expected with same-gender age-mates and had very close to expected values for within-matriline play partner choice. Although, or because, their play profiles were totally opposite, these two males were able to form a strong male social alliance that allowed them to remain in the troop. The former became troop beta male; the latter became the alpha male. It is very probable that their social play experience as youngsters contributed to this lasting and compatible social relationship as adults.

CONCLUSIONS

Early opportunities for rhesus monkey social play with individuals outside of the immediate family is probably essential for youngsters to learn about the intricacies of troop social structure and their place in it. Prior to 1 year of age young rhesus monkeys appear to make play partner choices relatively freely, without regard for social or gender roles and with a clear preference for play with peers. But by the time rhesus monkeys are juveniles, their social play partner choices begin to reflect the social boundaries maintained by the troop dominance hierarchy. Furthermore, the social divergence between males and females required to maintain a matrilineal system of social organization is reflected in the choice of play partners by the time young monkeys reach 3 years of age. It is not surprising, then, that play partner choice relative to the gender of young monkeys corresponds to the separation of adult gender roles as early as 1 year of age for males and by the age of 3 for both males and females. The results of this study also show unique variations in play preferences for 3-year-old males, which may have implications for the study of individual differences in social play development.

ACKNOWLEDGMENTS

This research has been supported by intramural funds of the National Institute of Child Health and Human Development. Acknowledgment is extended to Amanda Alexander, Ellen Byrne, Carrie Mckenna, and Joshua Schneider for data collection.

REFERENCES

Altmann, S. (1962). Social behaviors of anthropoid primates: Analysis of recent concepts. In E.L. Bliss (Ed.), *Roots of behaviour* (pp. 277–285). New York: Harper.

Baldwin, J. (1986). Behavior in infancy: Exploration and play. In J. Baldwin (Ed.), *Comparative biology: Behavior, conservation and ecology* (pp. 295–326). New York: Alan R. Liss, Inc.

Bekoff, M. (1978). Social play: Structure, function, and the evolution of a cooperative social behavior. In G.M. Burghardt & M. Bekoff (Eds.), *The development of behavior: Comparative and evolutionary aspects* (pp. 367–383). New York: Garland Press.

Bernstein, I. (1988). Kinship and behavior in nonhuman primates, *Behavioral Genetics, 18*, 511–524.

Biben, M. (1989). Effects of social environments on play in squirrel monkeys: Resolving Harlequin's dilemma, *Ethology, 81*, 72–82.

Caine, N. G., & Mitchell, G. D. (1979). The relationship between maternal rank and companion choice in immature macaques *Macaca mulatta* and *Macaca radiata*. *Primates, 20*, 583–590.

Cheney, D. (1978). The play partners of immature baboons, *Animal Behaviour, 26*, 1038–1050.

Colvin, J. (1983). Influences of the social situation on male emigration. In R.A. Hinde (Ed.), *Primate social relationships: An integrated approach*. Oxford: Blackwell.

French, J. (1981). Individual differences in play in *Macaca fuscata*: The role of maternal status and proximity. *International Journal of Primatology, 2*, 237–246.

Gard, G., & Meier, G. (1977). Social and contextual factors of play behavior in sub-adult rhesus monkeys. *Primates, 18*, 367–377.

Lee, P. C. (1983). Play as a means for developing relationships. In R.A. Hinde (Ed.), *Primate social relationships* (pp. 83–89). Sunderland, MA: Sinaur Associates.

MacKenzie, M. M., McGrew, W. C., & Chamove, A. S. (1985). Social preference in stump-tailed macaques (*Macaca arctoides*): Effects of companionship, kinship, and rearing. *Developmental Psychobiology, 18*, 115–123.

Moore, J., & Ali, R. (1984). Are dispersal and inbreeding avoidance related? *Animal Behaviour, 32*, 94–112.

Owens, N. (1975). Social play behaviour in free living baboons. *Animal Behaviour, 23*, 387–408.

Poirier, F. E., Bellisari, A., & Haines, L., (1978). Functions of primate play behavior. In

E. Smith (Ed.), *Social play in primates* (pp. 143–167). New York: Academic Press.

Pusey, A. E., & Packer, C. (1987). Dispersal and philopatry. In B. Smuts, R. Cheney, R. Seyfarth, R. Wrangham, & T. Struhsaker (Eds.), *Primate societies* (pp. 250–266). Chicago: University of Chicago Press.

Quiatt, D.D. (1967). Social dynamics of rhesus monkey groups. *Dissertation Abstracts, 28*, 1325.

Rhine, R., & Hendy-Neely, H. (1978). Social development of stumptail macaques (*Macaca arctoides*): Synchrony of changes in mother-infant interactions and individual behaviors during the first 60 days of life. *Primates, 19*, 681–692.

Symons, D. (1978). *Play and aggression: A study of Rhesus monkeys.* New York: Columbia University Press.

Tartabini, A., & Dienske, H. (1979). Social play and rank order in rhesus monkeys (*Macaca mulatta*). *Behavioural Processes, 4*, 375–383.

Tartabini, A., Genta, M., Bertacchini, P. (1980). Mother–infant interaction and rank order in rhesus monkeys. *Journal of Human Evolution, 9*, 139–146.

Walters, J. R., (1986). Transition to adulthood. In B. Smuts, D. Cheney, R. Seyfarth, R. Wrangham, & T. Struhsaker (Eds.), *Primate societies* (pp. 358–369). Chicago: University of Chicago Press.

Part III

Social–Cognitive Connections to Play

8

The Relationship between Creativity and Cognitive Abilities in Preschoolers

Robyn M. Holmes and Christine J. Geiger

In 1987, Brian Sutton-Smith delivered a keynote address at the 10th Conference of the International Association for the Child's Right to Play. In that speech, he noted that the relationship between play and creativity is relatively unexplored in play research in comparison to other dimensions of this phenomenon. Sutton-Smith (1988) contended that creativity emerges in all types of children's play because all play involves some form of refined problem solving (see also Sutton-Smith, 1986).

In a more recent work, Sutton-Smith (1997) discussed the modern rhetorics of play and returned to the notion that the relationship between play and creativity is still inadequately explored. He noted that substantial distinctions emerge between play and creativity. First, play is often viewed as "progress" oriented (B. Sutton-Smith, personal communication, January 4, 2000). In this instance, attention is focused upon the play activity itself rather than on the player's objective or outcome (Johnson, Christie, & Yawkey, 1999). In contrast, creativity is always directed toward achieving a goal. In creative endeavors, the ends justify and outweigh the means.

Second, play is often viewed as flexible or creative (B. Sutton-Smith, personal communication, January 4, 2000). Sutton-Smith (1997) argued that what is overlooked or ignored is the idea that play possesses "adaptive variability" (p. 221). In this respect, play shares parallels with Gould's model of evolution. For example, the possibilities that emerge in play and creativity allow individuals to adapt to the situation at hand by providing flexibility in their behavior. Thus, although past studies on play and creativity have contributed to our understanding of these phenomena, there are new avenues to pursue. Rather than concentrating on the function of play and creativity, researchers may wish to focus on the variability and possibilities these activities produce (Sutton-Smith, 1997).

The current study plans to explore the relationship between different domains of creativity and cognitive abilities in young children. Studying the relationship between creativity, play, and children's cognitive abilities may have implications for educators given the importance of play in children's lives and development (see, e.g., Isenberg & Jalongo, 1997; Johnson, Christie, & Yawkey, 1999). The National Association for the Education of Young Children (NAEYC) acknowledged the importance of play in their curricular guidelines for young children (Bredekamp, 1987; Bredekamp & Copple, 1997; Bredekamp & Rosegrant, 1992). Other early childhood educators have produced works to provide teachers and caregivers with the knowledge to design child-centered, play-based curricula (e.g., Isenberg & Jalongo, 1997). It is believed such frameworks and paradigms are effective in nurturing and enhancing children's creativity.

In addition, some researchers have posited a relationship between play and creativity in young children and its relevance to their competency in future work endeavors (e.g., Bartolini, 1996). It seems plausible that contemporary children will need to possess social, cultural, academic, and critical and creative thinking skills to meet the challenging demands of an increasingly complex and technologically advanced world and become competent and successful adults in it (Darling-Hammond, Ancess, & Falk, 1995).

Finally, Sutton-Smith (1988) noted that defining and assessing creativity is also problematic. For example, he recommended that a better understanding of the relationship between play and creativity might be achieved if researchers refrain from the reliance upon existing standardized psychological and behavioral measures. Rather, he recommended that inquiries into creativity should also examine both the irrational and rational aspects of play. The inclusion of these aspects will lead to plausible suggestions about the links between play and creativity. He suggested the use of dreams, fantasies, and artwork to accomplish this task.

Other researchers have acknowledged the multitude of definitions that exist for creativity. This term is often difficult to define precisely and existing definitions have included such phenomena as temperamental characteristics, specific behaviors, and cognitive abilities. Among the definitions proffered, Parnes (1963) noted that creativity is a cognitive process that involves an individual's ability to generate at least one novel association based upon his or her prior experiences. Isenberg and Jalongo (1997) noted four critical criteria that must be present to categorize a behavior or action as creative. First, the behavior must be original. This includes behaviors or actions that are uncommon, that are atypical, and that rarely occur. Second, the behavior or action should be appropriate. This requires that the individual's responses be related to the goals of the problem that needs to be solved. Third, the behavior or action must be fluent. Fluency refers to the ability to produce alternative and new ideas to solve a problem. Fourth, the behavior or action should be flexible. Flexibility is linked to divergent thinking insofar as the individual is able to use uncommon or "nontraditional" means to solve a problem.

In addition, Russ (1996) contended that an important element in creativity is "transformational abilities" (p. 32). This skill allows individuals to reorganize and modify existing material to depart from traditional ways of thinking. Sutton-Smith (1997) noted that the symbolic transformations that take place in play facilitate the cognitive processing that leads to increasing mental flexibility. It is this ability that enhances an individual's potential to adapt and discover atypical, original, and creative responses to situations. Finally, a defining criterion of creativity is that it is always goal-oriented (B. Sutton-Smith, personal communication, January 4, 2000).

CONTEMPORARY CREATIVITY RESEARCH

As Meador (1992) noted, there is a connection between creativity and children's cognition such that creative ideas and behaviors begin to emerge in preschoolers as they experiment with their newfound cognitive abilities. Cobb (1977) went so far as to suggest that childhood is a period of the life span in which individuals experience heightened creativity, a trend that appears to be a cultural universal.

Research on creativity in young children has explored cognitive styles or ways of thinking. The two dominant styles are divergent and convergent thinking (Guilford, 1967), and the former is often linked to creativity. Divergent thinking is defined as a cognitive ability often viewed as a component of creativity in which one produces alternative routes or unique solutions to a particular problem (Wallach, 1970). Russ (1996) defined divergent thinking as "thinking that goes off in different directions" (p. 32). An analogy can be made between divergent thinking and the way numerous branches emerge from a tree's trunk. In contrast, convergent thinking is viewed as a single, traditional, or typical route to solving a problem.

Studies that have examined the relationship between young children's creative abilities and divergent thinking include Dansky (1980), Pepler and Ross (1981), and Singer and Singer (1990). In this research paradigm, typical studies often employ alternate uses tasks or associative fluency to establish a connection between divergent thinking and creativity (see, e.g., Dansky & Silverman, 1973, 1975; Pellegrini, 1984–1985). For example, Pellegrini and Greene (1980) measured this aspect of creativity in preschoolers via an alternate uses task. In this study, preschool-aged children from middle-income families were randomly assigned to one of three conditions: control group, play group, and children who received "guided exploration questioning" (p. 192).

Children were then asked for alternative uses for target objects. Children in the group who were allowed to explore the features of the object through verbal questions performed better (i.e., provided more creative responses) than the play and control groups. In addition, children who had the opportunity to manipulate the objects provided more creative uses for them than did children in the control group.

In response to the extensive literature produced on creativity and cognitive style, Saracho (1992) examined the relationship between cognitive style and pretend play. In this work, one particular relatively unexamined aspect of cognitive style—field dependence/independence—was explored. Field-independent individuals are expected to be more analytical and less socially oriented. In contrast, field-dependent individuals engage in more social participation and less analytical tasks.

The participants were 300 preschool-aged children. Play behaviors and creativity were measured respectively using the Play Rating Scale and Preschool Embedded Figures Test. Play was also observed for frequency of play area occupation, communicative abilities, social play, and dramatic play. Multivariate analysis revealed a significant main effect for the relationship between cognitive style and play. Field-independent children (boys and girls) engaged in more play than did field-dependent children. Field-independent children demonstrated greater cognitive flexibility and communication skills. The authors suggested that future research endeavors pursue the notion that creativity is not measured by cognitive style on dimensions of social play.

Another line of research on children's creativity has focused on its relationship to play. Numerous publications have posited a relationship between creativity and play. These include object play and the manipulation of props and objects (Hughes, 1987; Sutton-Smith, 1992). However, the greatest proportion of studies that link creativity and play have focused on pretend play in both indoor (see, e.g., Dansky, 1980; Fein, 1981; Pepler, 1986; Russ, 1996; Singer, 1973; Singer & Singer, 1990) and outdoor environments (Susa & Benedict, 1994).

A recent review by Mellou (1995) summarized the major findings on the relationship between dramatic play and creativity in young children. She examined theoretical stances, empirical studies, and particular aspects of dramatic play that may assume a critical role in training programs aimed at facilitating and promoting creative thinking in children. One significant finding consistently emerges—the ability to perform transformational operations on roles and play objects contributes to and helps establish creative skills. This is supported by Vygotsky's theory on creativity as well (see, e.g., Smolucha, 1992a, 1992b).

In relation to the literature produced on the relationship between play and creativity, interestingly, few studies have examined the link between playfulness as an internal state (a predisposition to be playful) and creativity (Lieberman, 1977; Wallach & Kogan, 1965). Barnett and Kleiber's (1982) classic study was conducted in response to studies that examined the relationship between intelligence, divergent thinking, and play patterns, with little regard for controlling intelligence as a factor or considering the effects of sex on play behaviors.

Barnett and Kleiber (1982) examined the relationship between playfulness as an internal state and divergent thinking in preschoolers. The participants were 106 European American children of normal intelligence. Three measures were employed: (a) playfulness was assessed using Lieberman's Playfulness Questionnaire; (b) verbal intelligence was assessed using the Peabody Picture Vocabulary Test (PPVT)—a measure of receptive speech; and (c) creativity was measured using the Novel Uses Test—a measure of associative fluency.

Their results confirmed that playfulness was significantly correlated with verbal intelligence and creativity. However, when segregated by sex, a positive relationship for playfulness and divergent thinking emerged only for females. It appears as though playfulness as a measure should be explored for gender differences since it has been documented that boys and girls, perhaps as a result of socialization, engage in different forms of play.

In a recent study, Russ (1996) explored the link between creativity and affect in play. She designed and developed the Affect in Play Scale (APS), a measure with demonstrated reliability and validity. This scale focuses on make-believe play and measures frequency and categories of affect displays in such play. Three categories are emphasized: "affect states," "affect-laden thought," and "cognitive integration of affect" (p. 37). These three domains are believed to be criteria associated with creativity.

By and large, the link between playfulness and creativity has been studied primarily in Western cultures. However, this topic has been explored cross-culturally (see, e.g., Qiying, 1988). For example, Taylor (1992) examined the relationship between playfulness and creativity in Japanese preschoolers aged 5–6 years. This design included qualitative and quantitative methods. Teachers rated children's playfulness using the Children's Behavior Inventory (CBI), creativity was operationally defined as artistic creativity and assessed through the Creativity Thinking Drawing Production Test (Jellen & Urban, 1986), and data were supported by teacher interviews and observations of the children at play. Teachers rated 164 children using the CBI and placed them into categories of high and low playfulness. The sample was further reduced to 6 children from each of the six classrooms and the final sample included 12 children (6 boys and 6 girls from the two categories). Statistical analyses (t-tests) revealed no significant differences between the genders and the relationship between playfulness and creativity.

The current study examines the relationship between three different domains of creativity and cognitive abilities in preschoolers. These three domains were selected based upon the operational definition of creativity because they share the possibilities for actions and behaviors that are novel, flexible, fluent, transformational, goal-oriented, and used in problem solving (Amabile, 1989; Isenberg & Jalongo, 1997; Runco, 1996; Sutton-Smith, 1997).

In the present study, creativity is operationally measured in the domains of playfulness, artistic drawings, and construction activities. These three expressive domains have all been linked to creativity. First, Vygotsky (1930/1990) viewed children's play as a premature form of creativity and the predisposition to be playful has been linked to highly creative individuals (Taylor, 1992). Second, artistic (two- and three-dimensional) products have been employed to measure creativity in numerous studies (e.g., Amabile & Gitomer, 1984; Runco, 1989; Taylor, 1992).

In addition, creativity can be studied in a variety of ways by focusing on creative individuals, the creative process, or the final products. In this study, creativity is operationally measured by the quality of the final product rather than emphasizing the creative process or the common traits that appear in creative individuals (e.g., Isaksen, 1992). Finally, cognitive abilities apply to one particular aspect of cognition—language ability. This was selected for two reasons. First, the child participants are preschoolers and language and cognition are intricately linked in young children. Second, Vygotsky (1932/1978) believed language was an essential mechanism through which children "learn to think" and acquire more complex thinking patterns, such as those involving the use and manipulation of concepts (Thomas, 1996).

The present study plans to contribute to the existing literature on the relationship between creativity and children's cognitive abilities by exploring this relationship in three different domains. Creativity is expressed through different mediums such as art, playfulness, and constructive activities. All three of these areas share criteria associated with creative behaviors (Isenberg & Jalongo, 1997; Parnes, 1963; Runco, 1996; B. Sutton-Smith, personal communication, January 4, 2000). Yet each is uniquely different and may require both common and specific abilities. The ability to think creatively and generate numerous possibilities to solve problems may be beneficial to children who will need such flexibility to succeed as adults in an increasingly complex world (Bartolini, 1996; Darling-Hammond et al., 1995).

For example, playfulness is an internal state (a predisposition to be playful). In contrast, art and building demonstrate creative behaviors in two and three dimensions. Based upon existing literature, it was expected that: (a) older children would perform better than younger ones as a consequence of cognitive maturity (see, e.g., Cacciari, Levorato, & Cicogna, 1997); (b) more playful children and children with enhanced drawing and building skills would have greater language abilities than those children who had lesser skills (see, e.g., Barnett & Kleiber, 1982); and (c) gender would influence creativity.

For example, boys are expected to be more creative on the building task, whereas girls are expected to do better on the drawing tasks, due in part to American socialization practices and toy preferences (Eisenberg, 1983; Tracy, 1987). In addition, it is possible that such relationships might suggest multiple forms of creativity that would parallel Gardner's (1993) notion of multiple intelligences. Thus, particular kinds of creative abilities may be linked to particular cognitive gains.

Finally, the current work is theoretically aligned with the tenets of Vygotskian (1932/1978) psychology. This Russian theorist and advocate of social reform suggested that learning takes place in a social and cultural context. For example, his applied psychology focused upon how cultural practices and institutions (particularly social interactions with adults) affected children's development.[1] In this view, the creative process and its products are a reflection of interpersonal and intrapersonal interactions and the social and cultural traditions in which they occur. Thus, learning and creativity do not take place in a vacuum; rather, they are also subject to external forces (see also Smolucha, 1992a). Finally, Vygotsky focused on a child's potential to learn and the ability to acquire knowledge rather than the traditional psychometric tests that revealed what the child already knows.

METHOD

Participants

Forty-six preschool children participated in the project. There were 26 girls and 20 boys. The children's ages ranged from 51 to 70 months, with a mean age of 58.90 months and standard deviation of 5.14 months. Ethnic composition of the sample included 36 European American, 5 African American, and 5 children from other ethnic groups.

The children were enrolled in two different preschools. In the first preschool, there were 18 children (9 girls, 9 boys). Five children were African American, 8 were European American, and 5 were from other ethnic groups. The mean age was 59.61 months. Socioeconomic status of the children's families ranged from lower to upper-middle incomes. Family structure ranged from single- to two-parent households.

In the second preschool, there were 28 children (17 girls, 11 boys). All were European American with a mean age of 58.19 months. Socioeconomic status of the children's families ranged from lower to upper-middle incomes. Family structure ranged from single- to two-parent households.

Stimulus Materials

The stimulus materials employed for the drawing task were Crayola SO BIG crayons (eight primary colors) and 9 × 11-inch manila drawing paper. The stimulus materials for the building task were Floamworks by Tinker Toys. As Davidson (1988) suggested, child art and block building are two activities that should be considered when seeking to understand children's creativity. Both are goal-oriented processes that allow the child to come to know about the world through curiosity, manipulation, and experiential actions. Also in both activities, creativity emerges as the child's imagination adapts, modifies, and creates a novel product (Vygotsky, 1930/1990, 1932/1978).

The two creative tasks utilized in this project were selected with this in mind. Toys and the interactions children engage in with them have been viewed by some theorists as creative agents (Sutton-Smith, 1992) and a way in which children begin to learn about abstractions (Vygotsky, 1932/1978). Others have noted the value of object play in stimulating and nurturing creativity (e.g., Trostle & Yawkey, 1982). Building with blocks and other similar materials is a goal-oriented activity that leads to multiple novel possibilities, allows for flexibility, and has been classified as a divergent play material. The link between divergent thinking and creativity has been clearly established in the literature (Barnett & Kleiber, 1982; Guilford, 1981). In addition, art and building respectively tap children's experiences in two and three dimensions.

As other researchers have noted (e.g., Taylor, 1992), three-dimensional and experiential materials are developmentally appropriate for preschoolers and young children. The inclusion of two tasks in the present study seemed less limiting than using one task, which has occurred in prior research studies (e.g., Amabile & Gitomer, 1984; Acharyulu & Yasodhara, 1984; Taylor, 1992; Wallach & Kogan, 1965). Isenberg and Jalongo's (1997) contention that children's creative abilities are evident in play, manipulative tasks, pretend play, and drawings and artistic works also supports the selection of stimulus materials employed in this project.

Design and Procedure

This study employed a qualitative and quantitative design to support Vygotsky's contention that learning and creativity are socially and culturally constructed. For example, the senior author engaged in participant observation in both preschools during the school year. She visited the children one day a week for three hours a session. The data collection period ran from summer 1998 to spring 1999. Her relationship with the children approximated what Fine and Sandstrom (1988) termed the "friend role" (p. 18). She had a trusting and respectful relationship with the children, who viewed her as a nonauthoritarian adult playmate.

Children were continuously monitored but focal observations occurred during free-play time. Fieldnotes included what and with whom children played, verbatim phrases and conversational material while the children were playing, remarks made while the children were engaging in the study's designated creative tasks, queries posed by the researcher, and sketches of the children's buildings. These were used to discover patterns of play behavior and linguistic and conceptual categories that emerged while the children were performing the tasks and responding to researcher queries. Both authors administered all tasks.

Quantitative measures were employed to analyze the children's drawings and buildings. These included the ratings of the drawings and the buildings that were accomplished using specific criteria. These were scored using a Likert scale (see Appendices B, C, D, and E). The Peabody Picture Vocabulary Test—III

(PPVT—III) is also a quantitative measure because it is considered a standardized test for receptive speech. The order of completing the drawing and building tasks was varied and based upon the child's choice of which he or she wanted to complete first. The PPVT—III was administered last in every case. The tasks were administered one week apart.

The creative tasks were modified versions of what Vygotsky termed a "double stimulation method" (Thomas, 1996, p. 275)—a method that combines clinical interviewing while the child is completing a task-oriented goal. In this situation, the researcher may explicitly state the goal or the child may draw inferences about the goal from the situational context. The child is obliged to obtain a goal using the objects provided; the researcher's goal is to listen to and observe the child during the task to draw conclusions about the child's patterns of thought. This methodology reflects Vygotsky's concern with how and why children learn to think rather than whether or not the child correctly solved the problem (Thomas, 1996).

In the current study, the children performed two independent tasks (drawing and building) that required them to problem-solve and attain a goal with the aid of provided objects. In each case, the goals were stated explicitly for the children, and the researchers listened to and observed the children while they were performing the task. During the task the children were asked queries such as "What are you building?" and "Can you please tell me about your building?"

The Drawing Task

For the drawing task, children were asked to create drawings of an imaginary person. First, the children were asked if they could draw a person. If they were able to do so, they were asked to draw an imaginary person. This was clarified by telling the children this was a person who was "pretend, make-believe, or not real." Children drew individually at a table in the classroom during their free-play period. Children were allowed to place the paper in either a horizontal or vertical fashion and could use any of the colored crayons available. Children created as many drawings as they desired and no time limit was imposed on them.

The Building Task

For the building task, Floamworks by Tinker Toys were employed. This building set contains 53 pieces, including: (a) assorted colors of connecting and spinning spools, (b) straight and curved rods of various lengths, (c) two pairs of eyes, and (d) assorted foam pieces such as arrows, stars, circles, and wavy bars.

Several sets were combined to allow the children access to more pieces. Children were asked to build "anything they wanted for as long as they wanted" during their free-play period. Children constructed their products on an individual basis. Children unfamiliar with the Floamworks building toys were allowed to interact with and familiarize themselves with the toys for approximately 10 minutes before their buildings were recorded. Artistic renderings of the buildings were made in the field by the authors and these were later reconstructed using the Floamworks for the raters. The more elaborate and complex constructions were kept intact until they were rated because of the difficulty of drawing them in the field and the threat of inaccurate representation.

As Vygotsky (1932/1978) contended, children learn how to think in more complex ways through the "transmission of words" (Thomas, 1996, p. 271). The PPVT is a receptive speech test that measures children's ability to recognize vocabulary words. This test can be administered to individuals ranging from toddlers to adults. The PPVT—III was administered individually to the children in one session. The test is divided into 17 sets; with a total of 204 items; a child's chronological age determined the set in which he or she began the test.

Prior to the actual testing, children were given an explanation of the test and a few practice trials to be certain they understood the instructions. First, the researcher read to the child the appropriate target word from the scoring sheet. Next the child was shown a page that was divided into four quadrants. Each quadrant contained a black-and-white illustration, one of which illustrated the target word. The child was then asked to point to the picture that corresponded to the target word. The children completed the test in a quiet room, removed from their classroom.

The PPVT—III is scored in the following manner. First, the child must complete a set in which he or she records no or only one error, which is considered the basal set. Then the child continues through the vocabulary list until he or she reaches a set in which he or she records eight or more errors. The total number of errors in all sets is subtracted from the last correct item number, which yields the child's raw score. The raw score is then converted into a standard score using tables provided by the testing company. The raw form can also be converted into other scores such as percentile ranks and an age equivalent.

Finally, the head teachers completed the Children's Playfulness Scale for each child (see Appendix A). Barnett (1990) designed the scale to assess playfulness as an "internal predisposition to be playful" (p. 319). She accomplished this by revising an earlier playfulness scale introduced by Lieberman. Barnett renamed this scale the Children's Playfulness Scale (CPS). The 23-item questionnaire included five discrete features of playfulness: ". . . physical spontaneity, social spontaneity, cognitive spontaneity, sense of humor, and manifest joy" (p. 333).

Individual items were scored using a Likert scale. This has proven to be a valid and reliable tool with which to measure and assess children's playful interactions with their environment in Western societies (see, e.g., Barnett, 1991). However its assessment value may not hold true cross-culturally (see, e.g., Bundy & Clifton, 1998; Li, Bundy, & Beer, 1995).

Coding

A combination of assessment and subjective measures were used to evaluate the children's drawings and buildings. Three artists and two nonartists served as independent raters. Each group viewed each drawing and Tinker Toy building and rated them independently using specific criteria. The use of both artists and nonartists was employed for several reasons. First, many existing studies (e.g., Acharylulu & Yasodhara, 1984; Amabile & Gitomer, 1984; Taylor, 1992) have typically utilized only artists' ratings. The inclusion of both evaluations was employed to add power to the assessments. Second, given the subjective nature of the creative process, it seemed reasonable to separate the assessments of the creative products into two dimensions—subjectivity and objectivity. Thus, individuals trained in the arts rated the products for subjective content and nonartists rated the products for objective content.

Interrater reliability was .91 and .96 for artists and nonartists, respectively. As employed by Taylor (1992), subjective and objective measures were taken from Torrance (1962) and Acharyulu and Yasodhara (1984). Sample coding sheets appear in Appendices B, C, D, and E.

Scoring

Prior to scoring the products, the senior author explained to the artists and nonartists the ranking system that appears on the coding sheets (see Appendices B, C, D, and E). After this explanation, the raters performed several practice ratings to familiarize themselves with the system. Next, drawings were placed in the center of a rectangular table (3 × 6 feet). The three artists were seated in a triangular pattern so that they could not see each other's coding sheets. The senior author rotated each drawing so that each artist could view it clearly. The artists independently rated all the drawings. After the coding sheet was completed, each artist was instructed to place his or her initials in the upper right-hand corner of the page for identification purposes. The nonartists were placed opposite one another at the table and the senior author rotated the drawing so that each viewed it right side up. Ratings from both groups were completed in four sessions, and each session ranged from one to two hours in length.

The process of rating the buildings was similar to that of the drawings. The artists and nonartists were seated in the same pattern at the same table. One building at a time was placed in the center of the table and rated independently. The senior author rotated the buildings so that each individual could view it in its entirely. Raters were also allowed to stand if they wished to view the building from above. Simple buildings were reconstructed from fieldnote sketches made immediately after the children completed their creations. The fieldnote sketches were later turned into color sketches to ease the reconstruction process. Complex buildings were kept intact. Ratings from both groups were completed in six sessions, and each session ranged from one to two hours in length. Children received individual scores for each item on the coding sheet and a total score for the drawing and building tasks.

RESULTS

Correlation analyses were performed using the Pearson r correlation coefficient. T-tests were performed for age and gender on the creativity domains. The creativity measures were artist and nonartist ratings (individual items and total scores) of drawings and buildings, and total and subscale scores for playfulness from Barnett's Children's Playfulness Scale. Subscales were devised using the five criteria set forth by Barnett (1990, 1991). They were social spontaneity, cognitive spontaneity, physical spontaneity, manifest joy, and sense of humor. Other variables included the child's age, sex, and language abilities as measured via the standard scores on the PPVT—III.

The analyses revealed several significant relationships. These appear in Table 8.1. For example, several significant correlations emerged for the relationship between a child's age and the drawing and building tasks. Older children included more characteristics of a person and details and features of a person than did younger children. Also, older children tended to score higher on the building total scores for both artists and nonartists than did the younger children.

With respect to gender, boys included more detail in their buildings, received higher building total scores from both raters, and used a greater variety of pieces than did girls. Girls displayed more originality in their buildings than did boys. With respect to creativity, cognitive spontaneity (playfulness subscale) was correlated with several aspects of the drawing task for both boys and girls. Interestingly, social spontaneity (playfulness subscale) and complexity of drawing were negatively correlated. As social spontaneity increased, complexity of building decreased. Finally, PPVT—III scores were correlated with aspects of the building task. However, there was no relationship between the PPVT—III scores and either drawing or total and subscale playfulness scores.

DISCUSSION

In this particular sample of children, it seems reasonable to suggest that certain creative activities are related to specific cognitive abilities. In this study, the first and third hypothesis was supported and the second was partially supported. As confirmed by developmental norms (see, e.g., Gesell & Ilg, 1946), older children, due in part to increasing cognitive maturity, performed better on aspects of the drawings and building tasks than did the younger children. Findings reported by Cacciari, Levorato, and Cicogna (1997) also support the notion that chronological age affects performance on certain creative tasks such as drawing.

With respect to gender, boys tended to do better on specific aspects of the building task. This may be partially explained by the literature on the sex typing

Table 8.1

Correlational Analyses for Creativity, Playfulness, Language Abilities, and Child Characteristics

Correlation	Pearson r	Alpha
Maturity		
Age/features, characteristics of a person	$r = .31$	$p < .05$
Age/details of drawing	$r = .37$	$p < .05$
Age/# of features of the person	$r = .43$	$p < .01$
Age/# of different categories/drawing	$r = .36$	$p < .05$
Age/building total	$r = .30$	$p < .05$
Gender		
Sex/detail for building	$r = .39$	$p < .05$
Sex/building total	$r = .45$	$p < .01$
Sex/originality of building	$r = .42$	$p < .01$
Sex/different pieces/building	$r = .32$	$p < .05$
Creativity		
Cognitive spontaneity/features/characteristics of person	$r = .35$	$p < .05$
Cognitive spontaneity/different categories in drawing	$r = -.33$	$p < .05$
Cognitive spontaneity/# of features in drawing	$r = .31$	$p < .05$
Cognitive spontaneity/atypical features in drawing	$r = .32$	$p < .05$
Social spontaneity/complexity of building	$r = -.32$	$p < .05$
Physical spontaneity/# of buildings	$r = .37$	$p < .05$
Physical spontaneity/# of different categories in building	$r = .33$	$p < .05$
Sense of humor/atypical features in drawing	$r = .36$	$p < .05$
Playfulness total/# of drawings	$r = .30$	$p < .05$
Language		
PPVT/elaborate details of building	$r = .34$	$p < .05$
PPVT/originality of building	$r = .36$	$p < .05$
PPVT/# of different pieces in building	$r = .31$	$p < .05$

of toys and American socialization practices. Boys tend to request and play more with construction toys that are sex-typed as masculine (Eisenberg, 1983; Tracy, 1987). Thus, boys may have had more exposure to and experience with the toys than did girls due to their own toy preferences and parental, adult, and peer approval for the use of gender-appropriate toys.

However, it should be noted that the girls in this sample enjoyed playing with the constructive toys, and many played with the toys even after the project ended. These findings contrast with those of Taylor's (1992), who reported no gender differences for the relationship between playfulness and creativity. This may be partially explained by the different measures employed in the respective studies. Taylor used the Test for Creativity Thinking—Drawing Production, whereas the current study allowed the children to draw an imaginary person. Also, Taylor measured the relationship between playfulness and creativity and viewed playfulness as a separate and independent variable. In the current study, playfulness was viewed as an inclusive domain of creativity.

With respect to playfulness, there was no significant correlation to the PPVT—III scores. This domain of creativity was correlated only with the drawing task. As expected, children who scored higher on the cognitive spontaneity subscale created more detailed and elaborate drawings than those children who scored lower. Children who scored higher on the physical spontaneity subscale also constructed more buildings with different categories than those children who scored lower. Finally, there was also no correlation between the drawing task and the PPVT—III scores (cognitive abilities). The PPVT—III scores were significantly correlated only with the building task. Children who scored higher on the PPVT—III constructed more elaborate and original buildings than children who scored lower.

It seems plausible that the skills employed in constructive activities such as sequential patterning are similar to those used in speech and thus may enhance certain language abilities, that is, those used in receptive speech. It also seems reasonable to suppose that this relationship may be bidirectional. However, unlike the results obtained by Barnett and Kleiber (1982), these children did not reveal a relationship between playfulness, verbal intelligence, and creativity. The difference may be explained by the fact that in the current study, playfulness was considered to be a domain of creativity rather than a factor correlated with it. In addition, the playfulness scale was assessed in terms of subscales in the current study and these were not a part of the Barnett and Kleiber study.

It is also worthy of mention that certain subscales of the Children's Playfulness Scale were correlated with certain cognitive abilities. For example, cognitive spontaneity was linked to more detailed and imaginative drawing behaviors, whereas physical spontaneity affected both the content and quantity of the children's building behaviors. Interestingly, more social children tended to build less complex buildings than did less social children, perhaps because the former engage in more social kinds of play rather than in building tasks, which can range from solitary to cooperative kinds of play. It seems reasonable to suggest that certain aspects of playfulness may facilitate or enhance certain creative behaviors and that these relationships are bidirectional.

A limitation of this study is the challenge to external validity. The findings from this small, relatively homogeneous sample with respect to ethnicity and socioeconomic status should not be generalized to a broader population. Also, Pellegrini and Greene (1980) concluded that the children in their study who were allowed to explore and manipulate the target object were able to supply more creative or alternate uses for it. Similarly, the children in the current study became more creative with the building materials after the opportunity and increasing exposure to play with them.

Future research might employ a larger, more diverse sample with respect to ethnicity, socioeconomic status, and other creative mediums. Other studies might consider investigating the relationship between the playfulness subscales and creative behaviors. Such research will have applied value in young children's early childhood educational experiences since certain creative behaviors such as constructing, drawing, and playfulness may contribute to specific cognitive abilities in a bidirectional nature.

SOME FINAL THOUGHTS FOR EARLY CHILDHOOD EDUCATORS

The findings of the current study suggest that particular cognitive abilities may be enhanced or increased through activities performed in certain creative domains. The possibilities and mental flexibility that are generated by creative endeavors may have implications for children's future social, cultural, academic, and work-related success (Bartolini, 1996; Darling-Hammond et al., 1995). It seems prudent to begin with teacher–child interactions and the settings in which they occur, given the importance Vygotsky (1932/1978) placed upon child–adult social interaction as a context for learning. Other researchers have also acknowledged the impact early childhood educators have on stimulating and instigating children's creative development. This may be influenced by such factors as a teacher's interactive style, playfulness, classroom arrangement, and curricular activities (Isenberg & Jalongo, 1997; Tegano et al., 1991).

First, the findings suggest a positive relationship between block building and language abilities. Children who constructed more diverse, elaborate, and novel buildings had a more varied and expansive vocabulary than children who did not. Play researchers and early childhood educators have long recognized blocks as agents that inspire creativity (Hughes, 1995; Isenberg & Jalongo, 1997; Sutton-Smith, 1992). The possibilities and alternatives children create when building with blocks may enhance divergent thinking skills in other cognitive domains. For example, it is possible that these children were able to apply the flexibility and variability they acquired through block building to their language development when they were building their vocabularies. Perhaps flexibility in building activities can be extended to language skills. Vygotsky (1932/1978) acknowledged the relationship between language and thought.

As Isenberg and Jalongo (1997) suggest, teachers of young children can foster block play in their classrooms using the following strategies. They may equip their classrooms with (a) an ample supply of blocks (determined by age and class size); (b) adequate play time and space for block play; (c) additional props to enhance pretend possibilities; and (d) promotion of block play via adult approval for the activity.

Gender differences also arise in the children's constructive creations. My own observations over the years in early childhood classrooms confirm that boys and girls enjoy playing with blocks, although boys clearly show a preference for them (Eisenberg, 1983). The boys in this group tended to include more detail and variety in their creations than did the girls. This may be due in part to American socialization practices in which boys tend to play more with toys that promote spatial abilities. Perhaps social learning theory can be utilized to increase block play frequency for girls. Since most early childhood teachers are female, adult female approval and reinforcement may encourage the girls to engage in more constructive activities. Other suggestions might include class activities that incorporate block play and the availability of props that can also be integrated into constructive play (see also Van Hoorn, Scales, Nourot, & Alward, 1999). The possibilities that children can generate with blocks are endless.

Finally, the drawing task was positively correlated with the cognitive spontaneity playfulness scale. The cognitive spontaneity subscale includes inventiveness at play, leadership abilities, unconventional use of objects, taking on different play roles, and engaging in different activities. This subscale reflects the diverse and variable nature of creativity because it focuses on unconventional, variable, and divergent behaviors and actions (Sutton-Smith, 1997). Children who scored higher on the cognitive spontaneity subscale tended to include in their drawings more features and characteristics of a person, more uncommon features, and different categories. The qualities that emerge in cognitive spontaneity may help children develop more flexibility and variability in other activities. Thus, early childhood teachers might provide space and time, pretend play props, and a variety of play choices to enhance these cognitive abilities in children (Isenberg & Jalongo, 1997; Van Hoorn et al., 1999). In conclusion, creative abilities and cognitive abilities appear to share a bidirectional relationship that serves to equip children with the mental flexibility and variability to adapt to potential situations. Such skills will be necessary for them to succeed and become culturally, socially, and academically productive adults.

APPENDIX A: THE CHILDREN'S PLAYFULNESS SCALE

Child's name _____
Age _____
Sex _____
Ethnic group _____

Please answer the following 23 sentences about the child's daily behaviors using the scale below. Your help is very much appreciated.

Not at all	Not very much	A little bit	Frequently	Always
0	1	2	3	4

1. The child's movements are generally well coordinated during play activities. _____
2. The child is physically active during play. _____
3. The child prefers to be active rather than quiet in play. _____
4. The child runs, skips, hops, jumps a lot in play. _____
5. The child responds easily to others' approaches during play. _____
6. The child initiates play with others. _____
7. The child plays cooperatively with other children. _____
8. The child is willing to share playthings (toys). _____
9. The child assumes a leadership role in playing with others. _____
10. The child invents his or her own games to play. _____
11. The child uses unconventional objects in play. _____
12. The child assumes different character roles in play. _____
13. The child is interested in many different kinds of activities. _____
14. The child expresses enjoyment during play. _____
15. The child demonstrates exuberance during play. _____
16. The child shows enthusiasm in play. _____
17. The child is restrained in expressing emotions during play. _____
18. The child sings and talks while playing. _____
19. The child enjoys joking with other children. _____
20. The child gently teases others while playing. _____
21. The child tells funny stories. _____
22. The child laughs at humorous stories. _____
23. The child likes to clown around. _____

Items 1–4 refer to physical spontaneity, items 5–9 refer to social spontaneity, items 10–13 refer to cognitive spontaneity, items 14–18 refer to manifest joy, and items 19–23 refer to sense of humor.

The original version was single spaced and contained on one page.

APPENDIX B: ARTIST CODING SHEET

Child's name: _____   Age: _____
Ethnicity: _____   Date: _____
Artwork:
PART 1—Subjective Ratings: Please rate each drawing as either creative or not creative using your own definition of creativity.

                         Creative   Not creative

Basis for rating:
PART 2
Children were asked to draw an imaginary/pretend/make-believe person.
Please rate each drawing using the scale placed alongside each criterion. A 0 is the lowest rating; 4 is the highest rating.

1. The details that appear in drawings (0,1,2,3,4).
2. The use of unusual pictures, use of color, or placement (0,1,2,3,4).
3. The number of meaningful features or characteristics of a real person (0,1,2,3,4).
4. The number of different kinds/classes/categories found in the picture (0,1,2,3,4)
5. The number of drawings (0,1,2,3,4)—ONE DRAWING WAS REQUESTED

APPENDIX C: RATER CODING SHEET

Child's name: _____   Age: _____

Ethnicity: _____   Date: _____

Artwork:

PART 1

Children were asked to draw an imaginary/pretend/make-believe person.

Please rate each drawing using the scale placed alongside each criterion.

1. The elaboration of details. This is the number of details in a drawing. Please give 1 point for each detail.
2. The meaningful characteristics or features of a real person. Please give 1 point for each.
3. The inclusion of atypical features. Please give 1 point for each.
4. *Originality*. This is the percentage of children drawing the same picture. Please rate 0,1,2,3,4 from highest to lowest percentage.
5. *Flexibility*. The number of different kinds/classes/categories found in the picture. Please give 1 point for each.
6. *Fluency*. This is the total number of pictures drawn.

APPENDIX D: ARTIST CODING SHEET

Child's name: _____   Age: _____

Ethnicity: _____   Date: _____

Tinker Toys:

PART 1—Subjective Ratings: Please rate each building as either creative or not creative using your own definition of creativity.

                    Creative   Not creative

Basis for rating:

PART 2

Children were asked to build anything they wanted.

Please rate each building using the scale placed alongside each criterion.

1. The details included in the building (0,1,2,3,4).
2. The complexity of the constructed product: Height and depth—dimensional building (0,1,2,3,4).
3. The use of different pieces (0,1,2,3,4).
4. The number of buildings (0,1,2,3,4).
5. The number of different categories/kinds/classes of buildings (0,1,2,3,4).

APPENDIX E: RATER CODING SHEET

Child's name: _____   Age: _____

Ethnicity: _____   Date: _____

Tinker Toys:

PART 1

Children were asked to build anything they wanted.

Please rate each building using the scale placed alongside each criterion.

1. The elaboration of details in the building. Please give 1 point for each detail.
2. Was it a partial building or complete whole? Please give 1 point for complete whole.
3. *Originality.* The percentage of children building same picture. Please rate 0,1,2,3,4 from highest to lowest percentage.
4. *Flexibility.* The number of different kinds of pieces found in the building. Please give 1 point for each.
5. *Fluency.* The total number of buildings. Please give 1 point for each.

ACKNOWLEDGMENTS

The authors warmly thank the children, parents, teachers, and centers that participated in this project. Special thanks are extended to the artists who kindly rated the children's creations—Jennifer Malone, Stacie Melillo, and Veronica Scarpellino. Finally, we thank the editor, Professor Jaipaul Roopnarine, and the reviewers for their helpful and insightful comments and suggestions. Requests for reprints may be addressed to Professor Robyn M. Holmes, Department of Psychology, Monmouth University, West Long Branch, NJ 07764–1898.

NOTE

1. Vygostky (1978) placed an emphasis upon learning that occurs through social interaction, particularly those between children and adults. I also acknowledge the learning that takes place in child–child interactions.

REFERENCES

Acharyulu, S., & Yasodhara, P. (1984). Assessment of creative thinking abilities of preschool children through spontaneous drawings. *Psychological Studies, 29,* 192–196.

Amabile, T. (1989). *Growing up creative.* New York: Crown.

Amabile, T., & Gitomer, J. (1984). Children's artistic creativity: Effects of choice in task materials. *Personality and Social Psychology Bulletin, 10,* 209–215.

Barnett, L. (1990). Playfulness: Definition, design, and measurement. *Play and Culture, 3,* 319–336.

Barnett, L. (1991). The playful child: Measurement of the disposition to play. *Play and Culture, 4,* 51–74.

Barnett, L., & Kleiber, D. (1982). Concomitants of playfulness in early childhood cognitive abilities and gender. *The Journal of Genetic Psychology, 141,* 115–127.

Bartolini, V. (1996). On-the-job training: Children's play and work. In A. Phillips (Ed.), *Playing for keeps: Supporting children's play. Topics in early childhood education* (Vol. 2, pp. 1–10). St. Paul, MN: Red Leaf Press.

Bredekamp, S. (1987). *Developmentally appropriate practice in early childhood programs serving children from birth through age eight.* Washington, DC: National Association for the Education of Young Children.

Bredekamp, S., & Copple, C. (1997). *Developmentally appropriate practice in early childhood programs* (Rev. ed.). Washington, DC: National Association for the Education of Young Children.

Bredekamp, S., & Rosegrant, T. (Eds.). (1992). *Reaching potentials: Appropriate curriculum and assessment for young children* (Vol. 1). Washington, DC: National Association for the Education of Young Children.

Bundy, A., & Clifton, J. (1998). Construct validity of the Children's Playfulness Scale. In S. Reifel (Ed.), *Play & culture studies, Vol. 1: Diversions and divergences in fields of play* (pp. 137–148). Greenwich, CT: Ablex.

Cacciari, C., Levorato, M., & Cicogna, P. (1997). Imagination at work: Conceptual and linguistic creativity in children. In T. Ward, S. Smith, & J. Vaid (Eds.), *Creative thought* (pp. 145–177). Washington, DC: American Psychological Association.

Cobb, E. (1977). *The ecology of imagination in childhood.* New York: Columbia University Press.

Dansky, J. (1980). Make-believe: A mediator of the relationship between play and associative fluency. *Child Development, 51*, 576–579.

Dansky, J., & Silverman, I. (1973). Effects of play on associative fluency in preschool-aged children. *Developmental Psychology, 9*, 38–43.

Dansky, J., & Silverman, I. (1975). Play: A general facilitator of associative fluency. *Developmental Psychology, 11*, 104.

Darling-Hammond, L., Ancess, J., & Falk, B. (1995). *Authentic assessment in action: Studies of schools and students at work.* New York: Teachers College Press.

Davidson, S. (1988). Creativity and play. In *Play and creativity: Report of the 10th Conference of the International Association for the Child's Right to Play* (No. 15, pp. 46–49). Stockholm, Sweden: International Association for the Child's Right to Play.

Eisenberg, N. (1983). Sex-typed toy choices: What do they signify? In M. Liss (Ed.), *Social and cognitive skills: Sex roles and children's play* (pp. 45–70). New York: Academic Press.

Fein, G. (1981). Pretend play: An integrative review. *Child Development, 52*, 1095–1118.

Fine, K., & Sandstrom, S. (1988). *Knowing children: Participant observation with minors.* Thousand Oaks, CA: Sage.

Gardner, H. (1993). *Multiple intelligences.* New York: Basic Books.

Gesell, A., & Ilg, F. (1946). *The child from five to ten.* New York: Harper & Row.

Guilford, J. (1967). *The nature of human intelligence.* New York: McGraw-Hill.

Hughes, F. (1995). *Children, play and development* (3rd ed.). Boston, Allyn & Bacon.

Hughes, M. (1987). The relationship between symbolic and manipulative object play. In D. Gorlitz & J. Wohlwill (Eds.), *Curiosity, imagination and play: On the development of spontaneous cognitive and motivational processes* (pp. 141–165). Hillsdale, NJ: Erlbaum.

Isaksen, S. (1992). *Nurturing creative talents: Lessons from industry about needed work-life skills.* Buffalo, NY: The Creative Solving Group.

Isenberg, J., & Jalongo, M. (1997). *Creative expression and play in early childhood.* Upper Saddle River, NJ: Prentice-Hall.

Jellen, H., & Urban, K. (1986). The TCT—DP (Test for Creative Thinking—Drawing Production): An instrument that can be applied to most age and ability groups. *Creative Child and Adult Quarterly, 11*, 138–155.

Johnson, J., Christie, J., & Yawkey, T. (1999). *Play and early childhood development.* New York: Addison-Wesley Longman.

Lieberman, J. (1977). *Playfulness: Its relationship to imagination and creativity.* New York: Academic Press.

Li, W., Bundy, A., & Beer, D. (1995). Taiwanese parental values toward an American evaluation of playfulness. *Occupational Therapy Journal of Research, 15,* 237–258.

Meador, K. (1992). Emerging rainbows: A review of the literature on creativity in preschoolers. *Journal for the Education of the Gifted, 15,* 163–181.

Mellou, E. (1995). Review of the relationship between dramatic play and creativity in young children. *Early Child Development and Care, 112,* 85–107.

Parnes, S. (1963). Development of individual creative talent. In C.W. Taylor & T. Barron (Eds.), *Scientific creativity, its recognition and development. Selected papers from the first, second, and third University of Utah Conferences: The identification of creative scientific talent* (pp. 225–255). New York: Wiley.

Pellegrini, A. (1984–1985). The effects of exploration and play on young children's associative fluency. *Imagination, Cognition and Personality, 4,* 29–40.

Pellegrini, A., & Greene, H. (1980). The use of a sequence questioning paradigm to facilitate associative fluency in preschoolers. *Journal of Applied Developmental Psychology, 1,* 189–200.

Pepler, D. (1986). Play and creativity. In G. Fein & M. Rivkin (Eds.), *The young child at play* (pp. 143–154). Washington, DC: National Association for the Education of Young Children.

Pepler, D., & Ross, H. (1981). The effects of play on convergent and divergent problem solving. *Child Development, 52,* 1202–1210.

Qiying, Z. (1988). Creativity through play: A dream to be realized. In *Play and creativity: Report of the 10th* Conference of the International Association for the Child's Right to Play (No. 36, pp. 96–99). Stockholm, Sweden: International Association for the Child's Right to Play.

Runco, M. (1996). Personal creativity: Definition and developmental issues. In M. Runco (Ed.), *New directions for child development: Creativity from childhood through adulthood: The developmental issues* (pp. 3–30). San Francisco: Jossey-Bass.

Russ, S. (1996). Development of creative processes in children. In M. Runco (Ed.), *New directions for child development: Creativity from childhood through adulthood: The developmental issues* (pp. 31–42). San Francisco: Jossey-Bass.

Saracho, O. (1992). Preschool children's cognitive style and play and implications for creativity. *Creativity Research Journal, 5,* 35–48.

Singer, D., & Singer, J. (1990). *The house of make-believe: Children's play and the developing imagination.* Cambridge, MA: Harvard University Press.

Singer, J. (1973). *The child's world of make-believe: Experimental studies of imaginative play.* New York: Academic Press.

Smolucha, F. (1992a). A reconstruction of Vygotsky's theory of creativity. *Creativity Research Journal, 5,* 49–68.

Smolucha, F. (1992b). The relevance of Vygotsky's theory of creative imagination for contemporary research on play. *Creativity Research Journal, 5,* 69–76.

Susa, A., & Benedict, J. (1994). The effects of playground design on pretend play and divergent thinking. *Environment and Behavior, 26,* 560–579.

Sutton-Smith, B. (1986). The spirit of play. In G. Fein & M. Rivkin (Eds.), *The young child at play. Reviews of research, Vol. 4* (pp. 3–16). Washington, DC: National Association for the Education of Young Children.

Sutton-Smith, B. (1988). Creativity through play. In *Play and creativity: Report of the 10th* Conference of the International Association for the Child's Right to Play (No. 36, pp. 16–21). Stockholm, Sweden: International Association for the Child's Right to Play.

Sutton-Smith, B. (1992). The role of toys in the instigation of playful creativity. *Creativity Research Journal, 5,* 3–12.

Sutton-Smith, B. (1997). *The ambiguity of play.* Cambridge, MA: Harvard University Press.

Taylor, I. (1992). The relationship between playfulness and creativity of Japanese preschool children. *Dissertation Abstracts International, 15* (10a), 3440.

Tegano, D., Moran, J., & Sawyers, J. (1991). *Creativity in early childhood classrooms.* National Education Association. (ERIC Document Reproduction Service No. ED 338 435)

Thomas, M. (1996). *Comparing theories of child development.* Pacific Grove, CA: Brooks/Cole.

Torrance, E. (1962). *Thinking creatively with pictures.* Besenville, IL: Scholastic Testing Service.

Tracy, D. (1987). Toys, spatial ability, and science and mathematics achievement: Are they related? *Sex Roles, 17,* 115–138.

Trostle, S., & Yawkey, T. (1982). Facilitating creative thought through object play in young children. (ERIC Document Reproduction Service No. ED 221 301)

Van Hoorn, J., Scales, B., Nourot, P., & Alward, K. (1999). *Play at the center of the curriculum* (2nd ed.). Upper Saddle River, NJ: Prentice-Hall.

Vygotsky, L. S. (1978). *Mind in society: The development of higher psychological processes.* Cambridge, MA: Harvard University Press. (Original work published 1932)

Vygotsky, L. S. (1990). Imagination and creativity in childhood. *Soviet Psychology, 28,* 84–96. (Original work published 1930)

Wallach, M. (1970). Creativity. In P. Mussen (Ed.), *Carmichael's manual of child psychology* (Vol. 1, pp. 1211–1272). New York: Wiley.

Wallach, M., & Kogan, N. (1965). *Modes of thinking in young children: A study of creativity-intelligence distinction.* New York: Holt, Rinehart & Winston.

9

The Play of Early Writing

Phyllis Neves and Stuart Reifel

What is the contribution of play to early literacy development? How do the processes of classroom play interaction serve the emergence of early writing? Educators from a developmental perspective have explored these questions, usually reflecting a desire to promote the construction of literacy knowledge in kindergarten- or primary-aged children (Christie, Enz, & Vukelich, 1997; Galda, Pelligrini, & Cox, 1989; Morrow, 1990; Neuman & Roskos, 1992; Pelligrini & Galda, 1990; Schrader, 1991). The connections between symbolic aspects of play and early graphic expression have been a dominant avenue for study (Dyson, 1997; Vygotsky, 1978). The purpose of this study was to explore how preschool children create the earliest forms of writing (graphemes) in a context of classroom play at a writing center.

Much research in the literacy acquisition field has dealt with oral language to examine the development of reading and writing in young children (e.g., Teale & Sulzby, 1986), although there have been numerous examples of acquisition of conventional and preconventional writing (e.g., Chomsky, 1971; Clay, 1975; DeFord, 1980; Schickedanz, 1990). A common strand in this approach to literacy is the recognition that children combine drawing and writing on their paths to acquisition of compositional skills. These authors and others have found that drawing is an important part of a story's message, and that drawings could be used to help children gain greater understanding about how to convert visual images into alphabetic images or words. In fact, Ferreiro and Tebrosky (1982) found that young children do not differentiate between drawing and print, even when they could separate pictures from print during tasks. The developmental origins of graphic notational systems and their social origins have become an established field of inquiry (see, e.g., Dyson, 1982, 1986, 1991, 1997; Rowe, 1994), frequently reflecting the contextual theory of Vygotsky (1932/1978) and others.

Although using a rather broad definition for literacy and social context, these researchers look only at the semiotics involved in early literacy, not at the unique play context that could be an intrinsic part of that literacy. And literacy re-searchers who have linked play to early reading and writing have conceptualized play as an intervention of sorts, as materials to play with prior to engaging in more formal literacy (Christie et al., 1997; Frost, Wortham, & Reifel, 2001; Galda et al., 1989; Morrow, 1990; Neuman & Roskos, 1992; Pellegrini & Galda, 1990; Schrader, 1990). Again, Vygotsky (1932/1978) appears to influence this work, although his views of early literacy rather than his views on play tend to hold sway in this scholarship.

In an effort to connect ideas about meaningful classroom activities (such as literacy) and meaningful classroom play, Reifel and Yeatman (1993) constructed a model of play, building on Vygotsky's (1932/1978) play theory and Bateson's (1972) theory of play and fantasy. From Bateson, the notion of play frame was borrowed, to help identify the shared meanings that are created in play. From Vygotsky, the idea of pivots, or play objects around which meanings are con-structed, was adapted. Reifel and Yeatman described classroom play as a mean-ingful context that is shaped by physical and social pivots. Such an approach provides an alternative manner for understanding the relationship of literacy and play, situating literacy in play rather than as an outcome of it. Play pivots allow children to create a pretend context, in this case a literacy acquisition context.

The research reported here was a naturalistic, qualitative investigation of a prekindergarten writing center—a traditional constructive play center. The site of the study was a public school prekindergarten classroom, and the participants were the children in the class who were eligible to attend because they are economically disadvantaged. Collected data included observation notes, audio recordings of the children as they wrote at the center, and the children's graphic products.

This study built on the theories of Vygotsky; research from the literacy ac-quisition field that indicates that drawing is a child's earliest form of writing; the work of Christie and Johnson (1987) and that of Reifel and Yeatman (1993), which specify how children can use symbolic processes during constructive play frames; and Dyson's research, which demonstrated that young children inter-weave writing, oral language, and symbolic play as they construct their stories within a classroom context. Taking some of the phenomena Rowe (1994) ob-served in her preschool study and then interpreted from a semiotic perspective, this study will refract those same phenomena through the semiotics of symbolic/

constructive play and analyze them using the lens of the Reifel and Yeatman classroom play model to answer the question: What is the relationship between constructive and constructive/symbolic play in a preschool classroom and the children's production of graphemes?

METHODS

The site of this project was a self-contained, suburban, public preschool classroom. The classroom is in a school that serves 961 children, from the 3-year-olds in a program with disabilities, to the 10- and 11-year-olds in the fifth grade. The school is set in the midst of middle- and professional-class housing subdivisions. Although the number of children from these surrounding subdivisions increases each year, this school has so many students from the poorer areas of the school district that the school qualifies as a federally funded Chapter I school. The makeup of the school is largely white, with the rest of the student population coming from the Mexican American and African American communities.

The data for this project were gathered during the investigator's classroom writing-center time. The writing center is one of several learning centers in this classroom of 20 children. The children attend a 3-hour afternoon program, which has a theme play-based curriculum. They spend 15 to 25 minutes in a circle, where they do calendar and weather activities, songs, and finger plays based on the theme of study, and read stories concerning the current topic of study. Their lunch takes about 30 minutes. Outside play, restroom breaks, a 45- to 55-minute play-center time, and a good-bye circle take the rest of the 3 hours. Because of the number of children and the limited number of adults who work with these children, small-group time takes place during the play-center time each day. Small groups focus on math, science, and art projects. The children are free to come and go as they please in the play centers. At the writing center, they write in whatever manner they choose about any subject. Their graphics are accepted as the children label them by the adult in the room.

Children in this classroom are eligible for this program because they are economically disadvantaged. All the children spoke English as their first language and ranged in age from 4 years 3 months to 5 years 3 months. One child was enrolled in a program for children with disabilities and came into the class as part of inclusion during his extended school day. There were 11 males and 9 females in this group. Among the children, 16 were white, 3 were Mexican American, and 1 was African American.

Data Collection

Over a three-week period, data were gathered during the play-center time for 20–35 minutes a day. To accommodate the recording equipment used for this project, the writing center for the afternoon session was moved into the classroom next door for four weeks. The only writing materials available for the children to use were colored markers and copier paper, different from the variety of writing materials available in the usual writing center.

Three types of data were collected: audio recordings of the children's spontaneous talk while they were at the writing center, handwritten observation notes, and the children's graphics. The audio recordings were made to capture the speech the children used and to determine the nature of their play, writing, and oral language. Analysis of speech and how it was employed during play were key indicators of children's entry into play frames. Two portable cassette recorders were placed in the middle of the table used for the writing center. The teacher/investigator sat at one end of the table. The children arranged themselves according to their own wishes and the availability of seating. Since the children's choices of centers varied daily, the number of children at the center fluctuated from day to day.

Nine audio recordings and complete transcripts from those recordings were made. One tape was recorded each day. The transcripts were coordinated with the graphics of the children for analysis. During the writing sessions, the investigator made notations on sticky notes, which were placed on the children's graphics as she gathered the papers. After the transcripts were typed, she used a numbering system to correlate the graphics to the speech that surrounded the graphic's creation and, using the notations on the sticky notes, cross-referenced the children's speech in the transcripts with the numbered graphics, which followed each transcript.

The observation notes provided background information on the activities and conversations of the children as they wrote. The coming and going of the children were noted to give an idea of the flow of events during this center time. The written products of the children were collected daily so they could be part of the data analysis.

Categories of Analysis

Based on the theories of Vygotsky (1932/1978) and Bateson (1972) and the model of classroom play proposed by Reifel and Yeatman (1993), data were organized into categories of the pivots (i.e., meaningful sources) during play that prompted and transformed the graphics the children produced. Table 9.1 lists the coding categories for the pivots for the writing.

In a similar manner, the children's graphics were evaluated. Bridging the work of Dyson (1982, 1983) and modifying categories taken from Carroll and Wilson (1993), who all base their work on Vygotsky's theory for written development, categories for the graphemes the children used were established. The coding categories for the graphemes are found in Table 9.2.

Analysis

These categories were used to generate a two-tiered coding system. Working with a teacher who had several years of experience working with emerging

Table 9.1
Coding Categories for the Pivots (Sources) for the Writing

1. **Classroom environment**: The classroom pets, decorations, toys, etc.
2. **Writing center materials**: The writing materials: paper and markers; the sticky notes used by the teacher, and the tape recorder.
3. **Peer social interaction**: Conversation and play among the children.
4. **Peer graphics**: The scribbles, drawings, or writing of one child serving as the source for another child's graphics.
5. **Teacher–child interaction**: Social interaction between the child and the teacher or interaction between them focusing on the child's graphics.
6. **Ambiguous**: Pivots that cannot be readily explained using the classroom environment, class materials, peer social interactions, peer graphics, or teacher–child interactions.
7. **Peer social interaction and peer graphics**: When these two pivots together provide the source of the child's writing.
8. **One's own graphics**: When an individual's own graphics provide the pivot.

Adapted from Reifel & Yeatman, 1993; Vygotsky, 1932/1978.

Table 9.2
Coding Categories for the Graphemes

1. **Scribbling**: Random marks combined with speech/gesture that do not represent or denote a pictograph, ideograph, or writing.
2. **Scribble-writing**: Scribbling combined with speech/gesture that indicates "writing": simple letters or conventional adult writing.
3. **Pictograph**: A drawing combined with speech/gesture that denotes a person, object, or gesture known but not necessarily seen. Several drawings can be on one page. Generally, the child orally labels the drawing or parts of the drawing. This category includes scribbling/pictographs.
4. **Ideograph**: A drawing combined with speech/gesture that tells a narrative or that represents an idea or a relationship. This category includes scribbling/pictographs.
5. **Symbolic drawing**: A drawing combined with speech/gesture that directly denotes what is seen by the child—that is, the child does not see the drawing as a representation, but as a similar object.
6. **Letter writing**: Individual letters or strings of letters that combined with the child's speech indicate they do not represent words.
7. **Invented spelling**: Individual letters or strings of letters that combined with the child's speech/gesture indicate that they represent words.
8. **Conventional name or word writing**
9. **Number writing**: Individual numbers or strings of numbers that combined with the child's speech/gesture indicate that they represent numbers.

Adapted from Carroll & Wilson, 1993; Vygotsky, 1932/1978.

writers in her own classroom, a preliminary transcript and its paired graphic products was assessed to establish coding reliability. The reliability of the coding on that particular transcript was an agreement of 95 percent for the pivots and an agreement of 91 percent for the graphemes. The computation for the results was done by placing the number of agreements over the total numbers of codes

Figure 9.1
Joint occurance of pivots and graphemes

Pivots	#1	#2	#3	#4	#5	#6	#7	#8	Total #
Grapheme									
#1		3	1			3		3	10
#2			2			1	5	3	11
#3			3	46	3	47	70	41	210
#4			1	4		8	8	15	36
#5				3		6	4	8	21
#6			5		1	1	12	5	24
#7			1				4	5	10
#8			3				2	1	6
#9			2			2	1	4	9
Total #		3	18	53	4	68	106	85	337

and then dividing. The same method was used to determine the successive re-liability during the following procedures.

With the reliability of the coding system established, the first author coded all nine remaining transcripts and the accompanying graphic products. The findings of the coding results are presented in Figure 9.1. From this basis, patterns of congruence between play pivots and graphemes could be explored qualitatively.

RESULTS

The information gathered from the summary tables and data from the transcripts show some telling examples, which suggest that constructive and constructive/symbolic play offer the transformational basis for much of children's earliest forms of written language. During the writing sessions of this project, children were playing at several levels and using many levels of graphemes as they created their play frames within the social context of the writing center. Some general observations from the data are offered first; then the discussion centers on pivots and graphemes separately. Although the discussion of the results from the summary table and the transcripts examine pivots and graphemes individually, they are intertwined and furnish the means and the context for the playful graphic activity that occurs. Finally, a number of double codes that were generated are briefly discussed, and a summary of the results is offered.

General Observations

There were a total of 337 codes each for pivots and graphemes over the 9-day period. The individual ranges for pivots and graphemes generated by a child went from as high as 56 pivots over 6 categories and 56 graphemes over 7 categories, to 2 children who did not generate any codes. The average number of codes per child fell between 6 and 18 pivots/graphemes over no fewer than 3 categories. There were great variations both in the number of pivots in the production of graphemes and in the ranges of the categories for pivots and graphemes, as reflected in Figure 9.1. This was due to several reasons.

Two of the most important reasons for the number of depictions were the amount of time a child spent in the writing center and the level of development that child had reached. Raymond (a pseudonym, as are all names in the following sections), who was one of the oldest children, spent much of his time at the writing table. As a flexible thinker and very experienced with writing materials, he used 56 pivots across 6 of the categories and produced 56 graphemes across 7 categories. Bob, who also constantly processed creatively and fluently and was well practiced with writing materials but who spent only part of 2 days at the center, nonetheless used 30 pivots across 5 categories and produced 30 graphemes in 7 categories. Kelsey, who was not nearly as experienced as either Raymond or Bob, but who spent most of her center time at the writing table with Raymond and Amy, used 35 pivots across 7 of the categories and created 35 graphemes in 7 categories. Linette, who was as inexperienced as Kelsey but spent only part of 2 center times at the writing table, produced only 6 graphemes and used 6 pivots in 2 categories.

Another reason for the number of depictions was the amount of oral language surrounding the pivots and the graphemes. For example, Chase, who spent only part of two days at the center, was still exploring the materials by scribbling. He made no comment on his graphic even when the teacher made a remark about his scribbles, so no code was recorded. Lydia, on the other hand, scribbled and made comments to herself about what she was doing, which resulted in a subsequent code. K.B. and Amy both composed some very detailed pictographs as well as ideographs. They possessed quiet natures, which did not provide ready access to the pivots used to construct these graphemes, and this fact produced fewer codes for both of them than for children such as Raymond who were more verbal.

Graphemes

Far and away the most numerous graphemes, as reflected in Figure 9.1, were the pictographs (210, or 62 percent of the total number of graphemes), followed by the ideographs (36, or 11 percent), letter writing (24, or 7 percent), and symbolic drawing (21, or 6 percent). Pictographs and ideographs are what Dyson

(1983) called graphic writing. These children with very few exceptions did not give indications that they yet understand that speech can be written. They still operated with what Vygotsky (1932/1978) labeled as first-order symbols, which directly denote the object or the action depicted. Even children who on occasion wrote letters or letter-like forms, for the most part still used graphic writing. K.B. and his friends wrote his name, but they treated his name as a graphic depiction of him. At one point, K.B. hid his name as if it were an object in one of his pictures for his teacher to find. Later on, in another play frame, Concordia adds "eyes" to the letters of his name. Micah, Bob, and Rod at various times offered to "draw" their names for peers or the teacher. For these children, writing and drawing are interchangeable. The most common subjects for pictographs, ideographs, symbolic drawing, and letter or scribble writing were drawn from those familiar to the children, such as houses, people, and animals.

Pictographs for this group of children generally had pivots from peer social interaction and peer graphics (70 instances). There is logic in this result. What makes a difference between a pictograph and an ideograph is the oral language surrounding the graphic and encoding its meaning. When K.B. just labels a picture, "House, star, me," his oral language encodes the graphic as a pictograph. However, later in the same session when he says about a very similar graphic, "My dad is making a spaceship," his oral language encoded the graphic as an ideograph. When a child pivots his own grapheme, as happened 84 times, his ideas may become more complex as he goes through mental transformations about the meaning of his graphics.

Oral language and gesture combined with a graphic also can be encoded as an ideograph. Micah used gestures as he marked on the paper and orally depicted first finger plays and then a moving machine to create an ideograph. Raymond said "Bong!" and ran his fingers across his guitar pictograph to generate an ideograph.

Among this group of children, there were those who would first draw or scribble a graphic and then assign a meaning to create a grapheme. Pivoting on her peer's conversation and graphics, Kelsey drew something and named it a guitar. Amara's drawing became a refrigerator with food in it as she discussed her graphic with the teacher. This phenomena occurred also when the children used scribble-writing to "write" like adults. Rod scribble-wrote and then declared that he had written a "Chinese restaurant," implying, of course, that he had written what he had seen on a menu. Trevor scribbled vigorously and then decided that his graphics had to be a note from his mother.

The children who had more experiences with drawing and writing would state what they had intended to represent graphically and then proceed to create that representation whether in the form of a drawing, a letter, or a scribble. This is in keeping with what Buhler (1935) called "constructive work" and what is more commonly called constructive play, as children repeatedly said what they intended to make. (See the episode presented below about the birdie cat as an example of this.) One day toward the end of data collection, as the teacher was closing the writing center for the day, Raymond told her that he was going to build one more, meaning that he wanted to draw one more picture.

Just as Halliday (1973) demonstrated that young children tune their oral language to accomplish their goals, an overview of the use of graphemes in these transcripts confirms that this group of children tuned their graphic symbols to suit their needs for particular notations. They made letter or letter-like symbols when they wrote names or "letters" that were to be sent to someone else. Scribble-writing was used to indicate grown-up writing. Numbers, which appeared less frequently, were used for math notations.

Not only did the children tune their graphics to suit their needs, but they also tuned their graphics to the implicit themes that appeared some days. While these themes were not discussed overtly by the children, the themes provided a context for the graphics that were produced, whether pictographs, ideographs, letter writing, symbolic drawing, or scribbling. For example, early during data collection, a theme of houses was played out in a variety of ways. Some children—Micah, Libby, and Amy—drew houses; others such as Mason drew parts of houses (windows or doors). Things inside houses were represented graphically, for example, refrigerators, bedrooms, guitars, a little baby, and crying people who have no money to buy food. Raymond's garage takes on the form of a "noctopiggy." Before this particular transformation, Raymond used gesture, sound, and the marks of a blue marker to "drive" a car around his paper. All this activity supports the observation of Reifel and Yeatman (1993) that "classroom play is a frame, created for simulative behavior that is given its meaning as play in the course of its creation" (p. 353).

Some of the children had their own individual theme(s), which they used each time they were at the writing center. For example, each day Amy and K.B. invariably drew at least one picture with a house. These houses were similar each day. Some individuals would tune their own frame of reference to the group's implicit frame. Early during data collection, when almost everyone at the table was engaged in getting the letters of the alphabet committed to paper, Amy added letters to her usual house pictures. The letters in her pictures were later changed into squares that led to bigger squares that represented a bridge over water.

The motivating question for this analysis was the play associated with the depictions just described. Virtually all of the graphemes created by children in this study were tied to play. That play will be described in the following sections in terms of play pivots.

Play Pivots

The most frequent pivot for all categories of graphemes was the combination of peer social interaction and peer graphics (#7, 106, 32 percent). The next most numerous pivot was one's own graphics (85, 25 percent), followed by ambiguous (68, 20 percent) and peer graphics (53, 16 percent). While many of the conversations throughout the transcripts concerned the classroom environment (#1), this pivot did not prompt children to create any graphemes. There seemed to be an ebb and flow during these writing sessions, where the children talked about the environment or other topics as they played individually or in groups with their graphemes. This time was followed by discussions of their own or others' graphemes and sometimes statements of what they would create next. A very brief pause in the talk resulted as they depicted, and another general conversation ensued as the cycle repeated itself.

Among the other less frequent pivots, writing center materials (#2) resulted in scribbling and encompassed functional play, as children who did not have much experience with writing materials explored the color of the markers. On two occasions, Lydia scribbled with the markers for their colors. Once she likened the color pink to one of her nightgowns and to her mother's fingernail polish; on another, she said as she scribbled with the brown marker, "Chocolate, chocolate." However, in more sophisticated hands, the writing center materials sparked ideographs and some intricate symbolic play frames, as when Raymond and Micah popped marker lids into place and pretended that they were airplanes; they then used the markers to extend this concept, by drawing mouths that curved up in the manner that airplanes fly up (i.e., marker lids). Later in the play frame, their drawn mouths became airplanes themselves.

The pivots of peer social interactions (#3), peer graphics (#4), or teacher–child interaction (#5) separately also did not induce many graphemes, 75 when the 3 are totaled. While these pivots are associated with grapheme play, they do not account for much of the data collected.

Peer Interaction/Peer Graphics

When peer social interaction and peer graphics occurred together (pivot #7), the number of graphemes created jumped to 106. Consistently throughout these transcripts, a child would use this pivot to incorporate into his/her grapheme aspects of the object, in the case of a pictograph, or the subject of an ideograph about which another child had drawn and spoken. For example, Concordia, Kismet, Bob, and K.B. were among children at the writing table. Kismet drew a cat which she pointed out to Concordia:

K: This is a cat. A cat's head.

C: You know how to make a good cat. [*pause*] I'm gonna make a cat right here.

K.B.: [*laughs*] A birdie cat.

C: A birdie cat.

B: I'm going to make a rabbit.

K: A birdie cat. [*laughs*] I'm going to make a birdie cat.

B: I made a cat.

K.B.: It's a birdie cat.

B: Uh huh.

K.B.: It . . .

C: That looks like a doggie cat.

B: Nope. IT'S—A—CAT!

K.B.: It's a birdie cat. [*laughs*]

B: It's not no birdie cat.

C: It's a doggie. Wait. This is a dinosaur.

B: I can make dinosaurs.

C: Yeah. Now I am going to make a dinosaur.

In this vignette, using pivot #7, Bob's drawing of a rabbit takes on the attributes of a cat as K.B., Kismet, and Concordia discuss the birdie cats they are going to make. Afterward, Bob negotiated the meaning of his grapheme as a cat, not a birdie cat or a doggie cat, with K.B. and Concordia. Then using the pivot of peer social interaction and peer graphics, the group begins to construct dinosaurs together.

At another time, a whole group of children at the writing table employed this pivot at the same time, but on an individual level. An implicit topic developed when a house theme in graphemes was created. As children talked about the houses, garages, house elephants, and rooms they were creating, other children drew refrigerators filled with food or members of their families. No one spoke of this theme, but it impacted every grapheme the children produced that day.

It was when the children used pivot #7 that scaffolding often occurred spontaneously. One day, the group at the table discussed snakes and snails, arguing over whether snakes were "straight" and snails were "circles." Although Kismet took no part in the discussion, she created a circled graphic that had stripes. Raymond pivoted with no comment on the graphic that Kismet had made. He dubbed his creation a "snail stripper." Kelsey, who mostly just scribbled, wanted to make some, so Raymond told her how as he demonstrated. Kelsey used his scaffolding to draw above her usual ability and produced a very fine "snail stripper" of her own.

One's Own Graphics

One's own graphics (#8) provided the pivot for 85 graphemes. Children used this pivot to clarify what their graphemes meant. An episode illustrating this occurred among Mason, Micah, and the teacher:

Ma: That's, that's a head.

T: A head?

Ma: A face—.

T: And that's a face.

Ma: That's a triangle in the face.

T: And a triangle in the face. I wonder if this person is happy.

M: I know what a triangle is. It has four corners.

Ma: It's me.

When Mason pivoted on his own grapheme as he and the teacher talked, the intended meaning of his grapheme emerged.

At other times, a child would use this pivot to add more elaboration to his or her graphemes and sometimes to change the encoding as she talked. The children who utilized their own graphics as pivots used those graphics as objects to reflect their own mental transformations. One of the results of this reflection was that a grapheme, which started as a pictograph, could be transformed into a symbolic drawing. For example, when Raymond depicted a moustache, Micah remarked: "Sometimes dad gets moustaches." Raymond's graphic then becomes just a curly circle, and Raymond transforms the "hair" into a beard, which later becomes his dad.

Ambiguous Pivots

Surprisingly, the pivot that prompted a large number of graphemes was the ambiguous (#6) with 68 codes. The large number of pivots that are ambiguous may support the notion that while writing for young children may take place within a social frame, their play allows the individual to create independently in that frame. That independence cannot be tracked to any source other than the child's imagination, creating ambiguity in terms of the cues that can be interpreted by adults. This particular group of children used this pivot mostly when a child created his/her first grapheme for the day at the writing table, or after the silent pauses that occurred between the conversations the children conducted as they were working independently on their graphics. This ambiguous pivot suggests that aspects of associative social play (Parten, 1932) are involved in the group process of the writing center.

Double Codes

There were 12 codes for pivots that had double codes—for example, a child used both writing center materials and peer social interaction simultaneously as a pivot to produce an ideograph. For instance, Micah used the lid popping off a marker and flying through the air (pivot #2) and his conversation with Raymond (pivot #3) to create an ideograph representing an airplane: "And poof! And the airplane goes backwards. How about that!" After Micah laughs, he pivots on his own grapheme, saying, "I grow up to the tip where it goes backwards." Children with all levels of development used these double pivots. There were not enough of these codes to analyze for patterns. Perhaps a greater number of longer transcripts would yield a greater number of these double codes for examination.

DISCUSSION

There were two important factors causing the differences in the number of pivots a child used and of graphemes that a child produced: the amount of time a child spent in the writing center and that child's level of development. The amount of a child's oral language that surrounded a pivot and grapheme also affected the number of codes an individual generated.

The findings on play pivots demonstrated that the classroom environment (#1) did not generate any graphemes. This was most probably due to the children writing in a different classroom from their own. Children who were less experienced used the writing center materials (#2) to create scribbling and functional play. More experienced children used the same pivot to create ideographs and symbolic play. When peer social interaction and peer graphics occurred together (pivot #7), the children used it most often to produce graphemes. This pivot was also employed by individuals to tune their graphics to the implicit graphic themes that the group developed. Scaffolding among peers came about most often when the children used this pivot. The large number of pivots that sprang from ambiguous sources (#6) suggests that while the writing center provided a social frame, the children's constructive and constructive/symbolic play was often created independently within the group context. The children were more likely to utilize this pivot when they created their first grapheme for the day or after conversations with peers that did not center on graphics. One's own graphics (#8) served as pivots when a child clarified the grapheme's meaning, added more elaboration to the grapheme, or used her grapheme as an object for mental transformations.

The results of the graphemes establish that for this group of children the most common grapheme was the pictograph. This result demonstrates that these children, for the most part, still operated with first-order symbols, supporting Vygotsky's theory (1978). Their uses of letter writing and scribbling also denote these graphemes as first-order symbols. These children did not yet understand that speech could not be written down. The results indicate that the difference between a pictograph and an ideograph rested on the oral language a child used to encode the meaning of a graphic. Pictographs' most common pivot was peer social interaction and other peer graphics (#7), while the ideograph's most numerous pivot was one's own graphics (#8). Some children drew or scribbled a graphic and then assigned a meaning to create graphemes. Other, more sophisticated children would first state what they intended to represent and then produce a grapheme. The oral language reflected the language often heard at traditional constructive play centers.

Grapheme results also demonstrated that children tune their graphics to suit their play needs and in response to the implicit graphic themes that developed in the social context. Individual children, too, had their own themes that they played out daily. The intrinsic playful nature of the graphemes was reflected in how fluid the meaning of the graphics were. The process of creation took priority over the final product, confirming the essence of play involved. These transformations were embedded in the social context of the writing center.

What is remarkable and strongly suggests the intrinsic nature of play in these earliest forms of written language is how fluid these graphics are and how the children transform them during their interactions. This observation is reminiscent of those made by Werner (1948). Process always takes precedence over the final product. Thus, letters can be given eyes and depict more than one person. The letter "M" can become a monster's claw. Dots become windows, and houses become house elephants. These transformations are embedded within the specific contexts the children created at the writing center. The participants must negotiate the unspoken rules of what can be, in these specific frameworks. Water must be blue, as when Kelsey tried to draw it; however, similar blue marks on Raymond's paper can represent a driven car.

This study points to a dichotomy that exists in the fields of early education and literacy acquisition. Scholars such as Rowe (1994) and Dyson (1989, 1991, 1994, 1997) are firmly planted in the literacy field and use the theory of traditional semiotics as the basis of young children's literacy acquisition in early childhood classroom writing centers. These researchers acknowledge various communications systems and social bases for literacy acquisition, but they do not include play as a formal construct that young children use to communicate on several levels as they create literacy. Our evidence reveals patterns of early literacy that are like those found in earlier studies, but our data establish that graphemes are firmly situated in the pretend and construction play of young children. Graphemes are not just communications for young children; they are communications that pivot around play meanings, within frames that children create at the writing center.

Our findings also provide a slight contrast to the position taken by a number of scholars who argue for a play basis for early literacy (e.g., Christie, 1994; Christie et al., 1997; Hall, 1991; Levy, Schaefer, & Phelps, 1986; Morrow, 1989, 1990; Schrader, 1989, 1991; Sulzby, 1985, 1986; Vukelich, 1991; Zalusky, 1982). Planning play activities, whether with specific dramatic play materials or other forms of support for play, may indeed enhance early literacy (Frost et al., 2001). But as our findings show, literacy materials in the classroom provide a context for play, and the play that children create with literacy materials provokes increasing literacy. Children use their own play with paper and markers as pivots for literacy acquisition by making literacy (at a level that is meaningful to them) into play.

REFERENCES

Bateson, G. (1972). *Steps to an ecology of mind*. New York: Ballantine Books.
Buhler, C. (1935). *From birth to maturity*. London: Routledge and Kegan Paul.
Carroll, J.A., & Wilson, E. (1993). *Acts of teaching: How to teach writing*. Englewood, NJ: Teacher Idea Press.

Chomsky, C. (1971). Write now, read later. *Childhood Education, 47,* 296–299.

Christie, J. (1994). Literacy play interventions: A review of empirical research. In S. Reifel (Ed.), *Advances in early education and day care* (Vol. 6, pp. 3–24). Greenwich, CT: JAI Press.

Christie, J.F., Enz, B., & Vukelich, C. (1997). *Teaching language and literacy: Preschool through the elementary grades.* New York: Addison-Wesley.

Christie, J. F., & Johnson, E. P. (1987). Reconceptualizing constructive play: A review of the empirical literature. *Merrill-Palmer Quarterly, 33,* 439–452.

Clay, M.M. (1975). *What did I write?* Auckland, New Zealand: Heinemann Educational Books.

DeFord, D. (1980). Young children and their writing. *Theory into Practice, 19,* 157–162.

Dyson, A.H. (1982). The emergence of visible language: Interrelationships between drawing and early writing. *Visible Language, 26,* 360–381.

Dyson, A.H. (1983). The role of oral language in the early writing process. *Research in the Teaching of English, 17,* 1–30.

Dyson, A.H. (1986). Transitions and tensions: Interrelationships between the drawing, talking, and dictation of young children. *Research in the Teaching of English, 20,* 370–409.

Dyson, A.H. (1989). *Multiple worlds of child writers: Friends learning to write.* New York: Teachers College Press.

Dyson, A.H. (1991). *Social worlds of children learning to write in an urban primary school.* New York: Teachers College Press.

Dyson, A.H. (1994). Framing child texts with child worlds: The social use of oral and written narratives in an urban K/1 classroom. In S. Reifel (Ed.), *Advances in early education and day care* (Vol. 6, pp. 25–60). Greenwich, CT: JAI Press.

Dyson, A.H. (1997). *Writing superheroes: Contemporary childhood, popular culture, and classroom literacy.* New York: Teachers College Press.

Ferreiro, E., & Tebrosky, A. (1982). *Literacy before schooling.* Exeter, NH: Heinemann.

Frost, J.L., Wortham, S., & Reifel, S. (2001). *Play and child development.* Upper Saddle River, NJ: Merrill/Prentice-Hall.

Galda, L., Pellegrini, A.D., & Cox, S. (1989). A short-term longitudinal study of preschoolers' emergent literacy. *Research in the Teaching of English, 23,* 292–309.

Hall, N. (1991). Play and the emergence of literacy. In J. Christie (Ed.), *Play and early literacy development* (pp. 3–25). Albany: State University of New York Press.

Halliday, M.A.K. (1973). *Learning how to mean: Explorations in the development of language.* New York: Elsevier North-Holland.

Levy, A., Schaefer, L., & Phelps, P. (1986). Increasing preschool effectiveness: Enhancing the language abilities of 3- and 4-year-old children through planned sociodramatic play. *Early Childhood Research Quarterly, 1,* 133–140.

Morrow, L. (1989). *Literacy development in the early years.* Upper Saddle River, NJ: Prentice-Hall.

Morrow, L. (1990). Preparing the classroom environment to promote literacy during play. *Early Childhood Research Quarterly, 5,* 537–554.

Neuman, S.B., & Roskos, K. (1992). Literary objects as cultural tools: Effects on children's literacy behaviors during play. *Reading Research Quarterly, 27,* 204–223.

Parten, M.B. (1932). Social participation among preschool children. *Journal of Abnormal and Social Psychology, 27,* 243–369.

Pellegrini, A.D., & Galda, L. (1990). Children's play, language, and early literacy. *Topics in Language Disorders, 10*, 76–88.

Reifel, S., & Yeatman, J. (1993). From category to context: Reconsidering classroom play. *Early Childhood Research Quarterly, 8*, 347–367.

Rowe, D.W. (1994). *Preschoolers as authors: Literacy learning in the social world of the classroom.* Creekill, NJ: Hampton Press.

Schickedanz, J. (1990). *Adam's righting revolution: One child's literacy development from infancy through grade one.* Portsmouth, NH: Heinemann.

Schrader, C. (1989). Written language use within the context of young children's symbolic play. *Early Childhood Research Quarterly, 4*, 225–244.

Schrader, C. (1991). Symbolic play: A source of meaningful engagements with writing and reading. In J. Christie (Ed.), *Play and early literacy development* (pp. 189–213). Albany: State University of New York Press.

Sulzby, E. (1985). Kindergartners as writers and readers. In M. Farr (Ed.), *Advances in writing research. Vol. 1: Children's early writing development* (pp. 50–89). Norwood, NJ: Ablex.

Sulzby, E. (1986). Writing and reading: Signs of oral and written language organization in the young child. In W. Teale & E. Sulzby (Eds.), *Emergent literacy* (pp. 50–89). Norwood, NJ: Ablex.

Teale, W., & Sulzby, E. (1986). *Emergent literacy.* Norwood, NJ: Ablex.

Vukelich, C. (1991). Material and modeling: Promoting literacy during play. In J. Christie (Ed.), *Play and early literacy development* (pp. 215–231). Albany: State University of New York Press.

Vygotsky, L.S. (1978). *Mind in society: The development of higher psychological processes.* Cambridge, MA: Harvard University Press. (Original work published 1932)

Werner, H. (1948). *Comparative psychology of mental development.* New York: International Universities Press.

Zalusky, U.L. (1982). Relationships: What did I write? What did I draw? In W. Frawley (Ed.), *Linguistics and literacy* (pp. 91–124). New York: Plenum Press.

10

Parental Scaffolding during Joint Play with Preschoolers

Maureen Vandermaas-Peeler, Catherine King,
Amy Clayton, Mindi Holt, Kristen Kurtz, Lisa Maestri,
Erica Morris, and Emily Woody

As Rogoff (1990) observed, children's implicit and explicit learning in social context is influenced by the nature of the social interaction. Rogoff described a process of guided participation, in which children participate in loosely or formally structured ongoing routines and special events that are guided by other, more competent members of the culture. Moreover, Rogoff and others (Whiting & Edwards, 1988) found considerable cultural variation in the kinds of activities in which children participate. In many cultures, guided participation focuses on the acquisition of skills that contribute to the economic gain of the family, as children perform daily chores and other family responsibilities such as child care. By contrast, in middle-class families in the United States, guided participation is focused on the acquisition of academically oriented cognitive and social skills, in preparation for school (Rogoff, Mistry, Göncü, & Moisier, 1993).

Beliefs about who is considered an appropriate social partner for young children also vary cross-culturally. For example, Farver (1993) indicated that young children in Mexico spent the majority of their time under the supervision of their older siblings. In the United States, middle-class parents, particularly mothers, considered themselves appropriate social partners for their young children (Farver, 1993; Haight, Parke, & Black, 1997).

Furthermore, cross-cultural variation has been discovered both in the nature of the activities parents engage in with their children and in the goals and strategies that guide their interactions. In the United States, middle-class parents tend to be involved in many aspects of children's play activities (for a review, see Haight et al., 1997). Tamis-LeMonda, Bornstein, Cyphers, Toda, and Ogino (1992) found that American mothers tended to use play as a context for teaching world knowledge, while in contrast, Japanese mothers focused more on social interactions and communication in play with their toddlers. However, the middle-class Taiwanese mothers studied by Chin and Reifel (2000) did use joint play as a context for teaching.

Gender variation in parental approach is also evident, in that mothers more often choose intellectual activities, while fathers choose social-physical activities (Clarke-Stewart, 1973; Parke, 1996). Fathers tend to engage in more physical play, while mothers' play tends to focus more on the use of objects, social games, and pretend play (Lamb, 1981; Langlois & Downs, 1980; MacDonald & Parke, 1986). It should be noted that these gender differences are largely differences in degree, in that fathers have been demonstrated to support their young children's pretend play (Farver & Wimbarti, 1995) and not all studies have found gender differences in parental approach (Haight et al., 1997). The gender of the child also influences the nature of play, as persistent gender differences in child preferences and activities have been found. Typically, boys appear to be more physically aggressive during play, while girls generally prefer activities such as doll play, dress-up, and art activities (Fagot, 1978, 1994; Maccoby & Jacklin, 1974; Pellegrini & Smith, 1998).

In recent studies of parent–child pretend play, parent strategies also seem to vary by context. Shine and Acosta (1999) studied parents interacting with their children in a museum exhibit of a grocery store. In this setting, parents seemed to be oriented toward guiding their children's pretend play following a grocery store script rather than engaging in more imaginative make-believe play. In contrast, Chin and Reifel (2000) studied mothers in a toy-lending library, in which the parents seemed much more likely to engage in mutually interactive imaginative pretend play.

PERSPECTIVES ON THE NATURE OF PLAY

These specific cultural patterns of parent–child joint play raise questions concerning how parents' goals for their children's development are reflected in their play activities. Research from a psychological perspective has usually focused on one of two views of play. Piaget and others have viewed play as a reflection of children's current level of development. It is intrinsically motivated and allows for practice of currently developing schemes. Others (e.g., Vygotsky and Erikson) have described play as facilitating children's development. Play is used as a safe context for trying out new ideas and developing new skills and knowledge. Vygotsky emphasized play with skilled and responsive partners as an important source of learning for young children (Vygotsky, 1967, 1932/1978, 1990).

Although play may be intrinsically motivated in young children (play for its own sake), parents seem to view it in a more functional way (play for learning's sake). Given that parents in the United States use play as a context for guided participation, what kind of playmates do they make? If they focus on teaching their children, can they do so while maintaining playful experiences with them? Caldwell (1986) asserts that play should be mutually enjoyable, but that sometimes parents are so focused on their own goals for play that they can stifle children's creativity (e.g., by insisting on the "correct" use for a toy). Shine and Acosta (1999) call this the *as-if* approach to play, in which actions are tied to reality, in contrast to a *what-if* approach, which incorporates more fantasy elements. Caldwell and others (e.g., Levenstein, 1986) note a paradox of parent–child play: that adults who are generally *less* skilled at playing often take a didactic role with their children, who know quite well how to play already. Obviously, for many parents, children's learning is a primary goal of play interactions.

Bornstein and his colleagues (Bornstein, 1989; O'Reilly & Bornstein, 1993) have suggested that parents can assume a variety of roles during joint play with their children, some more social and others more didactic. Social interactions, according to Bornstein (1989), focus on the affective, mutual exchanges between parent and child. Didactic interactions, by contrast, have an extra-dyadic focus, and include attention to attributes of objects, events, and direct questions (Bornstein, 1989). Both research and theory strongly suggest that when social and didactic modes can be successfully integrated in parent–child play, there can be lasting social and cognitive benefits for the child (Bornstein & Tamis-LeMonda, 1989; Levenstein & O'Hara, 1993; Lindsay, Mize, & Pettit, 1997; McCune, Dipane, Fireoved, & Fleck, 1994).

SCAFFOLDING AND PLAY

The strategies that parents use to maintain or extend play activity have been described as providing a scaffold for the play (Farver, 1993). *Scaffolding* is a term used to describe actions by adults that structure children's participation in joint activity so that the child's level of participation is enhanced and learning is facilitated. Wood, Bruner, and Ross (1976) noted that adults used many different scaffolding strategies to keep children engaged in the ongoing activity, control frustration, model ideal performance, and simplify tasks so that children can participate at a higher level than if alone. By enhancing their children's participation in ongoing activities, parents provide a zone of proximal development that encourages a higher level of functioning in the future (Vygotsky, 1932/1978). Thus, scaffolding has two simultaneous goals: the enhancement of the child's participation in the current activity, and the facilitation of the child's development so that he or she can participate at a higher functional level in future activities (Griffin & Cole, 1984). As such, conceptualizations of scaffolding tend to include both "social" functions, such as maintaining the interaction, and "didactic" functions, such as assisting with task-related problem solving (Chin & Reifel, 2000).

Several studies confirm the theoretical position that scaffolding enhances children's performance on various tasks (e.g., Conner, Knight, & Cross, 1997; Pratt, Kerig, Cowan, & Cowan, 1988; Wood et al., 1976). In most studies of parental scaffolding, parents are asked by researchers to assist children in highly structured tasks (e.g., tower building with blocks and puzzle tasks), with the focus primarily on the didactic functions of scaffolding and a specific and "correct" outcome for the joint activity. Free play has fewer external goals and may provide more opportunities for social- or play-related emphases on the part of parents. Parents may be able to integrate scaffolding aimed at enhancing children's skills and knowledge while also remaining engaged in the mutual play activity.

GOALS OF THE PRESENT STUDY

In the present study, we were interested in ways in which parents guide their children's participation in dyadic interactions in free play with a variety of commercially produced toys. Two settings, laboratory and home, were included to measure the influence of the physical setting for observing joint play activity in parents and preschoolers. Play was defined as mutual engagement around a specific theme, for example, constructing a tower with blocks or pretending to shop at a grocery store. Following Singer and Singer (1990), we investigated play with preschool-aged children with the assumption that preschoolers (up to age 6) are at the pinnacle of make-believe play and are cognitively and socially ready to develop important play-related skills such as problem solving and creativity. Finally, in order to investigate gender differences in parental scaffolding during play, we observed mothers and fathers with either their son or their daughter.

We investigated scaffolding in two primary ways. First, we employed the coding system developed by Farver (1993) to categorize scaffolding as teaching, suggesting, commenting, or directing children's play. Given our interest in the dual focus of scaffolding as both social and didactic, and our questions about parental abilities to integrate teaching into play, we developed a new coding scheme to analyze parental teaching in more detail. Our observations of "teaching" included whether the child or parent initiated the teaching, how smoothly it was integrated into the play, and the focal orientation of the teaching (e.g., conceptual or procedural information).

Our specific research questions were as follows: (1) How do middle-class mothers and fathers and their preschool-aged children in the United States play in one of two physical settings with specified toys? (2) Does the research setting (laboratory or home) affect patterns of parent–child interaction in play? (3) What types of scaffolding strategies do parents most commonly employ in a free-play setting? (4) Are parents effective play partners, in terms of their responsiveness and ability to maintain children's focus on play? (5) How do parents' abilities to smoothly integrate the various functions of scaffolding into the joint play vary by the gender of parent and child?

METHOD

Participants

Forty-nine parents (28 mothers) and their 3- to 5-year-old children (27 girls) participated in the study. Parents who responded to interest forms circulated in daycare centers in a small community in the southeast were contacted by researchers. The sample consisted of middle-class Caucasian families (with the exception of one African American dyad). The mean age of the children was 4 years 4 months. The parents' mean age was 36 years.

Measures and Procedure

Families were randomly assigned to play in their home, or in the on-campus play laboratory. In both contexts, a standard set of toys was provided, including a doctor kit, booties and a "labcoat," pretend food, a cash register, a credit card machine, an apron, a grocery cart, a teddy bear, wooden blocks, a Mr. Potato Head, and a pretend phone. In the laboratory, there was a child-sized table and chairs in the room as well. In the home, the play occurred wherever the dyad was most comfortable. This was generally on the living room floor.

Parents were instructed to play with their children as they normally would, for 2 play sessions lasting 8 minutes each. Between the dyadic play sessions, parents completed demographics, typical-play, and toy-familiarity surveys designed by the researchers while the child played alone with the toys. All play sessions were videotaped. The current study focuses on the analyses of the videotaped play episodes.

Coding of Videotapes

Episodes of play in each session were defined as joint pretend play with a thematic focus or as nonpretend play with one set of materials (e.g., blocks). The two play sessions were combined into one unit for these analyses (16 minutes of play). The videotapes were fully transcribed, and coding was conducted using the transcripts while watching the videotapes. This enabled coding of both verbal and nonverbal behaviors. Type of play was coded continuously from the videotapes using a scheme employed by Stevenson, Leavitt, Thompson, and Roach (1988), which included "functional" (manipulation of toys as objects), "constructive" (building, generally with blocks), "physical" (rough-and-tumble play), "instructive" (teaching during play), and "pretend" (symbolic, dramatic, role-playing).

Table 10.1
Summary of Teaching Scaffolding Codes

Code	Definition	Example
Initiation		
Child	Child prompts teaching event	"Mom, can you show me how to put this on?"
Parent	Parent teaches spontaneously	"Do you know what this is used for?" (and then explains)
Smoothness		
Disruptive	Teaching event interferes	Parent asks many questions in a row, without considering child's interest in playing
Intermediate	Teaching neither completely disrupts nor facilitates play	Parent asks questions that neither inhibit nor facilitate play with an ongoing theme
Smooth	Teaching event supports play	Parent asks a question, accepts child's response, suggests or accepts a play activity
Focus		
Conceptual	Names and uses of objects	"That's what the doctor uses to check your heart"
Procedural	Physical uses of objects	"Look, you can scan it like this"
Linguistic	Child's language or number use	"Can you spell your name with these blocks?"
Mixed	Any combination of the above	"Here, let's fasten this. Do you know what this sticky stuff (velcro) is called?"

Scaffolding

Parent scaffolding codes, based on Farver (1993), were "suggest," suggesting activities for play (e.g., "Do you want to take my blood pressure?"); "comment," elaborating on play or labeling (e.g., "Remember the credit card machine in Grampa's store?"); "teach," responding to questions, modeling, giving instructions, and asking questions (e.g., "Do you know why doctors use this?"); and "direct," giving of commands (e.g., "Don't put that in my mouth"). Ratings using the four scaffolding codes were summed across episodes, resulting in a total score for each type of scaffolding for each parent.

Parental Initiation, Smoothness, and Focus of Teaching

Given our interest in the educational and social nature of parents' scaffolding, a more extensive coding scheme, presented in Table 10.1, was developed to investigate types of parental teaching. We were particularly interested in whether teaching interrupted or maintained ongoing play within the episodes. "Teach" scaffolds were thus coded for the following three features. Initiation was operationally defined by who initiated or was responsible for the teach (e.g., did the child ask a question that prompted the teach, or did the parent explain spontaneously) and was coded dichotomously. Smoothness was a measure of how well the teach was integrated into the play, and scored on a scale from 1 (teaching disrupted or ended the play) to 3 (teaching was extremely smooth and did not disturb the play sequence). The focus of the teach was coded by inferring the type of knowledge or skill the parent was attempting to teach using the following four categories: conceptual, when the parent named objects or explained their function (e.g., "This is used to take your blood pressure"), procedural, such as fine motor activities and demonstrations (e.g., showing how the credit card machine works), linguistic, such as in reading or spelling (e.g., "Can you spell your name with blocks?"), and mixed (some combination of the above codes).

Interrater Reliability

For each of the above coding schemes, 20 percent of the tapes were coded by a second coder in order to establish reliability. The interrater reliability for the play codes was established at 91 percent agreement. The reliability of the parental scaffolding coding based on Farver was 79 percent, and for this system the coding of one primary coder was used. The further coding of the teach scaffolds yielded 81 percent agreement.

RESULTS

Preliminary analyses of variance (ANOVAs) were conducted to examine the effects of laboratory versus home context on dyadic play and parental scaffolding. There were no significant effects for context in any of these analyses. Means are presented in Table 10.2.

With regard to the play categories, pretend and instructive play were the most frequent. Constructive and functional play were infrequent, and games and physical play were not seen in the context of this study. Means of the four dyadic play codes are presented in Table 10.3, but no further analyses of the play types were conducted given the low frequency of most codes.

Parental Scaffolding

The primary analyses were a series of 2 (child gender) × 2 (parent gender) ANOVAs performed on each scaffolding code. Means of the scaffolding codes are provided in Table 10.4. "Teaches" were the most frequent type of scaffolding performed by parents. "Directs" were far less frequent than any other type of scaffolding. Analyses of the scaffolding code "comment" yielded a significant interaction between parent and child gender, $F (1, 45) = 6.29, p < .02$. Interestingly, mothers made more comments to sons than fathers did, but there were

Table 10.2
Mean Parental Scaffolding and Dyadic Play Scores as a Function of Laboratory or Home Play Setting[1]

	Laboratory	Home
Parental Scaffolding (Mean number of events in 16 minutes of play)		
Comment	9.24	8.42
	(4.54)	(5.23)
Suggest	7.96	9.63
	(4.31)	(5.54)
Teach	15.08	14.75
	(6.90)	(9.12)
Direct	2.92	1.92
	(2.74)	(2.70)
Dyadic Play (Mean frequency in seconds)		
Instructive	335.00	329.88
	(186.95)	(235.06)
Pretend	513.44	482.88
	(230.55)	(277.61)
Constructive	27.52	25.54
	(76.99)	(54.56)
Functional	7.68	13.88
	(20.71)	(32.59)

1. Standard deviations are in parentheses. There were no significant differences due to play setting on any of the scaffolding or play variables.

Table 10.3
Mean Frequency in Seconds of Dyadic Play Categories

Category of play	Frequency
Pretend	481.41
Instructive	347.08
Constructive	41.29
Functional	11.07

Table 10.4
Mean Parental Scaffolding Scores as a Function of Parent and Child Gender (Number of Events Recorded in 16 Minutes of Play)[1]

	Mothers		Fathers	
	With Daughters	With Sons	With Daughters	With Sons
Scaffolding	(n = 16)	(n = 12)	(n = 11)	(n = 10)
Comment	7.75	12.08	8.91	6.60
	(4.20)	(5.16)	(4.23)	(4.72)
Suggest	8.25	12.08	7.82	6.70
	(3.79)	(5.98)	(4.94)	(4.00)
Teach	11.63	18.67	15.09	15.50
	(5.88)	(9.46)	(8.02)	(7.93)
Direct	3.44	2.33	1.46	2.00
	(3.52)	(2.64)	(1.92)	(1.89)
Number				
of Episodes	3.63	5.25	3.36	3.80
	(1.20)	(2.09)	(1.36)	(.789)

1. Standard deviations are in parentheses.

no significant differences for comments made to daughters. An analysis of "suggests" yielded a similar marginally significant interaction effect, F (1, 45) = 3.29, p < .08. Again, mothers made more suggestions to sons than did the fathers. There was also a main effect of parent gender, F (1, 45) = 4.54, p < .04, with mothers making more suggestions for play activities than fathers. Analyses of "teach" and "direct" did not yield any significant main effects or interactions between parent and child gender.

Parental Initiation, Smoothness, and Focus of Teaching

Although there were no gender differences in frequency of parental teaching, overall, the high degree of variability is noteworthy. On average there were 15.41 teaches per dyad (with a range of 0 to 34), 70 percent of which were initiated by parents. The average rating of smoothness of the teaching was 2.27 (on a scale from 1, disruptive, to 3, smooth). In order to examine parental teaching more carefully, we conducted a series of 2 (child gender) $\times$ 2 (parent gender) ANOVAs on the percent of initiation of the teaching by parents. There was a main effect of parent gender on initiation of teaches, F (1, 45) = 5.62, p < .02. Fathers initiated more teaches than mothers (M = .79 for fathers and .61 for mothers). A similar analysis was performed on the smoothness rating, with no significant results.

The smoothness of child-initiated and parent-initiated teaching was considered in the following analyses. When the child initiated the teaching, the average smoothness rating was 2.75. When parents initiated the teaching, the average smoothness rating was 2.11. To investigate the relationship between "smooth or disruptive integration of teaching into play," and the frequency of "parental initiation of teaching," a correlation was calculated between the number of teaches initiated by parents and the smoothness of the teaching, with r (47) = −.30, p < .05.

In order to examine the role of the gender of the child and the parent in the relationship between parent-initiated teaches and smoothness, we conducted separate correlations of these variables for mothers and fathers. For fathers, percent of parent-initiations was negatively correlated with the smoothness of parent-initiated teaches, r (47)= −.46, p < .03. The correlation for mothers was not significant, r (47)= −.32. This indicates that for fathers, more teaching is significantly associated with less smoothness in play, whereas this pattern did not emerge as statistically significant for mothers.

With regard to the focus of the teaching, we found that parental teaching was primarily focused on conceptual knowledge (60 percent), followed by procedural knowledge (20 percent), mixed (14 percent), and language (6 percent). A 2 (child gender) $\times$ 2 (parent gender) ANOVA was performed on each of the teaching focus variables separately. The only significant result that emerged was a main effect of parent gender, F (1, 44) = 5.18, p < .03, such that mothers focused more teaching on procedural knowledge than did fathers (25 percent for mothers and 15 percent for fathers).

In summary, parents initiated more teaching in play than did the children, and fathers initiated more teaching than mothers. Initiation of teaches was negatively correlated with smoothness of the teaching. However, subsequent analyses suggested that this pattern was only significant for fathers. In general, parents focused primarily on conceptual knowledge, and mothers taught more procedural knowledge than fathers.

Types of Teaching Strategies

In order to examine the parents' strategies for incorporating teaching into the ongoing play, we conducted a qualitative analysis of transcripts using those dyads in which parents were in the top quartile of frequency of parent-initiated teaching. These "high-frequency" parents were further divided on the basis of their overall smoothness scores. Two groups were formed, "smooth" and "disruptive," based on average smoothness scores above or below the midpoint of 2 on the smoothness scale. Descriptions of strategies used by parents with high smoothness scores and low smoothness scores are illustrated with summaries of transcript excerpts below.

Smooth Integration of Teaching

Parents who smoothly integrated teaching into play tended to provide information in an indirect way in the context of the play. This strategy served the didactic function of providing some instruction while simultaneously providing the social function of maintaining the play. The child's input was accepted and children were allowed to ignore or reject the parent's input. Parents often modeled the appropriate use of objects rather than verbally describing their use.

a) While father and son are exploring the contents of the doctor kit, the child holds up an X-ray, says, "Hey, look at this." The father says, "What is it?" The child says, "A big scratchy hand." Dad says "Whoa, a big scratchy hand," then goes on to see if the machine will work to "show you X-rays and stuff."

b) A child is building a tower of blocks. After he and his mother admire the height the tower has reached (10 blocks!), the child begins to take the tower down. The mother says, "Can you count how many blocks there are in your tower?" The child responds, "No." The mother suggests, "Want to count them together?" The child responds, "No, I want to do this." The mother says, "Okay."

c) While exploring the contents of the doctor kit, the child looks at the dental mirror. The mother says, "What's that?" to which the child replies, "I don't know." The mother then takes the mirror from him, tells him to open his mouth, and says, "I can see your teeth." Then she lets him look at her teeth and they talk about how pretty his teeth are.

Parents who smoothly integrated teaching into play created zones of proximal development for their children by providing help and encouragement at crucial points so that their children did not become frustrated with the play. These parents maintained a focus on the play itself, giving just enough and not too much help and information. Parents using this strategy fostered autonomy, allowing their children to discover properties of objects and explore their possible use.

a) The father and his son are working with the X-ray machine. The child is having difficulty getting the X-ray film into the machine in order to "read it" and the father says, "See if you can get it in again, just push it straight down, there you go, that's pretty neat."
b) While exploring the contents of the doctor kit, the child holds the face mask up to her mother, asking, "What's that?" The mother responds, "A mask, want me to put it on you?"

Parents frequently integrated teaching into the play by relating the ongoing activity to a child's own prior experience, rather than referring to adult experiences or abstractions.

a) While exploring the contents of the doctor kit, the mother says, "Do you remember when we had your blood pressure taken at the doctor? What did the nurse use?" Her son responds, "I don't know." The mother says, "She used one of these, a stethoscope. Do you remember when she let you listen to your own heart?"

Disruptive Teaching

Parents with lower smoothness scores tended to neglect the social function of scaffolding in favor of the didactic function. They often tried to engage their children in talk about objects apart from the context of the ongoing play. They frequently asked children questions about the real-world use of objects, and seemed more concerned about receiving correct answers than with playing.

a) While watching her son build a tower out of blocks, the mother asks a series of questions about the pictures on the blocks, asking him to name the animals and letters on the blocks, without waiting for a response from him.
b) While the father is pretending to buy food in the grocery store, he says to his daughter, "Can I buy some cherry juice? How much does this cost?" When the child doesn't seem to have an answer, her father holds out some play money, asking, "What's that?" The child responds, "Number." Her father then asks, "Number what?" to which the child responds "Number one." Her father says, "Not quite the number one, what number is that?" The child says, "I don't know." After this the father continues to point to the register and ask her to name several numbers. She does so, but then she says, "I'd rather beep!" and resumes pushing buttons on the register, making a loud beeping sound.

DISCUSSION

This study was designed to explore the nature of joint play between parents and their preschoolers in a laboratory or a home setting. How did middle-class parents play with their preschool-aged child? Somewhat surprisingly, there were no apparent differences in joint play or parental scaffolding in the home as compared with the laboratory. Although we had expected that play in the home setting would be more spontaneous and less guided by the parent than in the laboratory context, we found that our participants in both settings were highly engaged in play—primarily pretend play scenarios, such as grocery store and doctor's office. The lack of influence of the physical setting suggests high levels of engagement in the task and with the toys, and the relatively greater importance of familiar, ongoing patterns of dyadic interaction as compared with the potential artificiality of playing in either the laboratory or the home setting.

The primary focus of the present analysis was on the nature and focus of the scaffolding provided by the parents. We were interested in how the relatively well-educated, middle-class parents in the sample employed didactic and social strategies in joint play with a preschooler. Results indicated that parents engaged in "teaching" at a higher frequency than other forms of scaffolding, namely "commenting" on the play, "suggesting" activities for play, or "directing" their children's behavior in play. Parental directives of children's behavior were especially infrequent in our sample and focused almost exclusively on health and safety (e.g., not putting toys in mouths). Teaching usually occurred within the context of play, and was focused predominantly on conceptual knowledge. Parents identified objects and discussed their uses in the "real world" (e.g., "This is how the doctor takes your blood pressure"). Other teaching was oriented toward the use of the objects (e.g., sliding the credit card machine or putting the mustache on Mr. Potato Head). Some teaching involved both of these simultaneously. A relatively small number of the teaching episodes focused on the use of language and numeracy (e.g., showing the child how to spell his or her name with alphabet blocks).

Unlike Shine and Acosta (1999), who found that parents did not maintain play while teaching children in a museum display of a grocery store, we found considerable variability in the ways in which parents integrated teaching in the context of play. Some parents did not initiate any teaching but responded to questions from their children, while many initiated more than one teaching interaction per minute of play. Successful integration of teaching into ongoing play was a function of both the responsiveness of the parent and the interest and activity level of the child. Parent responsiveness includes many different factors. One important dimension is the inclusion of the social function of scaffolding: that of enhancing the child's ability to participate in the play activity. This involved accepting the child's suggestions (even the silly or seemingly irrelevant ones), not insisting that the child accept the parent's ideas, and continuing the established play roles. Responsiveness also involved the provision of instruction within the child's zone of proximal development. For example, parents provided the amount of help the child needed to maintain the play activity without interrupting play entirely or focusing exclusively on the new information. These findings—that parents were able to maintain play while simultaneously teaching their children—are consistent with Chin and Reifel (2000), who describe a number of interesting strategies Taiwanese mothers used to integrate teaching into play with their children.

Equally important to the social interaction during joint play was the child's level of engagement. Some children took a very active approach in initiating interactions and maintaining play. Others were quiet, passive, or more interested in solitary play or exploration. We assume that some of this variability has to do with the individual characteristics of the child as well as established patterns of interaction between parent and child. In addition, the effects of the somewhat artificial nature of the research setting are unknown. Future research should examine the influence of additional characteristics of both parents and children on parental teaching.

Gender did influence the nature and type of scaffolding observed in this study. Mothers made more comments to sons and more suggestions to both sons and daughters than did fathers. Mothers also focused more on procedural knowledge in teaching than did fathers. Although there were no gender differences in amount of teaching during play, fathers initiated more teaching than did mothers. Higher frequencies of teaching initiations by fathers were associated with lower smoothness of integrating teaching into play. That is, frequent teaching was associated with a greater disruption of the joint play. Fathers were highly engaged in pretend play scenarios; however, in those instances where fathers initiated the teaching event, they often disrupted the ongoing play activities. Mothers were better able to integrate teaching and play in both child-initiated and parent-initiated teaching events. These results are consistent with prior research suggesting that mothers tend to focus more on educational activities than fathers, and that fathers may play more (e.g., Parke & Tinsley, 1987). Our findings might reflect differential experiences of mothers and fathers in integrating the didactic and social functions of scaffolding in dyadic play with their preschoolers. Along those lines, it would be interesting to observe parental scaffolding in naturally occurring play episodes with their children, and assess how often the parents typically engage in free-play activities with their preschoolers.

In conclusion, our findings indicate that, consistent with Vygotsky's theory, parents seem to use play as a context for facilitating their children's cognitive and social skills. Parents vary in their ability to maintain the ongoing play activity in a mutually engaging, synchronous, and responsive way. We acknowledge the importance of interpreting our findings within the social context of our participants, namely a middle-class population of Caucasian parents in their 30s. Parents were relatively highly educated, and most of the children had daycare experience. Cross-cultural studies examining the nature of parental involvement in children's daily activities are needed to add to our growing body of knowledge concerning how parents scaffold their children's learning in formal and informal settings. It is also clearly important to assess the outcomes of the varying types of interactions on children's social and cognitive development.

ACKNOWLEDGMENTS

We gratefully acknowledge the support of the participating parents, children, and preschools. We are also indebted to our colleagues Maurice Levesque and Tom Henricks for their comments and suggestions. This research was supported financially by Elon University, with a research and development grant to the first author and several undergraduate grants-in-aid.

REFERENCES

Bornstein, M. H. (1989). Between caretakers and their young: Two modes of interaction and their consequences for cognitive growth. In M.H. Bornstein & J. S. Bruner (Eds.), *Interaction in human development* (pp. 197–214). Hillsdale, NJ: Erlbaum.

Bornstein, M. H., & Tamis-LeMonda, C. S. (1989). Maternal responsiveness and cognitive development in children. In M. H. Bornstein (Ed.), *Maternal responsiveness: Characteristics and consequences* (pp. 49–61). San Francisco: Jossey-Bass.

Caldwell, B. (1986). The significance of parent–child interaction in children's development. In A.W. Gottfried & C. C. Brown (Eds.), *Play interactions: The contribution of play materials and parental involvement to children's development.* Lexington, MA: D.C. Heath and Company.

Chin, J.-C., & Reifel, S. (2000). Maternal scaffolding of Taiwanese play: Qualitative patterns. In S. Reifel (Ed.), *Play & culture studies* (Vol 2). Ablex Publishing: Stamford, CT.

Clarke-Stewart, K.A. (1973). Interactions between mothers and their growing children: Characteristics and consequences. *Monographs of the Society for Research in Child Development, 38*(6 & 7).

Conner, D. B., Knight, D. K., & Cross, D. R. (1997). Mothers' and fathers' scaffolding of their 2-year-olds during problem-solving and literacy interactions. *British Journal of Developmental Psychology, 15*, 323–338.

Fagot, B. I. (1978). The influence of sex of child on parental reactions to toddler children. *Child Development, 49*, 459–465.

Fagot, B. I. (1994). Peer relations and the development of competence in boys and girls. *New Directions for Child Development, 65*, 53–65.

Farver, J. M. (1993). Cultural differences in scaffolding pretend play: A comparison of American and Mexican mother–child and sibling–child pairs. In K. MacDonald (Ed.), *Parent–child play: Descriptions and implications* (pp. 349–366). Albany: SUNY Press.

Farver, J. M., & Wimbarti, S. (1995). Indonesian children's play with their mothers and older siblings. *Child Development, 66*, 1493–1503.

Griffin, P., & Cole, M. (1984). Current activity for the future: The Zo-Ped. In B. Rogoff & J. V. Wertsch (Eds.), *Children's learning in the "zone of proximal development"* (pp. 45–64). San Francisco: Jossey-Bass.

Haight, W. L., Parke, R.D., & Black, J. E. (1997). Mothers' and fathers' beliefs about and spontaneous participation in their toddlers' pretend play. *Merrill-Palmer Quarterly, 43*(2), 271–290.

Lamb, M. E. (Ed.). (1981). *The role of the father in child development* (2nd ed.). New York: Wiley.

Langlois, J., & Downs, C. (1980). Mothers, fathers, and peers as socialization agents of sex-typed play behavior in young children. *Child Development, 7*, 1237–1247.

Levenstein, P. (1986). Mother–child play interaction and children's educational achievement. In A.W. Gottfried & C. C. Brown (Eds.), *Play interactions: The contribution of play materials and parental involvement to children's development* (pp. 293–304). Lexington, MA: D.C. Heath and Company.

Levenstein, P., & O'Hara, J. (1993). The necessary lightness of mother–child play. In K. MacDonald (Ed.), *Parent–child play: Descriptions and implications*. Albany: SUNY Press.

Lindsay, E.W., Mize, J., & Pettit, G.S. (1997). Mutuality in parent–child play: Consequences for children's peer competence. *Journal of Social and Personal Relationships, 14*(4), 523–538.

Maccoby, E.E., & Jacklin, C.N. (1974). *The psychology of sex differences*. Stanford, CA: Stanford University Press.

MacDonald, K., & Parke, R. (1986). Parent–child physical play: The effects of sex and age of children and parents. *Sex Roles, 15*, 367–378.

McCune, L., Dipane, D., Fireoved, R., & Fleck, M. (1994). Play: A context for mutual regulation within mother–child interaction. In A. Slade & D. P. Wolf (Eds.), *Children at play, clinical and developmental approaches to meaning and representation* (pp. 148–168). Oxford: Oxford University Press.

O'Reilly, A.W., & Bornstein, M. H. (1993). Caregiver–child interaction in play. In M. H. Bornstein & A. W. O'Reilly (Eds.), *The role of play in the development of thought* (pp. 55–66). San Francisco, CA: Jossey-Bass.

Parke, R. (1996). *Fatherhood*. Cambridge, MA: Harvard University Press.

Parke, R. D., & Tinsley, B. R. (1987). Family interaction in infancy. In J. Osofsky (Ed.), *Handbook of infant development* (2nd ed.). New York: Wiley.

Pellegrini, A. D., & Smith, P.K. (1998). Physical activity play: The nature and function of a neglected aspect of play. *Child Development, 69*(3), 577–598.

Pratt, M.W., Kerig, P., Cowan, P.A., & Cowan, C.P. (1988). Mothers and fathers teaching 3-year-olds: Authoritative parenting and adult scaffolding of young children's learning. *Developmental Psychology, 24*(6), 832–839.

Rogoff, B. (1990). *Apprenticeship in thinking: Cognitive development in social context*. New York: Oxford University Press.

Rogoff, B., Mistry, J., Göncü, A., & Moisier, C. (1993). Guided participation in cultural activity by toddlers and caregivers. *Monographs of the Society for Research in Child Development, 58*(8).

Shine, S. S., & Acosta, T. Y. (1999). The effect of the physical and social environment on parent–child interactions: A qualitative analysis of pretend play in a children's museum. *Play and Culture Studies, 2*, 123–139.

Singer, D. G., & Singer, J. L. (1990). *The house of make-believe: Children's play and the developing imagination*. Cambridge, MA: Harvard University Press.

Stevenson, M.B., Leavitt, L.A., Thompson, R.H., & Roach, M.A. (1988). A social relations model analysis of parent and child play. *Developmental Psychology, 24*(1), 101–108.

Tamis-LeMonda, C.S., Bornstein, M. H., Cyphers, L., Toda, S., & Ogino, M. (1992). Language and play at one year: A comparison of toddlers and mothers in the United States and Japan. *International Journal of Behavioral Development, 15*, 19–42.

Vygotsky, L. S. (1967). Play and its role in the mental development of the child. *Soviet Psychology, 5*, 6–18.

Vygotsky, L. S. (1978). *Mind in society: The development of higher psychological processes.* Cambridge, MA: Harvard University Press. (Original work published 1932)

Vygotsky, L. S. (1990). Imagination and creativity in childhood. *Soviet Psychology, 28*, 84–96.

Whiting, B.B., & Edwards, C.P. (1988). *Children of different worlds: The formation of social behavior.* Cambridge, MA: Harvard University Press.

Wood, D., Bruner, J., & Ross, G. (1976). The role of tutoring in problem-solving. *Journal of Child Psychology and Psychiatry, 17*, 89–100.

11

Increasing Play Competence for Very Young Children: How Two Early Head Start Home Visitors Conceptualize and Actualize Their Roles

Susan J. Welteroth

Both girls were dressed up in hats and grown-up shoes and long shirts. "It's time for a tea party," Beth announced. Out of her home visit bag came four little teacups, plates, spoons, napkins, and a tea kettle. As she pulled these play props out of the bag, she handed them to each girl, asking her to pass them around, one to each child, dad, and Beth. Tonya handed out the cups and plates, and Karla the napkins and spoons. Beth asked dad, "What do you think we need to have to drink at our tea party?" Dad responded, "We need make-believe tea." Beth agreed and began to pour tea into everyone's cup. As she poured, she changed her voice to have an exaggerated British accent and told the girls, "When we have a tea party, we need to talk with this silly voice, so everyone will know we are having a special tea party." When she was done pouring, Beth reached into her bag and pulled out real teacakes—one for each party-goer. "And," she continued in her outrageous accent, "We need to drink our tea with our pinkies out, like so!" And she demonstrated an overly extended pinkie. The girls and dad followed suit, putting their pinkies in the air. "Now," Beth declared, "we are ready for our tea party!" (fieldnotes, October 27, 1998)

The developmental period from birth to age 3 is a critical one, as change and growth during this time occur rapidly and establish the base for future development in many domains. Play influences all areas of a child's growth and development and can be a primary means of promoting a variety of develop-

Table 11.1

Developmental Trends in the Symbolic Play of Young Children 1–3 Years Old

Decentration	Decontextualization of Behaviors	Decontextualization of Objects	Integration
the degree to which the child focuses on himself in pretend play	the use of one behavior to substitute for another	the use of one object to substitute for another	the organization of play into patterns
child centers make-believe actions on the self (child brushes own hair or drinks from a cup)	child enacts familiar everyday experiences (drinking) detached from context (mealtime) and in the absence of need (thirst)	real objects are used in a realistic manner (child uses empty cup to take pretend drink)	child generally performs one pretend action or uses one object substitution during play sequence (child pretends to feed self)
child's pretense involves inanimate objects as recipients of make-believe actions (child gives bear a drink)	child begins to take role of a familiar person in pretense play (going to doctor)	objects are less realistic in terms of appearance and function (child uses shell to take pretend drink)	child may combine related activities in single-scheme combinations (child pretends to feed bear then hugs it)
inanimate objects are initiators as well as recipients of make-believe actions (child pretends to have bear take a drink)	child begins to enact roles he may not have experienced (cowboy)	substitute objects may bear no resemblance to what they represent and are used in a way that is far removed from their original function (child uses a toy car as a cup to take pretend drink)	child engages in multi-scheme combinations that may involve multiple transformations (child stirs pretend food in a cup with a stick, then feeds it to bear)

Adapted from Fein, 1981; McCune-Nicolich, 1981; Piaget, 1962; Rubin, Fein, & Vandenberg, 1983.

mental abilities, most significantly language and cognitive skills (Johnson, Christie, & Yawkey, 1999; Piaget, 1962; Rubin, Fein, & Vandenberg, 1983).

In particular, symbolic play reflects a child's ability to represent objects, actions, and experiences as symbols (Fein, 1981; McCune-Nicolich, 1981). The development of symbolic play begins to emerge during the second year of life and becomes more sophisticated with respect to four characteristics: the decontextualization of play behaviors (actions transformed to represent other actions), decentration (the shift from self-referencing to other-referencing), decontextualization of objects (the substitution of one object for another), and the sequential combination of objects or actions or both (Piaget, 1962). These four developmental trends in young children's symbolic play are summarized in Table 11.1. Children begin to exhibit these behaviors around 12 months of age. After the age of 3, the behaviors become more complex and more integrated, peaking around age 5, and gradually decreasing after that.

Pretend play with a young child is facilitated and encouraged by an adult's structuring role. A more capable play partner furnishes props, helps the child maintain a role, and models pretend transformations. The play that results is more frequent, of longer duration, and more sophisticated than that found in children who have not interacted with adults (Bornstein, Haynes, O'Reilly, & Painter, 1996; Vygotsky, 1978). Bornstein and his colleagues have concluded that play requires time, energy, resources, and intellectual commitment on the part of parents for children to benefit cognitively from the experience.

A concern about play at the toddler level is the quality of the adult–child interaction within the play situation. Many parents, especially those of low social or economic status or who have depressed educational levels, do not understand the importance of play for young children, nor do they know how to play with their children (Gottfried, 1984). Other concerns involve the types of play materials and play environments that are available to the child and how these should change over time. Previous research has revealed that the growth and development of young children can be influenced positively or negatively by the quality of their home environments (Bradley & Caldwell, 1984). Children who are of low social or economic status may be at risk for developmental delays due to the deficiency of materials in the home environment.

It is important to note that previous research on parent–child play has been completed with mothers who, for the most part, were college-educated and employed outside the home, and were in the middle to upper-middle socioeconomic range (Beizer & Howes, 1992; Bornstein et al., 1996; Bornstein & Tamis-LeMonda, 1995; Haight & Miller, 1993). Many of these families were also reported to live in large metropolitan areas. Research on the improvement of children's play sophistication using parent–child interactions with mothers who are not college-educated or who are of low social and economic status has yet to be completed on a wide-scale basis. It is unknown whether the research of Bornstein and others will generalize to families of poverty.

Programs designed to encourage parent–child play in families of poverty generally include family services geared to promote "positive parent–child interactions and the enhancement of each parent's knowledge about the development of their child within a healthy, safe environment" (Department of Health and Human Services, 1997, p. 60). Wasik, Bryant, and Lyons (1990) suggest that public care for families of poverty was practiced in the United States as early as colonial times. During the beginning of the 20th century, child and family services were developed to address the conditions associated with poverty in urban areas, with efforts being directed at changing social conditions. Historically, compensatory early childhood programs have served children ages 3 to 5, or those closest to school age.

More recently, research on brain development suggests that infants and toddlers are biologically ready for learning (Shore, 1997). The brain of a 2-year-old is as active as that of an adult. However, "early neurological development is shaped not only by physical conditions, but also by an individual's social environment" (Shore, 1997, p. 29). If a child's brain is not kept active enough during the early years, the neurological connections do not become permanent. "Given the crucial role of environmental factors in early brain development [children of poverty] are at particular high risk of developmental delays and impairments" (Shore, 1997, p. 48). These findings point to the importance of an active learning environment during the early years, especially for children of poverty.

In an effort to provide comprehensive child development and family support services to families with infants and toddlers who are of low social and economic status, Early Head Start was funded in 1994. The goals of Early Head Start are twofold (Department of Health and Human Services, 1994): (1) to provide safe and developmentally enriching caregiving and environments that promote the physical, cognitive, social, and emotional growth of children; and (2) to support parents, both mothers and fathers, in their role as primary caregivers and educators of their children. Throughout the years, there has been an abundance of evidence that demonstrates that intervention through high-quality programs enhances children's development and enables parents to be better caregivers and teachers to their children (Department of Health and Human Services, 1997). According to Early Head Start research, a chief characteristic of successful programs for families with young children is ongoing parent involvement that supports parents as primary nurturers, educators, and advocates for their children (Department of Health and Human Services, 1997). In many programs, parent involvement includes active parent training during a weekly home visit, so the family is able to carry out program goals during the remainder of the week.

During a home visit, a professional provides service to families in their own home (Wasik et al., 1990). Home visiting has been a long-standing means of enhancing children's development, playing a major role in programs for populations deemed to be educationally disenfranchised (Powell, 1990). A modern service delivery system, it was influenced by the establishment of Head Start in 1964. Home visiting has been encouraged and promoted over time because it affords the opportunity for the home visitor to learn firsthand about the conditions of life for children and parents and allows the intervention to take place in the most important setting for the child (Powell, 1990). The home environment is where the child's basic needs must be met. Working with the child and parent at home makes it possible to observe and enhance parent–child interactions and encourage family involvement.

Children of low social and economic levels tend to be at risk for developmental delays because of home environments that are unstimulating and impoverished. There tends to be limited parent education about child development. Early Head Start is charged with providing safe and enriching environments for young children at risk, as well as providing support to their parents. Play is the vehicle of this program and the home visitors, its drivers.

The purpose of this study was to better understand the conceptualization of children's play held by home visitors and how they utilize this understanding to facilitate parent–child play. The participants of this study, Michele and Beth, were Early Head Start home visitors, working with infants and toddlers in rural central Pennsylvania. For almost a year, I talked with them about their practice as educators of young children, accompanied them on home visits, and read their reflective journals. In this chapter, I have attempted to tell their stories about promoting the play of parents with their children, providing insights into how they support parent–child play during home visits, and describing successes and struggles with their practice.

The main question investigated in this study was What are the Early Head Start home visitors' understandings of play, and in what ways do the home visitors promote parent–child interactions to develop and encourage play competence in very young children? This research was concerned with one specific form of play—symbolic play—in a specific period of development—birth through age 3. This study focused on development during this period because of the dramatic changes that occur in those years. Related research questions included: (1) How do the home visitors perceive the importance of play competence in children? (2) In what ways do the home visitors facilitate parent–child play in order to encourage and support children's play skills? (3) How do home visitors articulate their practice of facilitating play?

DESCRIPTION

By examining the lives of two home visitors, this study looked at the inner dynamics of home visiting and how Michele and Beth made sense of their understanding of play and used that sense-making to facilitate parent–child play. The findings from this study attempt to tell Michele's and Beth's stories, using their own words in order to build a sense of context for the reader.

Within the theoretical context of symbolic interactionism, a case study research design was used as a means to communicate the context of the home visit and to illustrate emerging themes. Symbolic interactionism, the theory that the meanings of experience arise out of the social interactions one has with others, provides a framework for studying how individuals interpret events and people, and for studying how this process of interpretation leads them to behave in particular situations (Blumer, 1964; Jacob, 1987). This study was framed by symbolic interactionism because it focused on the interactions between parents and children, home visitors and children, and home visitors and parents, and the manner in which the meanings of play and the roles of the adult in play were modified through the interactive experience.

Early Head Start is a federally funded program operating within three rural counties of central Pennsylvania. Two home visitors, Michele and Beth, who serve the counties closest to my home, became the focus of the study, representing a convenience sample. Michele has been a home visitor with Early Head Start and its predecessor, Early Start, for almost seven years. She has an elementary education background, though her experiences over the last 12 years have been with infants and toddlers and their families. Beth has been employed by the child development agency for more than 20 years. She has worked as a center-based Head Start assistant teacher and teacher, after earning a Child Development Associate (CDA). Six years ago, Beth became a home visitor.

In order to gain a comprehensive and representative understanding of Michele's and Beth's practice as home visitors, they were followed through the program year as they visited with two families. From each home visitor's caseload of eight families, those who were considered "typical" (representing the basic elements of the majority of families) were selected for the participant pool through the use of key informants (Michele and Beth) (Patton, 1990). From the resulting pool, two families from each caseload were then chosen by drawing names. Ricky—2 years 3 months in age—was on Michele's caseload. He lived with both of his parents and was an only child. Both parents were generally present during home visits. Tina—2 years 1 month in age—was also on Michele's caseload. She lived with both of her parents and an older half-brother. During the course of this study, a baby sister was born. Dad, and sometimes Mom, was present during the home visits. Michele felt these families were typical of the families on her caseload (Michele, interview, 10/16/98). From Beth's caseload were twins, Tonya and Karla—11 year 11 months in age. They lived with their father and had an older sister who lived with their mother. The father was always present for home visits. Beth also worked with Nancy, who lived with both of her parents and had a younger brother, Sammy. When they were able to, both parents were present during the home visits. Nancy was 2 years 11 months in age, and Sammy celebrated his first birthday soon after the first home visit. Beth felt these families were the "less-needy" on her caseload (Beth, interview, 10/27/98).

Child play and parent–child interaction in play has most often been studied in its normal setting, the home. During this study, data were collected in the homes of the participating families. For Beth and Michele, visits tended to vary slightly from home to home. Plans were made at the end of each home visit for the following week, and a Parent/Home Visitor Plan was completed. When they came to the home, Michele and Beth talked with the parents first, catching up on what had been going on since the last home visit. This led into the plans for the current week's activity. Materials were gathered and the majority of the home visit was spent in the planned parent–child activity. After cleanup, the home visitor and parent reviewed and reflected upon the activity.

Naturalistic observations of home visits, interviews with home visitors, reflective journal entries dictated by the home visitors, and Parent/Home Visitor Plans were used to collect data. Michele and Beth were interviewed three times during the period of the research: at the beginning, about six months into the study, and upon exit. A standard, open-ended interview was used to provide the opportunity to ask each home visitor the same set of questions to assure attainment of all necessary data and comparability of responses. The addition of conversational items at the end of the question set allowed for the probing of topics that arose during the interview, as well as providing flexibility in exploring certain subjects unique to each home visitor (Patton, 1990). The interviews were tape-recorded and transcribed verbatim. Observations took place in the families' homes and focused on elements of the home visit relating to play. All home visit observation notes were transcribed into expanded fieldnotes.

Beth and Michele had not engaged in formal, written reflection of their practice as home visitors, but agreed to do so during the term of this study and provided reflective journal entries of their weekly home visits with the families included in the study. The focus of their reflections was parent–child interactions in play. Michele and Beth tape-recorded the journal entries after each home visit and the tapes were transcribed verbatim.

In order to answer the research questions about how home visitors understand play and in what ways they promoted parent–child interaction to develop and encourage play competence in very young children, data analysis proceeded in six phases: (1) initial reading; (2) second and third readings to begin to extract themes and patterns; (3) categorization of meaningful categories and subcategories; (4) construction of data displays; (5) development of the case study; and (6) cross-case analysis.

During the initial reading, all data were read in their entirety in order to develop a holistic sense of the data, as well as to check for missing data. The interview transcripts, observation fieldnotes, reflective journal entries, and Parent/Home Visitor Plans were reread to extract themes and patterns. A two-level scheme was used in developing the code system: a general system reflecting the theoretical orientation of symbolic interactionism and the research questions (i.e., interactions between parent and child, home visitor and child, and home visitor and parent, as well as home visitors' understanding of children's play); and codes that emerged from the data and were more closely related to the data.

During data reduction the themes and patterns of home visiting and play were examined together, placing like topics into categories to allow the search for patterns and themes within each category. With the literature of the facilitation of children's play in mind, the data were studied to identify subcategories. The original data were reread to check the adequacy of fit between the patterns and home visitors' expressed topics. The process was iterative, in that as categories came together, they were merged and altered. During this process, the categories were "held lightly" (Miles & Huberman, 1994) so that new ways of grouping and understanding data could be considered. Data displays were constructed and altered throughout the course of analysis, and concept maps were developed to help view the findings in context.

At the completion of the analysis phase, an outline was developed to frame the case study in an effort to help develop a clear sense of the case and paint a picture of Michele's and Beth's practice as home visitors. The findings formed the base for the outline, and data were cross-referenced to the outline. The outline provided the primary conceptual structure for the case study and was expanded to include narrative and excerpts from interviews, fieldnotes, and journal entries. Quotes, which were representative of the themes contained in the outlines and which provided the richest illustration, were chosen from the original data set. Throughout the writing of the case study, attempts were made to capture the dynamic ways in which Michele and Beth interacted with children and families to create opportunities for play. The outline constructed during the development of the case study was used to compare the dominant themes of each case.

In an effort to construct a valid and credible study, trustworthiness was attempted through the techniques of: (1) prolonged engagement; (2) methods triangulation; (3) adequate reference materials; and (4) member checks. Observations of home visits and collection of reflective journal entries and Parent/Home Visitor Plans took place throughout an entire program year (October 1997 through August 1998). Separately, these documents provided limited data. But presented together, they worked to validate and cross-check findings of the researcher (Patton, 1990). Thick description of the data provided a solid data base and allowed the reader to experience home visiting with Beth and Michele. In a continuous and informal manner, the home visitors were asked to verify data and preliminary interpretations. In addition to supporting the categories and changes identified in the analysis, the information gained from this activity also helped to clarify and refine the findings.

MICHELE'S AND BETH'S PRACTICE OF FACILITATING PLAY

Michele's and Beth's understanding of children's play was central to their roles as home visitors and influenced their practice of facilitating play. Their educational background, as well as in-service training, professional reading, and experience working and playing with young children formed their knowledge of child development. With this foundation in child development, Michele and Beth believed that play is how young children learn.

Play is all they do. It's how they explore their world, how they learn to trust the people around them, and how to express themselves. If a child is allowed to direct [the play], to follow their own lead, with some appropriate modeling, they are more likely to be learning. You start with letting them lead and then extend their play and gently direct them in the direction you want them to go. (interview, 10/9/97)

Play is their work. Play is important because it's how they learn everything in life. Every play activity, I try to focus the parent in on what's happening. I will say, "Look, there's language happening here; she's learning a new word." I use those [developmental] terms so they can understand, so they can see [the child] learning through play. (interview, 10/9/97 and 10/27/98)

Both Michele and Beth acknowledged the need for a strong foundation in understanding children's play within the context of child development and then

Figure 11.1
Michele and Beth—Understanding of Children's Play and Their Practice as Home Visitors

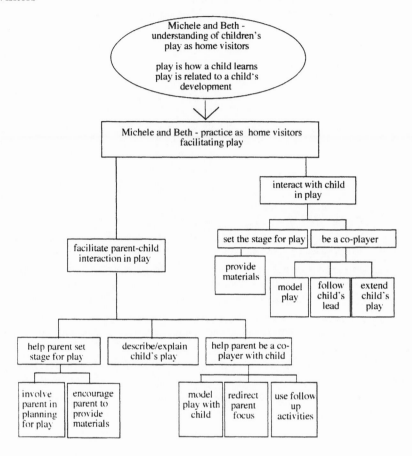

communicated their understanding of children's play to both children and parents. They not only used their knowledge to help scaffold a child's play skills to the next developmental level (Beth, interview, 10/9/97), but they were also prepared to answer parents' questions and provide information about their child's play and development (Michele, interview, 10/9/97).

Looking across the cases revealed that these home visitors used similar patterns of interaction to facilitate play in young children. These similarities in their practice also have the potential to inform others in the field of home visiting. Two primary patterns of interaction used by both Beth and Michele to facilitate play were brought to light during the data analysis. They are visually portrayed in Figure 11.1.

Interacting with the Child in Play

Michele and Beth utilized two main patterns of interaction during their home visit play with young children: setting the stage for play and being a co-player with the child. They set the stage for play by providing or supplementing play materials. Michele engaged in play using toys found in the home, as well as items she always had on hand.

I always have paper, crayons, a small bag of blocks, and books. I have balls in the back of the car, so if the weather is nice, we can go outside and kick the ball. Those are the basics I keep with me if we need something to extend what we have already planned. I bring things in to play with and I use materials in the home to play with. (interview, 10/9/97 and 10/16/98)

In order to provide a variety of appropriate play materials, Michele supplemented household items and the child's own toys with a collection of toys, which could be used to extend and support a variety of play activities. Beth generally brought play materials the family did not have available or specific materials to supplement toys the family already owned. By providing materials, she was able to expose the child to new toys and new play experiences and set the stage for play. "I try to read each child, think of each child's needs, think of how the child will respond, observing what the child likes to do and what the parents like to do with the child. That will determine what I bring" (interview 10/9/97). Beth tried to individualize this pattern of interaction in order to choose the most appropriate play materials.

For Michele and Beth, acting as a co-player with the child involved modeling play, following the child's lead in play, and extending the child's level of play. Beth liked to model play when showing a child how to use materials, so the child could see how to perform a new skill or play with a new toy appropriately (interview, 10/9/97).

She could handle the snowman [puzzle], the head, middle-sized body, and the big ball on the bottom. When we got into seven and nine piece puzzles, and I was quite sure that it would be more difficult, I showed her how to trace the design in her hand and look for the design on the puzzle. ("Nancy," journal entry, 2/3/98)

When a child was unsure of how to use a new toy or play materials, such as the more complex puzzle, Beth used modeling to help the child correctly use the toy or become more comfortable with the medium.

When playing with a child on the home visit, Beth liked to "read the child and go with what they are doing" (interview, 10/9/97). This involved having the child choose which materials to play with and how to play with them, and then Beth followed along. For Beth, following the child's lead often moved directly into play extension.

Beth brought cookie cutters, rolling pins, and a garlic press to use with the play dough. The girls tried using these utensils, but then began to make balls and roll them across the table. Beth shifted from using the utensils to enthusiastically engage the girls in turn taking; rolling balls of play dough back and forth. ("twins" fieldnotes, 11/17/97)

Because the twins had chosen not to play with the play dough in the manner in which Beth had planned, she moved quickly to adapt the simple play-dough-ball rolling to be a turn-taking activity. In this way, she was not only following the child's lead in play, but also providing an expansion on that play activity, making it a learning activity.

As home visitors, Michele and Beth believed it was their role to extend children's play and lead it in developmentally appropriate directions. Children chose the play experience and Michele and Beth then guided them to more sophisticated levels in order to improve the chances of learning through the play activity (Vygotsky, 1976, 1932/1978).

Michele talked about this pattern of interaction in her reflective journals. During a home visit, Michele worked on improving puzzle completion skills by expanding on Tina's interests and lead in the play.

When Michele arrived at the home, Tina came out to the car to greet her. She chose a puzzle from the back seat and carried it into the house. Once inside, she took all the pieces out and then stacked the pieces. Michele asked Tina, "Where does this piece go? Look at it." Tina moved the piece from place to place in a seemingly random manner. Michele gently placed her hand over Tina's and softly said, "Try turning it around." They turned the piece together and when the piece fit in the right spot, Michele quietly said, "Look how it fits. There you go!" Tina smiled and tried the next piece. (fieldnotes, 8/10/98)

Tina chose the toy she was interested in, and through some physical assistance and words of encouragement, Michele was able to help Tina complete the puzzle, which she had been unable to do on her own. Michele's use of extending the activity and verbal and physical prompts helped Tina to be successful in this play activity. Having a more competent player support and extend a child's play was an important component of home visiting for Michele and Beth (Vygotsky, 1976). Besides scaffolding the child's learning, they were also able to model how to be an effective co-player for the parent.

Facilitating Parent–Child Interaction in Play

On home visits, Michele and Beth attempted to facilitate parent–child interactions during play by utilizing several approaches: helping the parents to set the stage for play by involving them in planning for play and helping to provide materials; describing ways in which the child was playing and what he or she might be learning; and encouraging the parents as co-players by modeling co-playing behavior, involving them in follow-up activities, and directing the focus onto the child's play.

Helping Parents Set the Stage for Play

One way Michele and Beth actively involved parents in their child's play was to encourage them to help with planning the activity for the next visit. Through planning, Michele and Beth explained the developmental benefits of play and had the parents help decide which play materials to use. Michele reflected on some of the planning sessions:

I did like how in this visit at the end, when we were planning, Dad asked me about some memory games, trying to work on thinking skills and cognitive development. And, we were able to come up with a plan for Ricky next time that revolved around that planning. (journal entry, 3/19/98)

Michele used planning for the next home visit as a way to actively involve Ricky's dad in his child's play. Dad was able to make the connection between Ricky's play with memory cards and the development of cognitive and language skills.

Part of the planning process involved deciding which materials might be needed for play to occur and who would provide them. By encouraging the parent to provide the play materials, Beth attempted to involve the parent in his child's play.

Parent/Home Visitor Plan: Dad will provide play hut, babies, and related objects. Journal entry: Dad was very involved in putting [the cubes] together. I said, "On the plan we said about having receiving blankets and stuff the girls could use in their imaginative play." He had them right there. I said, "You also said you'd have dishes available." He went upstairs, brought the dishes down. ("twins," 1/12/98)

Beth involved this father by having him be responsible for the play props. When the parents were part of the planning process, they had some ownership in the play experience, whether to provide materials or to develop the activity. When they felt some ownership, the parents were more likely to actively engage in play with their child during the home visit (Hohman & Weikart, 1995).

Describing and/or Explaining the Child's Play

Some of the families did not fully understand the importance of play to a child's development (Klass, 1996). In order to help advance this understanding, Beth believed it was important for parents to understand the developmental nature behind the play activities she engaged in while in the home in order for them to see the value of children's play as a learning tool (interview, 10/27/98). As often as possible, she related what the child was doing in play to the child's developmental levels.

Dad didn't like Nancy squeezing glue all over the paper. I told him, "She needs to understand how to manipulate, how to squeeze, and that's what I'm concerned about for this activity." He said, "She's using so much glue." I replied, "Yes, but I don't mind that. As soon as children understand the flow of the glue, then the dots start to happen. So, I'm really comfortable about that. I think children need to experience and understand how the glue works before I expect them to [make dots]. She's doing exactly what every child her age does." ("Nancy," journal entry, 12/2/97)

Beth took the time during the play activity to explain to Nancy's dad, in terms he understood, why she chose to set the stage in a particular manner and what developmental skill she expected Nancy to demonstrate. By using this pattern of interaction in explaining Nancy's play relative to her development, she tried to help the parent see the value of his child's play and its connection to learning.

Beth also used the Parent/Home Visitor Plan to note for the parent what the intended developmental outcome of each planned activity would be: gross motor and sensory play and imaginative play—build a fort, crawl over things, and pretend play ("Nancy," January 13, 1998). By using the Parent/Home Visitor Plan in this manner, Beth left the parent with a clear written record of the developmental areas the play activities were designed to touch, and explained the child's play in terms of development.

Encouraging Parents to Be Co-players

Michele and Beth encouraged parents to be co-players with their children by modeling co-playing behavior, involving the parents in follow-up activities, and directing the parents' focus to the child's play. Michele tried modeling as a pattern of interaction during play with Ricky's parents and was successful when they were able to follow her lead.

I began picking out all the little yellow cars—it was Ricky's little matchbox cars that he loves. He lined up all the yellow ones and dad got real involved. He leaned in and asked Ricky to find the red cars. Ricky caught on a little to the [concept] "same," and I was trying to use the words, "This is the same," just to draw dad into doing that. And, he picked up on it a bit. I was trying to lead dad into working on the colors with the cars and, actually, it went pretty well. ("Ricky," journal entry, 12/18/97)

Michele used modeling in this instance to encourage Ricky's father to participate in the activity. Michele only needed to demonstrate, not explain, the behavior, and the father was able to understand, display the co-playing behavior with Ricky, and continue the play.

Beth and Michele often used follow-up activities and materials left in the home as a pattern of interaction to facilitate parent–child play. The Parent/Home Visitor Plan contained a section for follow-up activities. When Beth included an activity the parent and child could engage in during the week, she checked with the parent on the next home visit to see if the follow-up activity was completed.

Parent/Home Visitor Plan: I'm going to bring some puzzles here next week and leave them for her to work on [1/27/98]. Journal entry: They told me she really enjoyed doing the puzzles this week. It was nice to see they followed through. And, I could tell when I did the puzzles with her at the table, she was able to put (the pieces) in more readily. ("Nancy," 2/10/98)

While planning, Beth noted on the Parent/Home Visitor Plan suggestions for parent–child play and which materials were involved in the follow-up activity. On the next home visit, she asked the parents about the activity. In these examples, the parents reported playing with their children using the puzzles, and Beth noted improved skill on the part of the children.

Lastly, Michele and Beth used redirection of the parent's focus to facilitate parent–child play. They drew the parent's attention to the play activity in which the child was engaged, in an effort to have them become more involved in the child's play. Often, the parents had issues of their own to discuss and while Michele did not discourage this, she gently redirected the parents back to the child's play. Michele reflected on this issue with Ricky's family.

Sometimes in this home, I need to step back and reassess what it is I'm trying to do here, especially with drawing out play with Ricky, because we've kind of fallen in this pattern where mom and dad both feel like they're waiting for me to talk about their problems, their struggles. And, I've got to look at it and see how I can really get them to focus on what our goals are with Ricky, because they do like to plan, they like to look at what Ricky's doing, and plan how to draw it out. (journal entry, 3/19/98)

Ricky's parents came to use Michele as a sounding board for their own issues. While it was important for parents to feel valued during the home visits, these parents also wanted to be actively involved with Ricky's play, and Michele was generally able to gently refocus them during the home visits to the play activity at hand. This was an ongoing issue for this family, and Michele worked for several months to be able to develop a balance between adult conversations and child-focused play. Using redirection as a pattern of interaction allowed Michele to involve Ricky's parents more in play as co-players.

QUESTIONING THEIR PRACTICE

As part of the development of this research study, Michele and Beth agreed to record their reflections about home visits with the target families. The practice of reflection upon their role as a home visitor, and specifically as a facilitator of parent–child play, was new to them. The journals created opportunities to focus on the goals of the home visit and what could have been done differently.

The emphasis on reflection has really helped me to think about why I'm doing what I'm doing; looking at it more from the viewpoint, "Just what am I trying to do here?" It's helping me think about the visits . . . trying to focus on the main goal (and) am I being successful? (Michele, interviews, 3/26/98 and 10/16/98)

Michele and Beth questioned their practice when they found they were unable to influence parent–child play using usual patterns of interaction. Michele's style as a home visitor was quiet and soft-spoken. The ways in which she approached the facilitation of parent–child play tended to be nondirective and nonintrusive. She was comfortable with this style and it had worked in many homes for many years. However, it did not seem to be working with Tina's family. Tina's mother was not involved in play even when Michelle was present, and her father tried to focus most of the session on himself. Tina's parents would seldom interact with her during the play activity, even when Michele encouraged them to play. In March, Michele found it was necessary to almost start over with this family and become more direct about how to meet Tina's needs for co-players.

I've been giving it a lot more thought—about just exactly what I'm trying to do in there. Basically, what I think I need to do is try to get the focus off "self" and get us all focused on Tina. [Today] I think we did less with Tina than usual, but, at the same time, I feel like we restarted. I think I got him thinking about [the goal of the home visit] a little more. I wish I could get one or the other of them down, playing directly with Tina. They still say, "You do it with Michele," and I've got to figure out [how] I can move from that point so that I can get them doing it directly with her. Maybe I need to say, point blank, "YOU are going to do it with Tina, not me!" (journal entries, 3/10/98 and 3/17/98)

In reflecting upon her practice, Michele decided to be more direct in her attempts to focus the parents back onto Tina's play and their interactions with her. She wanted the parents to understand she was not there to play alone with Tina, that they should be playing with her as well. For Michele, the movement from a gentle, indirect style of interaction to a more direct and assertive style represented a significant shift in her practice, and one she seemed somewhat reluctant to make. The struggle between what Michele felt may need to be done to affect change and her own style was quite evident in her journal entries.

Finally, Michele's change of style began to yield positive results as Tina's parents slowly became a little more involved in play activities. Michele reflected on her last home visit with Tina:

I'm not sure if I should have addressed more directly some of his talking about other stuff instead of playing with Tina. That might be something I could have done. I could have directly said, "We can talk about that later. We need to do this now." I wish there were more time to work with this family. (journal entry, 8/10/98)

Although Michele recognized the need to change her style of interaction, she was not comfortable in being as blunt as she wanted to be. She had the thought of telling the parents to get on the floor and play, but could not actually say it.

There was even an element of wistfulness that this was the last home visit and maybe, if there were more opportunities and if she could be even more direct in her interactions, more gains could have been made with this family.

Beth worked for almost three years with the twins and their father. She tried all of her usual patterns of interaction to have the father be an active participant in play during the home visit. During some visits, her attempts appeared mildly successful; during others, they were not successful at all. Typically, Beth's style of interaction was to be direct and straightforward. In an effort to facilitate more parent–child play interactions, Beth decided in the early days of 1998 to be even more direct in asking him to be a partner in the play activity. Beth instituted her plan over several months and reflected on the home visits in her journal entries.

I told him, "I'm not going to cut [the pineapple] up. I'll need you to be a part of this." So, I waited him out. As he went to get their lunch, I think he thought I was going to take care of it. But, I didn't. I waited him out and I said, "I don't know how much longer the girls can sit here, touching the pineapple, without tasting it." (journal entry, 2/2/98)

Dad was on the phone a lot, so he was tuning me out, and I didn't like it. I waited him out and he hung up, and came over to help me with the mat and the corn. (journal entry, 3/2/98)

I moved over and said, "There's room here, dad. We'd love to have you come sit on the floor with us." Then, he joined us. He was able to focus more on the children. (journal entry, 3/4/98)

I want him to be participating with the children, so I try to help by asking him to do some things. I can let him know how he can be involved. So, I've been doing more and more of that. (journal entry, 3/9/98)

These February and March home visits showed Beth in the "waiting-him-out" phase. She had decided to stand her ground regarding her decision to have the father be more involved in the play activities. She gave him clear, specific directions and then a prolonged wait time to give him an opportunity to become involved. When the father did not move to the play activity, Beth provided verbal or visual prompts to encourage him a little further.

These incidents represented the most direct interactions Beth had with this father. She believed she was being honest with him about her concerns regarding his responsibility to interact with his children in play. Although Beth's style of interaction was generally very direct and straightforward, she felt frustrated and devalued by this father's lack of involvement and needed to be even more blunt.

It's frustrating and sometimes I wish [the home visit] would be looked upon as more important. I can't say I'm not disappointed. I am disappointed. I'd like to be valued more and [for him to] think that [playing] is as special as I know it is. And, I would just like it if he could be more a part of the visits than he is. I wish he would get it. I could wave my magic wand and, "Just get it, dad, just get it!" I'm just impatient. (interview, 10/27/98)

Michele and Beth have both struggled, and continue to struggle, with the ever-present tension of questioning and exploring the issue of "how hard should I push" for parent–child play, and "how hard is hard enough?" These questions must relate back to the relationship the home visitor has built with the family and how well she can read the parent's reaction to words she might say or things she might do. Michele and Beth also must rely on their experiences of working with families to know where "the line" might be, and when crossing it may mean the parent asks them to leave. Each situation is unique to that family, and so, it is almost a new struggle every time. Each struggle is also unique to the home visitor and becomes a learning experience as she builds a repertoire of patterns of interaction.

This tension is always lurking in their practice as home visitors; facilitating play and the nature of their job seldom affords the time or space to reflect upon their practice. As Michele and Beth left one home visit, their minds were already gearing up for the next visit, as they drove from home to home. There is almost an element of isolation to being a home visitor. Michele and Beth have noted:

[I'd like some] time to keep in touch with the other people that we work with. We work on our own quite a bit. [We need] more time to sometimes just vent, or get another opinion—especially at the end of the day when it's been one home visit after another. It's overwhelming. (Michele, interview, 10/19/97)

Where's the time for our mental health? We don't see each other enough. I have families with differing needs and I just need to talk about it sometimes. When we get together with other people, when you hear others saying the same thing, [it is] reflecting almost a support-like atmosphere. They are understanding and know because they are going through the same thing. (Beth, interview, 3/26/98)

Michele and Beth disclosed feelings of isolation when dealing with the struggles of their practice. Although there were other home visitors working within the agency, the nature of their job did not permit much time for staff interaction, and there was no one else to talk with who has similar experiences about how to decide what will work with one family or another.

DISCUSSION

The purpose of this study was to better understand how home visitors conceptualize children's play and actualize their conceptualization with families in order to promote play competence in very young children who are enrolled in Early Head Start. By giving voice to two home visitors, this study revealed the dynamics of facilitating parent–child play as experienced by them rather than an outside source.

Facilitating Parent–Child Play

Michele and Beth each followed the child's lead in play as a more sophisticated player, providing materials and attempting to scaffold him or her to the next developmental level (Vygotsky, 1976, 1932/1978). They sought to accomplish this by providing opportunities for play within the child's zone of proximal development (Vygotsky, 1976, 1932/1978). Their knowledge of child development aided them in determining which materials to provide, and in understanding what skills to encourage during the play activity with the child. While acting as co-players, they also facilitated parent–child play so that parents could learn how to be more effective players with their children (Bornstein et al., 1996).

An important goal in Early Head Start is to encourage parents to be partners in play with their child. Parents need to understand the developmental importance of play as a means of learning (Klass, 1996). The parent's current role in the child's play influenced Michele's and Beth's position as co-players during the home visit. A challenge that home visitors may face involves parents who do not enjoy or know how to play with their children (Klass, 1996).

Michele and Beth helped parents set the stage for play through planning play activities and providing play materials. Through co-planning, parents gained skills in setting appropriate expectations for their children. Including parents in planning tended to increase their commitment to participating in activities and carrying out activities between visits. Klass (1996) argues that parents should be active participants during home visits. Active involvement increases the likelihood parents will learn and remember information and strategies that have been part of the visit. Michele and Beth modeled being co-players, engaged parents in follow-up activities, and focused the parents' attention onto the child's play as means of facilitating parent–child play interactions.

Michele and Beth helped parents to understand the value of play by describing what the child was doing when he or she played and what skills the child might be learning or practicing. They also provided written documentation about the developmental domains they expected an activity to touch on during the play episode. Where they fell short was in being able to give parents the knowledge base to discover their child's zone of proximal development. The parents studied by researchers such as Beizer and Howes (1992) and Bornstein and colleagues (1996) were more highly educated and more economically secure than these Early Head Start parents typically were, and they were able to determine at what place to intervene and how to scaffold their child to the next level. While there appears to be some positive effect of working with Early Head Start parents, Bornstein (1995) demonstrated that merely having the parent present was not enough.

With the strain many Early Head Start families are under in dealing with issues of poverty, employment, and so on, could we, perhaps, be asking too much of them when we ask them to become competent co-players? If we move some parents from being nonplayers to appreciating the value of play and to being even marginal players, is that enough for them? Do we interact individually with each family as we do with each child—taking them from where they are—moving them as far as they can go? Or do we hold out for some predetermined level of competence? As educators, should we question our practice or should we question the federal mandates? Perhaps we need to question both.

IMPLICATIONS

The results of this study suggested several implications for the practice of home visitors facilitating parent–child play.

Professional Development Issues

Issues of Isolation and Tension

The foremost professional development issue is related to the feelings of isolation and tension that Michele and Beth disclosed as they questioned their practice. As educators, we need to understand this problem and provide support to home visitors to aid them in dealing with the tension of "how hard to push." Home visitors need to be allowed time and space to reflect upon their interactions with families, to question their practice, and to collaborate with each other as a means of support. Their feelings of isolation need to be combated by having peers and supervisors consult with them on a regular basis about these issues.

Michele and Beth also revealed that in addition to feelings of isolation, lack of time for reflection and lowered energy levels were present within the practice of home visiting.

I always think that [with] enough time, I could get it all in, but there is never enough time. You can always find three other things that need to get done. (Michele, interview, 10/16/98)

You have to be up, because if you're not up, the visit goes nowhere. I feel we have to set the tone for the home visit. So, when we are up, [the parents and children] are up. There's usually no problem unless my fuel tanks are a little bit low. You know, I have those days, too. I'm human. (Beth, interview, 10/28/98)

Lack of energy after a long day of home visiting and limited time for reflection can result in increased levels of stress. As Beth noted in an earlier interview, "This is a demanding, stressful position."

When home visiting staff is feeling isolated and under stress, it may lead to professional "burnout." In their book about home visiting, Wasik and colleagues (1990) report that professional burnout is a concern for home visitors: "Burnout can result from many conditions, including low pay, insufficient training, un-grateful (families), heavy caseloads, and political constraints and realities" (p. 212). These authors concluded that preventing burnout with home visitors was difficult because their personal characteristics often combine with the difficulties of their professions to create a feeling of being overloaded. Wasik and col-leagues suggested that setting realistic expectations, focusing on the process, and celebrating small successes represented some interventions for burnout. Equally important were that support opportunities, both formal from the admin-istration and informal from peers, be built into the program. Finally, the authors recommended improvement of the home visitor's own skills to counteract burn-out. Through self-development, "the home visitor can find successes in her own work, even at times when it may be hard to see successes in the [families'] lives" (p. 215).

One additional support for home visiting staff could be the sharing of occa-sional home visits. If two home visitors go together on a visit, it would help to validate the patterns of interaction they are engaging in, and perhaps show them some additional ways they could be interacting with families. Michele said of my presence during the visits, "I really liked being out in the home with a second person. You get so much more out of it. You can't do it all, and you benefit so much from someone else's perspective" (Michele, interview, 10/9/98).

Issues of In-service and Pre-service Training

Early childhood educators who work in homes are seldom trained for the work they are ultimately employed to do. Some, like Michele, have elementary education certification, which traditionally has provided minimal course work in early childhood (specifically, play) and little or no exposure to working with families, much less in homes. Other home visitors, like Beth, have received a CDA. This program can be more tailored for those working in the field of early childhood, and, specifically, within the context of the home. However, few in-dividuals receive a CDA prior to becoming home visitors and are inclined to earn it along with on-the-job training. The resulting predicament is that home visitors tend to come to the profession with a wide variety of skills and bases of knowledge and, currently, each employing agency must determine what skills/ knowledge each home visitor needs to have in order to be successful at what she does. One of the issues raised by this study was that Michele and Beth, even with all their training and years of experience, lacked a deep understanding of play theory, even though their Early Head Start program and curriculum promoted play as a tool for learning. For this agency in particular, as well as others like it, it is suggested that staff be exposed to a professional development program designed to increase their understanding of play theory.

If federal mandates continue to favor early childhood education within the home setting, teacher educators should evaluate their current training programs and consider the addition of course work and practicum experiences focusing on home visitor–family interactions, play in young children, and the facilitation of parent–child play.

Translating Play Theory into Practice and Larger Issues

Michele and Beth believed that play is how young children learn; play is their "work" and "all they do." Michele's and Beth's understanding of play represented an incomplete understanding of play theory. It tended to be superficial and more indicative of clichés of play rather than of theoretical knowledge. According to Piaget (1962, 1978), the child in play is primarily engaged in assimilation, or adapting the experience and making it fit his own meaning. Work, on the other hand, is primarily accommodative in nature, where the child makes an effort to accommodate himself to new objects or activities (Piaget, 1962, 1978). According to Piaget, children do not acquire new skills as they play, but instead, they practice skills they have newly acquired. Therefore, play itself is not learning, but a practice session of what has previously been learned by the child.

Researchers working in the field of early childhood education admit there is a challenge to the incorporation of play theory into the practice of educating young children (Johnson et al., 1999). Play is an important component of developmentally appropriate practice in early childhood programs and provides a context for children to practice newly acquired cognitive, social, and emotional skills (Bredekamp & Copple, 1997).

Van Hoorn, Nourot, Scales, and Alward (1993) propose two methods of weaving play and curriculum into early childhood education: curriculum-generated play and play-generated curriculum. In curriculum-generated play, the home visitor would provide play experiences that would enable a child to acquire developmental skills. Play with home-visitor-selected materials could occur first, allowing the child the opportunity to learn the skill without direct instruction. Play could also follow direct instruction, permitting opportunities for the child to practice the newly acquired skill. Curriculum-generated play would provide the home visitors with the means by which to fill in gaps in a child's developmental state. In play-generated curriculum, the home visitor would organize developmental experiences around the interests the child has demonstrated in his play activities. The home visitor would select stimulating materials and present them within the naturalistic context of play in the home environment.

Johnson et al. (1999) believe writes that transfer of learning is more likely when children are provided opportunities to assimilate and combine their experiences and are provided a place and time to play in order to attain authentic developmental gains. The facilitation of play competence in children by home visitors can be framed by play theory within developmentally appropriate practices.

It was not surprising to discover that Michele and Beth did not have a "deep understanding" of play theory. They have not had the benefit of the time and opportunity for study and contemplation about play, nor have they had access to scholarly works or experts in the study of play. Most home visitors, and for that matter, most early childhood teachers working in the field, have not had that advantage. I wonder if, after all, we are expecting too much of them. Are we expecting home visitors to have extensive knowledge and yet only compensate them the scant amount most early childhood teachers earn in this country? The fact that they have practical knowledge of the importance of play to child development and are willing to go into homes week after week, where sometimes they see little or no progress toward their goals, and continue their practice with inadequate compensation is admirable. And, as educators, we need to support them in what they do. I have worked in early childhood for more than 20 years and can say that almost all of the teachers and paraprofessionals I have known and worked with have not been part of this profession because of the salaries but because of their love of children. The same is true of Michele and Beth and others like them: "I have something that I really love and it's my job. I could cry that's how much I love my job" (Beth, interview, 10/9/97).

The National Association for the Education of Young Children reported in their 1995 position statement that "compensation is inadequate in most early childhood programs" (p. 1). And a recent update to that report (Whitebook, Howes, & Phillips, 1998) indicated that wages for most early childhood teachers have remained stagnant over the past decade, with wages averaging $7.50 to $10.85 per hour. If the political agenda is to provide quality education for young children, let's give some appropriate compensation to the staff in whose hands those young children are placed. Perhaps when they are adequately compensated and supported in the work they do, then we can ask home visitors to have a deep understanding of the theories they put into practice.

Implications for Research

In addition to its implications for practice, this study has only begun to ask and answer questions about home visiting. As mentioned previously, the research on home visiting in Early Head Start is virtually nonexistent. While this study did not evaluate the effects of Michele's and Beth's practice of facilitating parent–child play, other studies should certainly look at this issue. Additionally, future researchers may want to examine more closely how families feel when home visitors engage in various patterns and styles of interaction. Home visitors should consider engaging in pieces of action research with the families they visit to explore these and other issues. Continued research within the area of the tensions of interacting with families could aid further discussions for professional development.

CONCLUDING REMARKS

Symbolic Play

One of the surprising results of this study was the limited amount of symbolic play observed during home visits and discussed in Michele's and Beth's journal entries. I assumed there would be more pretense occurring on a regular basis than there actually was, particularly for Nancy, Ricky, and Tina, who were older than the twins.

Although Nancy had shown some consistent evidence of competent symbolic play throughout the data-collection period, the twins had been engaging in only precursors to this mode of play. Beth, along with the father's girlfriend, planned the playing-house activity for the twins. Beth extended this into the tea party for the last home visit I observed with that family. She told me:

I had discussed pretend play with the family ahead of time. I said I would just bring a few things and I would like you to get together some things you have—like shirts, shoes, and hats. We had done very little imaginative play [before this], but they were ready for it. Dad had bought them a tea set last year and we had that out twice over the past year and at first, they had no idea what to do and the second time it got better and by the third time today, you could see they understood. I didn't want to have everything pretend because I felt that they weren't quite there yet. (interview, 10/27/98)

Beth was able to see that the girls were heading toward make-believe and had even attempted some symbolic play with the same materials at an earlier time. Because she knew them so well, she anticipated they would be able to have a pretend tea party, but even she was surprised when they were able to pretend without some concrete objects.

I discussed the minimal amounts of symbolic play with Michele during the last interview and she agreed that most of what we had been observing with Ricky and Tina over the last year was the precursors to make-believe. When I asked why she thought families may not be as encouraging of their child to engage in make-believe, she said:

It's hard to get them to play with their children sometimes. And I think I can get them to focus a little more on paper-and-pencil kinds of things, because it is easier for them to see. It's very concrete. It's more school kinds of things. It's hard to get them to be playful sometimes. (interview, 10/9/98)

It seems as though engaging in pretend play is almost too playlike for some parents to promote. They cannot easily see the direct connection between the play and potential learning. "School" kinds of tasks were more readily accepted even when in a play mode. School tasks, such as paper-and-pencil activities and worksheets, can be important to parents who want their children to succeed, where perhaps they have failed.

Haight and Miller (1993) reported on several studies involving extensive interviews of parents of young children. They noted that with middle-class parents, both mothers and fathers rated pretend play as important to the child's development, and parental participation was believed to facilitate children's pretend play. On the other hand, mothers from the working class did not view pretend play as important and tended to participate with their child in other types of play.

The missing element of well-developed pretense in the play of children enrolled in Early Head Start could be a function of the culture of poverty. This issue should be further explored with the families who participated in this study. Parent training on the importance of pretend play, as well as practice sessions on how to engage the child in make-believe activities, should be considered.

REFERENCES

Beizer, L., & Howes C. (1992). Mothers and toddlers: Partners in early symbolic play: Illustrative study #1. In C. Howes (Ed.), *The collaborative construction of pretend: Social pretend play function*. Albany: SUNY Press.

Blumer, H. (1964). *Symbolic interactionism: Perspective and method*. Englewood Cliffs, NJ: Prentice-Hall.

Bornstein, M.H. (1995). Parenting infants. In M.H. Bornstein (Ed.), *Handbook of parenting: Volume 1. Children and parenting*. Mahwah, NJ: Erlbaum.

Bornstein, M.H., Haynes, O.M., O'Reilly, A.W., & Painter, K.M. (1996). Solitary and collaborative pretense play in early childhood: Sources of individual variation in the development of representational competence. *Child Development, 67*, 2910–2929.

Bornstein, M.H., & Tamis-LeMonda, C.S. (1995). Parent–child symbolic play: Three theories in search of an effect. *Developmental Review, 15*, 382–400.

Bradley, R.H., & Caldwell, B.M. (1984). 174 children: A study of the relationship between home environment and cognitive development during the first 5 years. In A.W. Gottfried (Ed.), *Home environment and early cognitive development: Longitudinal research*. New York: Academic Press.

Bredekamp, S., & Copple, C. (1997). *Developmentally appropriate practice in early childhood education programs: Revised edition*. Washington, DC: National Association for the Education of Young Children.

Department of Health and Human Services. (1994). *The statement of the Advisory Council on Services for Families with Infants and Toddlers*. Washington, DC: Author.

Department of Health and Human Services. (1997). *Federal Register*. Washington, DC: Author.

Fein, G.G. (1981). Pretend play in childhood: An integrative review. *Child Development, 52*, 1095–1118.

Gottfried, A.W. (1984). Home environment in early cognitive development: Integration, meta-analyses, and conclusions. In A.W. Gottfried (Ed.), *Home environment and early cognitive development: Longitudinal research*. New York: Academic Press.

Haight, W.L., & Miller, P.J. (1993). *Pretending at home: Early development in a sociocultural context*. Albany: SUNY Press.

Hohman, M., & Weikart, D.P. (1995). *Educating young children: Learning practices for preschool and child care programs.* Ypsilanti, MI: High/Scope Press.

Jacob, E. (1987). Qualitative research traditions: A review. *Review of Educational Research, 57,* 1–50.

Johnson, J.E., Christie, J.F., & Yawkey, T. (1999). *Play and early childhood development* (2nd ed.). New York: Addison, Wesley, & Longman.

Klass, C.S. (1996). *Home visiting: Promoting healthy parent and child development.* Baltimore: Brookes.

McCune-Nicolich, L. (1981). Toward symbolic functioning: Structure of early pretend games and potential parallels with language. *Child Development, 52,* 785–789.

Miles, M.B., & Huberman, A.M. (1994). *Qualitative data analysis: An expanded sourcebook.* Thousand Oaks, CA: Sage.

National Association for the Education of Young Children (1995). *Quality, compensation, and affordability.* Washington, DC: Author.

Patton, M.Q. (1990). *Qualitative evaluation and research methods* (2nd ed.). Newbury Park, CA: Sage.

Piaget, J. (1962). *Play, dreams and imitation in childhood.* New York: Norton.

Piaget, J. (1978). Response to Brian Sutton-Smith. In R.E. Herron & B. Sutton-Smith (Eds.), *Child's play,* New York: Wiley.

Powell, D.R. (1990, September). Home visiting in the early years: Policy and program design decisions. *Young Children,* 65–73.

Rubin, K.H., Fein, G.G., & Vandenberg, B. (1983). Play. In P.H. Mussen (Ed.) *Handbook of child psychology: Volume 4. Socialization, personality, and social development.* New York: Wiley.

Shore, R. (1997). *Rethinking the brain: New insights into early development.* New York: Families and Work Institute.

Van Hoorn, J., Nourot, P., Scales, B., & Alward, K (1993). *Play at the center of the curriculum.* New York: Macmillan.

Vygotsky, L.S. (1976). Play and its role in the mental development of the child. In J.S. Bruner, A. Jolly, & K. Sylva (Eds.), *Play: It's role in development and evolution.* New York: Basic Books.

Vygotsky, L.S. (1978). *Mind in society: The development of higher psychological processes.* Cambridge, MA: Harvard University Press. (Original work published 1932)

Wasik, B.H., Bryant, D.M., & Lyons, C. (1990). *Home visiting: Procedures for helping families.* Newbury Park, NJ: Sage.

Whitebook, M., Howes, C., & Phillips, D. (1998). *Worthy work, unlivable wages: The national child care staffing study: 1988–97.* Washington, DC: Center for the Child Care Workforce.

12

Finding the Humor in Children's Play

Doris Bergen

Britta, 11 months old, is crawling across the room. Her mother says, "Come here, Britta, you need to get dressed." Britta starts crawling away even faster. Mom says, "I'm gonna get you," and starts after her in a playful way. Britta shrieks (falsely) and crawls under the table. Her mother repeats again and again, "I'm gonna get you," and makes exaggerated stalking movements around the table. Britta laughs and crawls to the other side but her mother moves quickly, catches her, and swoops her up high. Both Britta and Mom are laughing.

Leah, 17 months old, is sitting in her high chair at the dinner table with the family. She has fed herself competently and tried most of the items served that evening. Her dad says, "Do you want a bean?" and Leah replies, "No," with a big smile. Dad repeats the question; Leah again says, "No," smiling even more broadly. Dad asks, in quick succession, "Do you want meat . . . milk . . . sweet potato . . ." to all of which Leah responds, "No," with increasing animation and giggles. Then Dad asks with a smile, "Do you want ice cream . . . candy . . . cookies . . . ?" to which Leah continues to respond, "No," "No," "No," as her laughter and Dad's laughter escalate.

Jason, 22 months old, is in the car, which is sitting at a light waiting to turn left while other cars whiz by on the right and go down a hill. Jason starts laughing loudly and repeats "cars downhill" as each one disappears.

Olivia, 22 months old, is playing with a blanket. Dad puts it over her head and she laughs. Then she puts it over Dad's head and laughs even more. This sequence is repeated three times with both Dad and Olivia laughing.

Connor, 24 months old, and his friend Jordan are chasing each other up and down the hall, each taking turns going into the closet and shutting the door on each other, saying "bye bye" and "be back." They repeat this turn-taking routine 10 times with increasing laughter and zest.

Sam, 26 months old, is with an older child who asks him what ducks drink. Sam answers, "Ducks drink water." The older child teases, "No, ducks drink orange juice." Sam laughs and reiterates, "Ducks drink water." This sequence is repeated four times, resulting in more and more laughter.

Mark, 33 months old, is running his battery car around the room and performing "tricks" with it, making it go over his toy train tracks, down the hall, and having the car end up on its back. Mom makes "reactive" faces and sounds as he shows one trick after another. His initial smiles become laughter and then great hilarity. Finally, he gives a "fake" laugh and says "I'm laughing."

Marissa, 34 months old, looks at the family dog and says, "Daisy is melling [smelling]." Mom says to the dog, "Daisy, are you melling?" Marissa laughs because she knows she has mispronounced the word, and she says, "Mommy, are you teasing me?" She also says, "I'm giggling and giggling."

Sam, 40 months old, tells a joke, "Knock-knock." Mom says, "Who's there?" and Sam says, "T." Mom says, "T, who?" and Sam replies, "Trex dinosaur," with exaggerated laughter. (He has heard about dinosaurs at preschool this week.)

Connor, 50 months old, is playing "rough-house" with Dad, and the play becomes increasingly boisterous. Dad teases Connor by pretending to take his ball, and Connor indicates mild distress. Dad says, "I'm just joking, Connor; you need to be able to take a joke." Connor manages a weak smile.

FINDING THE BEGINNINGS OF HUMOR DEVELOPMENT IN PLAY

Studying and writing about children's play has been an interest of mine for 25 years, but I never really thought much about the role of play in children's humor development until I started studying it about 15 years ago. In the first humor study I did, I asked parents to be participant–observers of their children's humor, and to record examples of what their children thought was funny (not what the adults thought was funny about what children said or did, but what the children thought was funny). Parents were also asked to record when and where the humor occurred and who was present at the time it occurred (e.g., parents, peers). Over 100 parents of children from age 2 to 12 initially agreed to participate in collecting these examples, and so I was able to get a good idea of humor over that age span and examine the cognitive and social-emotional implications of that development (see Bergen, 1989, 1998b, for descriptions of these findings).

Since that time, other parents have been asked to record their examples and the findings continue to be very similar. When analyzing the first data set, one of the things I discovered was how salient was the influence of the context in which these humor examples occurred. Many of the examples parents recorded occurred in playful social interaction situations with themselves or with siblings and friends. Moreover, the parents in this sample seemed to be unusually playful people, initiating many types of humorous interactions with their children during play. Obviously, these were parents who valued both humor and play. These results got me thinking about, theorizing, and testing the hypothesis that humor and play arise from similar sources, each facilitating the development of the other (Bergen, 1998a).

Play and humor appear to be conceptually connected from an early age of development. They both begin at a similar age period (about 6 months), and they are facilitated by common contextual sources. Parents, at least those parents who have participated in these humor studies, seem to know intuitively how to facilitate humor development through playful means. They are initiators of humor with their children, responders to the children's humor attempts, appreciators of children's developing modes of humor expression, and facilitators of humor–play connections. Just as adults initiate children into the "play frame" so that children can learn that certain verbalizations and behaviors signal "this is play" (Bateson, 1956; Sutton-Smith & Sutton-Smith, 1974), these parents also conveyed the meaning of "this is humor" through their verbal and behavioral signals that identified the "humor frame." As the examples presented earlier illustrate, the introduction to "this is humor" occurs during the first few years of life, through adult facial expressions and verbal exaggerations, interactive adult–child practice in using repetitive humor patterns, adult direct labeling of "joking" and "teasing" behaviors, and adult acknowledgment of child labeling of "teasing" and "laughing" modes of expression.

Play and humor have many qualities in common. They are both enjoyable, and they have similar features of internal motivation, control, and reality (Neumann, 1971). They both involve *as if* abilities, flourish in low-risk settings with people who are trusted, and have cognitive and social-emotional consequences. According to McGhee (1979, p. 61), "Humor develops as the child's playfulness extends to recently mastered ideas and images, as well as overt play with objects." Although most of the humor children exhibit in the first years of life is related to playful physical activity and, a little later, to playful verbal activity, even this early humor-related play has an element of recognition of incongruity, one of the major types of humor found throughout life (Pien & Rothbart, 1976). That is, the child knows what is supposed to happen and so finds the "surprise" facial expression, physical movement, or verbal utterances funny. By 9 months of age, this type of humor, with its recognition of incongruity within a playful adult–child interaction routine, is already well developed, as Connor and his mother demonstrate.

Connor, 9 months old, is lying on the floor, and his mother has lightly placed a blanket on his face so that he must pull it off to see her. She says, "Where's

Connor? Where's Connor? Where is that boy?" using a high speech register and emphatically articulated speech style. In a routine with which he is obviously already quite familiar, Connor pulls the blanket off his face and smiles at Mom. By this age, he is already in charge of the play, and so he pulls the blanket up again to cover his face, at which point his mother repeats her questions. As he connects and reconnects through the sequence of this "peek-a-boo" play, his smiles become laughs and his laughs become high glee. Mom is laughing too as she ends the sequence with a hug.

As the other examples cited earlier show, during the age period up to 4 years, knowledge about what humor is develops rapidly, with young children beginning to initiate humor with peers and adults. At that time they recognize that laughter can be promoted by certain deliberately playful actions, words, and sounds; labeling humorous behaviors and beginning to be socialized into some of the "conventions" of humor, such as understanding riddle and joke routine patterns (if not yet their point) and the meaning of "just joking." As Jason's observation of the cars going down the hill demonstrates, young children also independently notice various types of incongruity that they find funny. However, much early humor expression occurs within situations of playful social interactions, first with adults and then with peers and siblings.

THEORETICAL PERSPECTIVES ON THE PLAY–HUMOR CONNECTION

The hypothesis that play and humor are closely connected is not new, having been discussed many years ago in the work of psychoanalytic theorists who built on Freud's (1905) writings about the social-emotional role of joking behavior. Freud identified three stages in humor development; the first he called "play," which he said begins by age 2 and involves children "practicing their capacities." The second, beginning about age 4, he called "jesting," which involves knowing the distinction between "reasonableness" and "absurdity," but which is not really intended to provide meaningful communication of conceptual incongruity. The final stage, "joking," which begins about age 6 or 7, involves displaying meaning through humor—that is, making "sense" of "nonsense." One of the things tested in my first study was whether the progression outlined by Freud held up in the examples from parents. Although the age levels of the early stages were somewhat different, coming a little earlier than Freud predicted, the stages did follow that progression, with the ability to tell a joke or to use a "joking facade" (Wolfenstein, 1954) to express hostile and sexual humor arising primarily after age 6 or 7. By age 12, the use of humor to express hostile, sexual, or otherwise shocking ideas is well established, as the "insult" and "parody" jokes popular with children of this age period attest. (The earliest indicator of this type of humor is the "bathroom humor" of preschoolers, which appears gross because it is expressed without the cover of the "joking facade.")

A number of years ago, McGhee (1971) outlined the early stages of cognitive aspects of humor development, suggesting four types/stages, all of which were related to the use of incongruity in humor. They include: (1) observing and performing visual incongruity; (2) observing and performing verbal incongruity (both types beginning at about age 2); (3) understanding conceptual incongruity (about age 4); and (4) understanding multiple meanings or "word play" (about age 6). Those stages have held up well in later studies (e.g., Bergen, 1998b; Bergen & Brown, 1994). While psychoanalytical theorists see play as the first step in humor development, cognitive theorists see play as continuing to be allied with incongruity humor throughout life but becoming internalized and closely tied to linguistic ambiguity (phonological, syntactic, semantic, and pragmatic). That is, humor development parallels specific cognitive changes, resulting in "play" with ideas and multiple meanings at later ages.

If play and humor arise at similar times and from similar sources, a question of interest is why they are typically thought of as two different phenomena and when do they begin to diverge as conscious expressions. Some theorists hypothesize that it is at the age of pretense development that humor begins to diverge from play to become a separate entity. For example, Wolfenstein (1954) suggested long ago that at about the age of 18 months, pretense becomes differentiated into two strands, which she called "serious" make-believe and "joking" make-believe. In serious make-believe, the real world is simulated, and children try to make their actions resemble the real world as closely as their understanding permits. For example, they will take the role of "Mom" and "cook" dinner. On the other hand, in joking make-believe, children deliberately distort reality with the intention of getting a surprise effect or humorous response. For example, they will have "Mom" put the pan on her head or say they are "cooking" shoes for everyone to eat! In order to do this distortion of reality, they must have a good understanding of what "should" be so that they can distort it through pretending that it is something else. According to Bariaud (1989), incongruities expressed in humorous actions are not "incorrect," but of a pretend nature. That is, "there is a certain 'distancing' from the norms of reality, and a combination of being fooled and complicity required from the other" (p. 21).

Wolfenstein (1954) also suggests that humor assists children in mastering anxieties they encounter, because they tend to use joking make-believe in situations where they have just mastered some understanding or experience. For example, pretending not to know one's name or giving the "wrong" name to familiar people is humor that toddlers who are just gaining a clear sense of their identity find enjoyable. Similarly, older children tell "dumb" jokes or laugh at "stupid" antics of people on television when they are engaged in mastering anxieties about their own learning competence. Because play is also used to master experiences and emotions, there is a congruence of purpose between humor and play in this area as well. Bariaud (1989, p. 18) explains the necessity for playful social interaction as a catalyst for humor, thus, "[Humor] is only complete when it is set in social communication, the aim of which is to make others laugh." She further states that the purpose of humor is "to trigger laughter" (p. 23).

THE NEED FOR MORE RESEARCH ON THE HUMOR–
PLAY CONNECTION

Although the author's research with parents and toddler-age children supports the integral role that social play interactions have in fostering very young children's humor development, most research on play development and most research on humor development have focused on behaviors occurring after this crucial age period, and they have rarely combined the exploration of both play and humor dimensions in the same study. Drawing upon cognitive and social theory and research, many researchers of play have studied the development of young children's play and its relationship to their cognitive and social-emotional development (see Bergen, 1998c). Similarly, there is a body of research that describes young children's expression and appreciation of humor and relates it to cognitive and social-emotional development (see Bergen, 1998b). Researchers who study the sense of humor also have investigated the personality correlates of such behavior (Ruch, 1994). Few of the researchers who have studied play or who have studied humor have explicitly made humor–play theoretical connections, however.

In studies of the personality quality "playfulness," Barnett (1991) identified two factors in playfulness that are related to humor development. She labeled them "manifest joy" and "sense of humor." Knox (1997) also includes humor expression as a facet assessed in her play scale observation criteria. With the exception of the researchers on playfulness and play-based assessment, however, humor has rarely been mentioned in published works on children's play, and although the humor research indicates that humor often occurs in playful, low-risk contexts, few of the extensive numbers of naturalistic research studies on children's play in preschool have included descriptions of the humor being exhibited by the children during their practice, pretend, and gamelike play.

Because play seems to be a fertile medium through which humor develops, it is particularly surprising that, of the many researchers who have studied play, so few have studied how these playful behaviors and contexts may facilitate humor development. As a consequence, the picture of play presented by many researchers on play is of a "serious business." (Perhaps that is why the phrase "play is the child's work" is so often used.) Because play and humor are so closely allied, with both being fostered during early adult–child physical and vocal interaction, and flowering during the *as if* behavior of early pretense, it is important to examine the types of play contexts that promote children's use of humor, and to notice the types of humor that are typically exhibited by children during their play in preschool and early school-age programs.

To help remedy the knowledge gap, in the past two years I have been exploring the play–humor connection during the toddler and preschool years by revisiting 75 of the videotapes taken of young children's play, in order to search for the elusive "humor moments." I had no estimation of how many examples of humor would be found in the children's videotaped free-play behavior because that had not been a dimension initially coded. This investigation was designed to find some preliminary answers to questions such as these:

1. How much humor is spontaneously enjoyed by toddlers and preschoolers during their play in group settings?

2. During what types of play is humor most likely to occur: practice, pretend, or games?

3. In what social settings is humor most likely to occur: solitary, parallel, associative, or cooperative play?

4. Are some children more likely to exhibit humor than others—that is, is the "playfulness" quality and thus the "humor" quantity and quality greater in some children?

5. Are boys or girls more likely to exhibit humor in toddler and preschool settings?

6. What eliciting conditions are most likely to result in expressions of humor during play?

7. What is the role of teachers in encouraging or suppressing humor expression in preschool play?

STUDYING THE HUMOR MOMENTS DURING FREE PLAY IN GROUP SETTINGS

The subjects on the videotapes were children ages 2 to 5, attending 12 different toddler and preschool programs. Tapes of these children were collected in a number of previous studies of play, all of which used a similar method of data collection. Each focal child had been videotaped in 10-minute segments on at least 3 occasions, with a total time of observation for each child approximating 30 minutes. Because the author's past play research had focused on toddlers as well as preschoolers and on children with disabilities as well as typically developing children, there were 279 preschool records and 101 toddler records analyzed with the assistance of a psychology student research team, and of these records, 93 were of children with special needs.

Every humor event (i.e., play episodes in which smiles, laughter, or other indicators of humor were exhibited) was recorded, and these events were coded as to humor type (e.g., expression or recognition of incongruity, clowning, joy in mastery play, sound play, verbal reproductions, and elaborations of language patterns). The types of play (practice, pretend, games) in which the humor occurred and the social contexts (solitary, parallel, associative, cooperative) of the humorous episodes were noted, as well as how adults facilitated or tolerated children's expression of humor.

FINDINGS ON THE QUANTITY AND QUALITY OF HUMOR MOMENTS

The child records that contained a humor event outnumbered the records that had no evidence of humor. Of the 380 child records observed, 259 of the records had at least one humor event, ranging from smiles to boisterous laughter. Although many of the humor events were very brief and many of the expressions of humor were mild (approximately 75 percent smiles, 25 percent laughter), it was notable that evidences of humor were clearly present in many records. One instance of humor was noted in about 47 percent of the records that had humor events, while 28 percent of these records had 2 or 3 instances, and the rest (25 percent) had 4 to 10 instances. The records included examples of humor expression during all three types of play, with about 30 percent recorded during practice play, 17 percent during pretend play, and 27 percent during gamelike play (e.g., turn-taking routines), while the remaining records had a number of examples of humor events occurring in more than one of these types of play (26 percent). For example, a particular child's 10-minute record might have shown that child finding humor during both a practice play and a pretend play event.

The humor events did not occur equally in all social contexts. Especially for the younger children, milder forms of humor, such as exhibiting pleasure in mastery play, often occurred during solitary or parallel play situations. About 37 percent of humor events were under that condition. About the same amount (37 percent) occurred in associative and cooperative play events, while the remaining records (26 percent) were of children showing humor in more than one social situation. The presence of other children seemed to elicit more boisterous humor than did solitary play, especially among the preschool-aged children.

Much of the humor expression could be coded as joy in mastery play (35 percent), clowning (16 percent), or teasing play (14 percent). Expressing humor when observing or performing incongruous actions or verbalizations was also a common type, with each (observing/performing) being present in about 12 percent of the records (for a total of 24 percent of events having incongruity humor). A few examples may serve to illustrate the types of humor observed.

Joy in mastery play was observed in the record of Sandy, a 2-year-old child with special needs. Her older sister was visiting the class and engaged her in play with a balloon hanging from a string. As she pushed the balloon and then caught it again (it swung on the string so it was easy to catch), she initially smiled, but after pushing and catching it about three times, she was chuckling each time she caught it again. Another example of joy in mastery play was exhibited by Zoie (a special-needs child of 2 1/2 years), who watched other children slap their hand in the water table and then joined in, laughing as she splashed. Similarly, Joe (a typical child of age 3), who had climbed the "big" slide, smiled broadly as he went down. Five-year-old Bill also showed joy in mastery play when he succeeded in building a large structure with table blocks.

Jessie, a 19-month-old child with special needs, initiated a game of "peek-a-boo" with the teacher by lifting up the butcher paper that had been spread out for scribbling. She peeked under her side and the teacher responded by lifting the part on the other side of the table. Jessie and the teacher engaged in a repetitive peeking game, and Jessie laughed delightedly in this humor incongruity routine.

An example of teasing and incongruity observation occurred in a typically developing toddler classroom, in which Elizabeth (age 2) and another girl were loading a shopping cart with books. Elizabeth occasionally looked over her shoulder as if she anticipated seeing her friend Zach come around the room divider. When he did suddenly appear from behind the divider and he touched the shopping cart, Elizabeth gave an exaggerated shriek and the two girls "escaped" by pushing the cart quickly away while laughing.

Linda (4 years old) demonstrated laughter at observing incongruity when Craig began to take big cardboard blocks off the shelf, many of them tumbling down on him. After Craig saw her reaction, he began clowning, by piling more blocks and sprawling in them. John also joined in the clowning and more laughter ensued.

Shane and his friends (all age 4 to 5) were sitting at the table awaiting materials to be used in making an animal creation, but when they got the first material, a square of wax paper, one of the boys performed an incongruous act by beginning to "kiss" the paper. Then all the boys kissed their paper, laughing and looking around to get the teacher's reaction.

This same group of boys later engaged in verbal pattern/sound play when yellow butter was provided for the activity. Patrick said, "Yellow is smello," and Shane replied, "Red is bread," both boys thinking this was hilarious.

Allie (4 years old) demonstrated "joking" make-believe by shrieking that a snake was chasing her. She ran to two boys and engaged them in a "fight" to save her from the snake. This play was accompanied by much exaggerated vocalization and laughter.

Lucy (4 years old), in one 10-minute record, engaged in clowning (hopping in a "silly" manner and looking to see the effect), teasing (poking and hugging another child who was engaged in an activity), verbal/sound play (saying "baby, baby, baby" in an increasingly loud manner), and "joking" make-believe (pretending to "comb" the hair of the "baby" with a wooden rod and pretending to feed her in an exaggerated manner). During most of this variety of activities, Lucy was giggling or laughing expansively. The teacher intervened once to ask Lucy not to annoy the other child.

Finally, the humor–play connection occurred even during lunch time. For example, Jamie engaged in a series of food-related humor, the last of which was saying, "Yum, yum," and making chewing noises very loudly while he was eating his sandwich. Everyone at the table was laughing until the teacher said, "Jamie, don't play with your food!"

To answer the questions about differences in humor events among children of different age levels, genders, and disabilities, statistical analyses using analysis of variance (ANOVA) with these independent variables were conducted. The ANOVAs showed no significant differences between children with disabilities and typical children in the number of humor events, and there were no significant age differences or gender differences in the number of humor events. There were also no significant differences by age, gender, or disability condition in the types of humor that were expressed. For all children, joy in mastery, teasing, clowning, and observing or performing incongruity actions were the primary types. Although mild forms of humor were more prevalent overall than boisterous ones, humor of some type did occur about equally when toddlers, preschoolers, and children with disabilities played in group settings.

Adults also took a more initiating and responding role in humor–play facilitation with toddlers and with children with disabilities, with older children and typically developing children having more humor–play interactions with peers. The teachers in preschool classrooms, in fact, often took the role of "toning down" the humorous play. Adult tolerance of humor expression may have a major influence on how often it occurs in preschool settings. It is also possible that personality differences may be a factor in humor expression and understanding, since the records of some children showed much humor, while about one-third of the children's records showed no humor events.

NOTICING AND ENCOURAGING HUMOR DEVELOPMENT THROUGH PLAY

I have written elsewhere about the need for teachers to appreciate and foster children's humor understanding and expression, and especially to promote it as a coping skill for meeting life's problems (Bergen, 1992). Teachers should at least be as facilitative of humor as are the parents who helped to study this phenomenon. This closer look at the research videotapes has confirmed the importance of investigating humor development and the ways it can be fostered by teachers. At an earlier time period, I did conduct one study that asked kindergarten teachers to be participant observers of children's humor (Bergen, 1990), and received many interesting examples of the ways in which playful teachers demonstrated responsiveness to hearing the same riddle for the 10th time, or showed children how humor could help them cope with life's minor upsets. However, one teacher sent back her observation form with the comment, "I never realized how little time I allowed for play and humor in my classroom until I started this observation." She had recorded only three examples in three weeks, while other teachers had 20 or more examples in that same time period.

Researchers may miss an important element in their analyses of children's play if they don't note when humorous expression is an accompaniment to that play. Those who study play could make a contribution to the data base on humor as well if they would analyze the humor events in their observations of children (and youth) at play. Of special interest would be further study of the initial periods of pretend play when joking and serious make-believe may diverge, giving humor a "life of its own." For example, the question of whether this divergence seems to occur without adult modeling or whether adults are crucial to the process of humor development is an important one in need of further study.

Finally, theorists need to examine humor–play connections in order to expand upon earlier theoretical work and/or to create new perspectives that will enhance both the study of play and the study of humor. Although there has been a great deal of theoretical work in the area of adult humor, there are still only a few researchers and theorists focusing their work on children's humor development. Researchers who have studied adult play and its humor accompaniment might shed light on this phenomenon in children if they were to take a closer look at it through the lens of their theories of adult play and humor.

Humor expression and appreciation are important for both children and adults, and play has an integral role in fostering and nourishing such humor development. Play does not have to be studied only as "serious business." Rather, it is time to find out more about the ways in which play provides a medium not only for physical, cognitive, and social-emotional development, but also for children's humor development. Children's play can provide a rich context for studying the development of the "sense of humor."

REFERENCES

Bariaud, F. (1989). Age differences in children's humor. *Journal of Children in Contemporary Society, 20,* 5–45

Barnett, L. A. (1991). The playful child: Measurement of a disposition to play. *Play and Culture, 4,* 51–74.

Bateson, G. (1956). The message "This is play." In B. Schaffner (Ed.), *Group processes: Transactions of the second conference* (pp. 145–241). New York: Josiah Macy Jr. Foundation.

Bergen, D. (1989). Characteristics of young children's expression of humour in home settings as observed by parents. *International Journal of Educology, 3*(2), 124–135.

Bergen, D. (1990, July). *Young children's humor at home and school: Using parents and teachers as participant observers.* Paper presented at Eighth International Conference on Humor, Sheffield, England.

Bergen, D. (1992). Teaching strategies: Using humor to facilitate learning. *Childhood Education, 68*(4), 105–106.

Bergen, D. (1998a). Play as a context for humor development. In D. Fromberg & D. Bergen (Eds.), *Play from birth to twelve and beyond: Contexts, perspectives, and meanings* (pp. 322–337). New York: Garland Press.

Bergen, D. (1998b). Development of the sense of humor. In W. Ruch (Ed.), *The sense of humor* (pp. 329–358). Berlin: Mouton de Gruyter.

Bergen, D. (1998c). Stages of play development. In D. Bergen (Ed.), *Readings from play as a medium for learning and development* (pp. 71–93). Olney, MD: Association for the Education of Young Children.

Bergen, D., & Brown, J. (1994, June). *Humor development of children of three ages: 5–6, 8–9, 11–12.* Symposium presentation at the International Humor Conference, Ithaca, NY.

Freud, S. (1905). *Jokes and their relation to the unconscious.* New York: Norton.

Knox, S. (1997). Development and current use of the Knox preschool play scale. In L. D. Parham & L. S. Fazio (Eds.). *Play in occupational therapy for children* (pp. 35–51). St. Louis, MO: Mosby.

McGhee, P. (1971). Cognitive development and children's comprehension of humor. *Child Development, 42,* 123–138.

McGhee, P. (1979). *Humor: Its origin and development.* San Francisco: Freeman.

Neumann, E. A. (1971). *The elements of play.* New York: MSS Information Corp.

Pien, D., & Rothbart, M. K. (1976). Incongruity and resolution in children's humor: A reexamination. *Child Development, 47, 966–971.*

Ruch, W. (1994, June). *A state-trait approach to cheerfulness, seriousness, and bad mood: A progress report.* Paper presented at the International Humor Conference, Ithaca, NY.

Sutton-Smith, B., & Sutton-Smith, S. (1974). *How to play with your child (and when not to).* New York: Hawthorn/Dutton.

Wolfenstein, M. (1954). *Children's humor.* Chicago: Free Press.

Part IV
Playfighting

13

Perceptions of Playfighting and Real Fighting: Effects of Sex and Participant Status

Anthony D. Pellegrini

Play is in many ways a very easy construct to recognize and define. For example, children and adults alike have little difficulty recognizing it (Smith & Vollstedt, 1985). One form of play—fantasy or pretend play—is especially easy to recognize and define. Indeed, fantasy play is considered to represent the paradigm example of play (McCune-Nicholich & Fenson, 1984). As we move away from fantasy to other forms of play, ambiguity appears abruptly. Evidence of this ambiguity can be found in debates over definitions of play in the ethological (Burghardt, 1999; Martin & Caro, 1985) and child play literatures (Smith & Vollstedt, 1985).

The case of rough-and-tumble play (R&T), or playfighting, seems particularly problematic. Until rather recently, developmental psychologists have confused and conflated playfighting with aggression (e.g., Potts, Huston, & Wright, 1986). However, behavioral studies of human and nonhuman juveniles have delineated them as separate constructs, with different components, antecedents, and consequences (e.g., Smith & Boulton, 1990). R&T is a dimension of social play that is composed of physically vigorous behaviors (such as jumping and swinging) resembling real fighting, except for its play tenor. Consequently, R&T is sometimes labeled "playfighting." That is, R&T, unlike real fighting, is characterized by positive affect (as evidenced by a "play face," or smile), little or no contact from hits or kicks, reciprocity (where subordinates and superordinates alternate roles), and continued affiliation (juveniles stay together at the end of the bout).

Playfighting is more frequently observed in males—relative to females—of many primate species, including humans (Pellegrini & Smith, 1998). This is probably due to the fact that playfighting is related to subsequent hunting and fighting abilities. In the species where these sex differences are observed, males, not females, use aggression and fighting to establish and maintain dominance (deWaal, 1996). From this view, it has been proposed that playfighting in human males serves a dominance and practice-for-fighting function, especially during adolescence (Smith, 1982).

Motivational analyses from observational studies have helped us address possible functions of playfighting. These inferences are typically based on contemporaneous (Humphreys & Smith, 1987) and longitudinal correlations (Pellegrini, 1995) as well as sequential lag analyses (Pellegrini, 1988). These studies suggest that playfighting can serve at least two possible functions, and these functions vary developmentally. During the juvenile period, playfighting is associated with social competence and cooperative interaction, not dominance (Humphreys & Smith, 1987; Pellegrini, 1993). With the onset of adolescence, however, the tenor of playfighting seems to change for both human and nonhuman primates, such that playfighting seems to be used to establish and maintain dominance status (Fagen, 1981; Humphreys & Smith, 1987; Pellegrini, 1995).

Other methods besides behavioral observations have been used with human juveniles to gain further insights into differences between play and real fighting, as well as possible functions of each. Interviewing children about differences between videotaped play and real fighting bouts has been particularly productive in making inferences about youngsters' motives for engaging in playfighting (Costabile et al., 1991; Pellegrini, 1988). In one variant of this procedure, children are shown videotaped bouts of play and real fighting. They are then asked to differentiate between the two ("Is this playfighting or real fighting?") by making a smiling or frowning face. Preschool children reliably discriminate between the two, though aggressive youngsters have more difficulty than non-aggressive youngsters (Pellegrini, 1989). In this procedure, children are also asked why they engage in this form of behavior and are provided with various prompts, for example, "Are they having fun?" "Are they showing off?"

This latter form of questioning is most promising in terms of making inferences about possible motivations for engaging in each form of behavior and possible functions. These motives may not be readily observable, and youngsters can use their experience in these bouts as a basis for exposition. For example, in a cross-national study involving Brazilian, English, and Italian children, Smith, Hunter, Carvalho, and Costabile (1992) suggested that children engaged in playfighting for reasons associated with fun (e.g., "It's good fun"; "It makes me laugh") and dominance (e.g., "It's fun to show what you can do"; "You can keep them down and they don't have a chance").

Dominance is a construct referring to the social ordering of individuals for access to valued resources (Dunbar, 1988; Strayer, 1980). Dominance is established through a series of agonistic and affiliative behavioral strategies, such that when individuals first encounter each other, agonistic strategies (such as threats and physical aggression) are used to establish status. After status is achieved, more affiliative strategies (such as cooperation and reconciliation) are used by dominant individuals to form alliances and maintain group harmony (Pellegrini & Bartini, 2001; deWaal, 1989).

Dominance status is renegotiated with the onset of adolescence due to rapid increase in body size, sexual maturity, and abrupt changes in social group membership. In cases of children in the industrialized world, abrupt changes in social groupings occur when they move from primary to middle school. Consequently, it is a particularly important period to examine youngsters' perceptions of play and real fighting as well as possible motivations for engaging in it. It may be the case that functions in adolescence, compared to childhood, become more related to dominance. Adolescence does seem to witness an increase in physical aggression (Pellegrini & Bartini, 2001) and in the co-occurrence of play and real fighting (Pellegrini, 1995).

To date, the studies of play and real fighting among adolescents have been observational (e.g., Humphreys & Smith, 1987; Neill, 1976; Pellegrini, 1995), and these all suggest that playfighting may be used to serve a dominance function. For example, Neill (1976) found that play and real fighting co-occurred in his sample of boys. Similarly, both Humphreys and Smith (1987) and Pellegrini (1995) found that playfighting and peer-nominated dominance were significantly intercorrelated.

In the present study I used a videotape playback methodology to examine the extent to which male and female adolescents who were both participants and nonparticipants in the observed bout differentiated play from real fighting, and differences in possible motivations. That different individuals should have different perceptions of the same behaviors is typically studied in terms of individual differences. For example, and as noted above, aggressive children, relative to nonaggressive youngsters, are less accurate in their perceptions of ambiguous and provocative social information, such as playfighting, possibly due to social information-processing deficits (Dodge & Frame, 1982; Pellegrini, 1989). Importantly, and unlike previous research (with the exception of Smith & Pellegrini, 2000), in this study I also compared the perceptions of youngsters who participated in those bouts with those who did not.

In the only study of its kind, Smith, Smees, Pellegrini, and Menesini (1993) first observed and videotaped bouts of primary school children's play and real fighting during their morning breaktime on the school playground. These bouts, in turn, were shown to participants and nonparticipants in the afternoon of the same day on which the bouts were filmed and again one week later. There was greater concordance between participants' interpretations, relative to nonparticipants. These trends were maintained across the one-week interval. It was suggested that the differences may have been due to the fact that friends usually playfight with each other (Humphreys & Smith, 1987) and that this close relationship may help them more accurately interpret the meaning of this ambiguous social construct.

Based on these previous findings we expect differences between participants and nonparticipants in differentiating playfighting from real fighting. Playfighting can be ambiguous and participation in the event is probably an important factor in accurately differentiating it from real fighting.

Sex differences in play, fighting are robust (Pellegrini & Smith, 1998). Boys exhibit more than do girls, and these differences are due to a combination of distal (evolutionary history) and more proximal factors (hormonal and socialization events). In light of this different level of participation, we expect boys to be more accurate than girls in differentiating play from real fighting.

Perhaps the most fruitful use of the participant/nonparticipant paradigm relates to perceptions of function or motivations for engaging in playfighting. Typically, inferences about function for playfighting have been based on the observed consequences of playfighting. For example, if playfighting is followed by games, we would assume it served an affiliative function; if it were followed by dispersion, we would assume it served an aggressive function (Pellegrini, 1988). Participants' comments on their motives for engaging in play and real fighting has the potential to provide important information not directly available from observations. For example, observational research has documented that playfighting sometimes moves into aggression during early adolescence (Pellegrini, 1995). This can be due, according to Fagen (1981), to an "honest mistake" or to "cheating." In the former case, one youngster may accidently hit too hard, while in the latter case, this is done to exploit the playful tenor of the bout to "show off" one's status to peers for dominance-exhibit ends. The period of early adolescence may be particularly prone to "cheating" given the relation between playfighting and dominance and aggression during this period, unlike relations during childhood. Asking participants about intent provides access to motives about what may be especially ambiguous bouts.

We posit that there will be differences due to participation status in perceptions of playfighting and real fighting. Further, participation status should attenuate sex differences such that there should be no sex differences between participants but differences should exist between nonparticipants.

METHOD

Participants

A total of 95 (54 males, 41 females) youngsters took part in this study, which was part of a larger ongoing study. The participants were drawn from youngsters in their first year of middle school (6th grade) in two rural schools in the southeastern United States. The average age at the start of the study was 12 years.

Procedures

As part of an ongoing project, students were observed and videotaped at various locations across the school day, from breakfast in the morning, through changing classes and lunch time, to free time at the end of the day on Fridays. Additionally, youngsters were observed during a Friday evening dance held monthly.

Event sampling with continuous recording rules were followed for recording play and real fighting. Only those participants for whom we had informed consent were recorded. Tapes were reviewed by research associates trained to differentiate play from real fighting along the following criteria. Playfighting had positive affect, soft or exaggerated physical contact, and participants stayed together after the bout terminated. Real fighting, on the other hand, was characterized by negative affect, hard hits, and separation of peers at bout termination. From a corpus of tapes, a set of six bouts was chosen for each participant and edited into a sequence of three play and three real fighting bouts.

Participants viewed two sets of tapes. In one case they were participants and in other cases they were nonparticipants. They were asked, individually, the following series of standardized questions by an interviewer for each of the six bouts. Responses were audio-recorded and later coded. For the first question, responses to both play and real fighting were analyzed. For the remainder of the questions, responses to playfighting only were analyzed. First, they were asked, "What's going on?" Responses were categorized as play, teasing, fighting, dominance, don't know. Next, they were asked, "Why are you/they doing it?" Responses were coded as to play, to tease, to retaliate, to pick on/victimize, an accident, to hurt/aggress against, don't know/can't remember. Third, they were asked, "Is it fun?" and responses were yes, no. Fourth, they were asked, "Are you trying to hurt him/her?" Responses were yes, no. Fifth, they were asked, "Are you showing off?" with yes/no responses.

RESULTS

In this section I present results of boys' and girls' responses to the series of questions asked and how the responses varied according to participation status. The descriptive statistics are displayed in Table 13.1. All analyses were subject to gender by participant/nonparticipant by response level repeated measures analyses of variance (ANOVA) where the last two factors were within subject factors. Multiple comparisons were made using Student's Newman Keul criteria with a .05 *alpha* level.

What Is It?

In this first question we asked youngsters to categorize each of the 6 bouts they viewed (3 were play and 3 were real fighting). The 2 (sex) by 2 (participant)

Table 13.1
Descriptive Statistics for Responses to Interview Questions

Interview Question

	Participant				Nonparticipant			
	Male		Female		Male		Female	
	M	SD	M	SD	M	SD	M	SD
What is it?								
Play	3.42	1.57	3.30	1.80	3.60	1.52	3.04	1.77
Tease	.88	1.10	.75	.78	1.07	1.08	1.52	1.43
Fight	.19	.40	.30	.57	.10	.31	.09	.30
Dominance	.46	.90	.80	.69	.32	.66	.38	.58
Don't know	.19	.49	.25	.91	.10	.31	.04	.21
Why are you doing it?								
Play	1.73	1.15	1.65	.98	2.53	1.42	1.14	1.15
Tease	.19	.49	.15	.36	.21	.49	.28	.46
Retaliate	1.26	1.34	1.90	1.33	.60	.87	2.42	1.71
Pick on	.15	.46	.05	.22	.10	.31	.04	.21
Accident	.57	.85	.55	.75	.53	.88	.23	.53
Hurt	.03	.19	.00	.00	.07	.26	.00	.00
Don't know	.07	.27	.00	.00	.00	.00	.09	.30
Is it fun?								
Yes	3.30	1.34	3.55	1.82	3.96	.126	2.85	1.45
No	1.07	1.29	1.00	1.33	1.00	.86	1.66	1.06
Are you trying to hurt him/her?								
Yes	.50	.86	.10	.30	.46	.69	.47	.74
No	4.26	1.21	5.25	1.61	5.00	.90	4.90	1.37
Is it showing off?								
Yes	.15	.46	.00	.00	1.21	1.34	.90	1.30

by 6 (response level) repeated measures ANOVA revealed a main effect for response level, $F(5,455) = 119$, $p < .0001$. Bouts were considered play and real fighting most frequently, and each of these were more significant than teasing, dominance, cooperation, and don't know.

Why Are You Doing It?

The 2 by 2 by 9 (response level) repeated measures ANOVA revealed a significant main effect for response level, $F(8,728) = 58.75$, $p < .000$, as well as a significant interaction among response level, gender, and participant status, $F(8,728) = 3.82$, $p < .004$. While the main effect for response level indicated that the majority of responses fell into the first three categories (play, tease, and retaliation), the main effect will be interpreted in terms of the three-way interaction. Significant differences were observed only for two response categories, play and retaliation. For the play category, participant females, more than nonparticipant females, said they engaged in these bouts because they were playing. For males, however, nonparticipants, more than participants, gave a play response. Among nonparticipants more generally, males, more than females, gave play responses.

For retaliation responses, more were given by female nonparticipants than female participants. For males, more were given by participants than male nonparticipants.

Is It Fun?

The 2 by 2 by 3 (response level) repeated measures ANOVA revealed a significant main effect for response level, $F(2,182) = 128.75$, $p < .0001$, and a significant three-way interaction, $F(2,182) = 3.80$, $p < .03$. Significant differences were observed only within the yes category; this category also had the largest number of responses. For girls, participants said yes more than nonparticipants, and for boys, the pattern was reversed such that nonparticipants said yes more than participants.

Are You Trying to Hurt Him/Her?

The 2 by 2 by 2 (response level: yes/no) repeated measures ANOVA revealed a significant main effect for response level, $F(1,91) = 708.02$, $p < .0001$, and a significant three-way interaction, $F(1,91) = 4.90$, $p < .02$. While the vast majority of respondents said the participants were not trying to hurt each other, more males than females said that they were trying to hurt each other. The three-way interaction showed that participant males, more than nonparticipant males, said they were trying to hurt their peers.

Is It Showing Off?

The 2 by 2 by 2 (response level) repeated measures ANOVA revealed a significant main effect for response level, $F(1,91) = 378.26$, $p < .0001$, and a significant two-way interaction between response level and participant status, $F(1,91) = 13.30$, $p < .0004$. While the majority of youngsters said the bout was not showing off, the participants, compared to the nonparticipants, said it was showing off.

DISCUSSION

The results from this study convey a consistent picture, but the picture is different for males and females. First, in terms of differentiating play from real fighting, all youngsters could do so, and there were no differences due to participation or sex. While these findings were not hypothesized, they are consistent with data for younger participants where most children reliably differentiate the two; 70 percent accuracy at 5 years of age, and the figure increases to 90 percent accuracy for 8- to 11-year-olds (Smith et al., 1992). In short, young adolescents, like preschoolers, can reliably differentiate play from real fighting. This ability cut across participation status and sex.

The contrast between participants and nonparticipants should, however, come more clearly to the fore when we address more subtle questions, such as Why do you engage in this sort of behavior? and Are you doing it in an aggressive or playful way? These subtleties are especially important during early adolescence, when the tenor of playfighting becomes more serious and aggressive (Pellegrini, 1995), possibly to serve a dominance exhibition end. Boulton (1992), for example, showed that interviewing adolescents about their playfighting provided insight into possible uses of playfighting to show off to one's peers and to exhibit physical prowess to onlookers.

Results clearly show that boys and girls have very different views of play and real fighting and these views were moderated by participation status. I begin with girls. The playfighting bouts involving girls were interpreted as more fun for participants than for female nonparticipants. Further, participating girls did not consider these bouts to be dominance, or show off, exhibitions.

Interestingly, participant girls, more than nonparticipant girls, interpreted playfighting as playful. It may be the case that these girls were different from girls who did not engage in playfighting. Playfighting for adolescent girls, relative to males, is infrequent. When it is observed, it most often is playful and it often occurs in the context of girls initiating contact with boys, as part of early heterosexual contact (Pellegrini, 2001). Maccoby (1998) describes a similar phenomenon as "pushing and poking courtship" behavior. In such cases, young adolescents use playful overtures to initiate contact with members of the opposite sex. These sorts of overtures reduce the personal risk associated with making cross-sex interactions. Specifically, cross-sex interactions in public places are relatively rare during childhood, only beginning to change slowly during adolescence (Maccoby, 1998). However, at the start of adolescence, youngsters are motivated to do so, but they simultaneously want to minimize the risk associated with any possible rejection of an overture. They use play tactics, such as playfighting, to initiate contact. If there is uptake to the overture, they have succeeded in making contact. If they are rebuffed, they can dismiss it as play (Pellegrini, 2001).

The results for boys were quite different from girls. Boys, like males of many primate species, engage in playfighting with greater frequency than do females (Pellegrini & Smith, 1998). Playfighting is thought to serve as practice for dominance exhibition and maintenance. Females use other strategies, such as alliances with other females (Smuts, 1995) and manipulation of relationships (Crick & Grotpeter, 1995), to gain and maintain status in their groups. The results from the present study support the hypothesis that adolescent males use playfighting to assert dominance. Male participants, relative to nonparticipating males, saw playfighting as retaliatory. Further, males more than females, independent of participation status, said that they were trying to hurt their partner in playfighting. Males who did not participate, relative to males who did, said there was no intent to hurt. Thus, participation provided clear insight into possible cheating in playfighting.

In short, males use playfighting to exhibit dominance. These bouts are often retaliatory and cause physical pain to participants. When asked if they consider these bouts to be displays, or showing off, both boys and girls alike see them as such. Playfighting, then, seems to be serving an exhibition function, at least with some children.

In summary, this study adds to the small but growing literature on playfighting during early adolescence. Playfighting during this period, unlike during the period of childhood, is used by males to establish and maintain dominance in their peer groups. To this end, they used playfighting to retaliate and hurt peers. Uniquely, this study gains closer insight into intentionality by interviewing youngsters who participated in the playfighting bouts. Participation seems necessary to gain closer insight into behaviors that are ambiguous, like playfighting.

Future research using videotape interviews to gain insight into youngsters' cognitive processing of ambiguous and provocative social behavior should take note of differences associated with participation status. Differences in status yield different interpretations.

ACKNOWLEDGMENTS

This research was supported by a grant from the W. T. Grant Foundation. We also acknowledge the support of the superintendent of schools, Andy Byers, and director of research, Bob Covi, of the Jackson County (Ga.) Schools, as well as the youngsters, teachers, and staff of the East and West Jackson Middle Schools. Correspondence should be addressed to the author at the Department of Educational Psychology, 214 Burton Hall, University of Minnesota, Minneapolis, MN 55455; e-mail: pelle013@tc.umn.edu.

REFERENCES

Boulton, M. J. (1992). Rough physical play in adolescence: Does it serve a dominance function? *Early Education and Development, 3*, 312–333.

Burghardt, G. M. (1999). Conceptions of play and the evolution of animal minds. *Evolution and Cognition, 5*, 115–123.

Costabile, A., Smith, P., Matheson, L., Aston, J., Hunter, T., & Boulton, M. (1991). Cross-national comparison of how children distinguish serious and playful fighting. *Developmental Psychology, 27*, 881–887.

Crick, N. R., & Grotpeter, J. K. (1995). Relational aggression, gender, and social-psychological adjustment. *Child Development, 66*, 710–722.

DeWaal, F.B.M. (1989). *Peacemaking among primates.* Cambridge, MA: Harvard University Press.

DeWaal, F.B.M. (1996). *Good natured: The origins of right and wrong in humans and other animals.* Cambridge, MA: Harvard University Press.

Dodge, K., & Frame, C. (1982). Social cognitive biases and deficits in aggressive keys. *Child Development, 53*, 620–635.

Dunbar, R.I.M. (1988). *Primate social systems.* Ithaca, NY: Cornell University Press.

Fagen, R. (1981). *Animal play behavior.* New York: Oxford University Press.

Humphreys, A., & Smith, P. K. (1987). Rough-and-tumble play, friendship and dominance in school children: Evidence for continuity and change with age. *Child Development, 58*, 201–212.

Maccoby, E. E. (1998). *The two sexes: Growing up apart, coming together.* Cambridge, MA: Harvard University Press.

Martin, P., & Caro, T. (1985). On the function of play and its role in behavioral development. In J. Rosenblatt, C. Beer, M. C. Bushnel, & P. Slater (Eds.), *Advances in the study of behavior, Vol. 15* (pp. 59–103). New York: Academic Press.

McCune-Nicolich, L., & Fenson, L. (1984). Methodological issues in studying early pretend play. In T. D. Yawkey & A. D. Pellegrini (Eds.), *Child's play* (pp. 81–104). Hillsdale, NJ: Erlbaum.

Neill S. (1976). Aggressive and non-aggressive fighting in twelve-to-thirteen year old pre-adolescent boys. *Journal of Child Psychology and Psychiatry, 17*, 213–220.

Pellegrini, A. D. (1988). Elementary school children's rough-and-rumble play and social competence. *Developmental Psychology, 24*, 802–806.

Pellegrini, A. D. (1989). What is a category? The care of rough-and-tumble play. *Ethology and Sociobiology, 10*, 331–341.

Pellegrini, A.D. (1993). Boy's rough-and-tumble play, social competence, and group composition. *British Journal of Developmental Psychology, 11*, 237–248.

Pellegrini, A.D. (1995). A longitudinal study of boys' rough-and-tumble play and dominance during early adolescence. *Journal of Applied Developmental Psychology, 16*, 77–93.

Pellegrini, A. D. (2001). A longitudinal study of heterosexual relationships, aggression, and sexual harassment during the transition from primary school through middle school. *Journal of Applied Developmental Psychology, 22*, 119–133.

Pellegrini, A. D., & Bartini, M. (2000). Dominance in early adolescent boys: Affiliative and aggressive dimensions and possible functions. *Merrill-Palmer Quarterly, 47*, 147–162.

Pellegrini, A., & Smith, P. (1998). Physical activity play: The nature and function of a neglected aspect of play. *Child Development, 69* (3), 577–598.

Potts, R., Huston, A., & Wright, J. (1986). The effects of television forum and violent content on boys attention and social behavior. *Journal of Experimental Child Psychology, 41*, 1–7.

Smith, P.K. (1982). Does play matter? Functional and evolutionary aspects of animal and human play. *The Behavioral and Brain Sciences, 5*, 139–184.

Smith, P. K., & Boulton, M. (1990). Rough-and-tumble play, aggression, and dominance: Perception and behavior in children's encounters. *Human Development, 33*, 271–282.

Smith, P. K., Hunter, T., Carvalho, A.M.A., & Costabile, A. (1992). Children's perceptions of playfighting, playchasing and real fighting: A cross-national interview study. *Social Development, 1*, 211–229.

Smith, P. K., Smees, R., Pellegrini, A., & Menesini, E. (1993, July). *Playfighting and real fighting: Perspectives on their relationship.* Paper presented at the biennial meetings of the International Society for the Study of Behavioral Development, Racife, Brazil.

Smith, P. K., & Vollstedt, R. (1985). On defining play: An empirical study of the relationship between play and various play criteria. *Child Development, 56*, 1042–1050.

Smuts, B. B. (1995). The evolutionary origins of patriarchy. *Human Nature, 6*, 1–32.

Strayer, F. (1980). Social ecology of the preschool peer group. In W. A. Collins (Ed.), *The Minnesota Symposia on Child Psychology: Development of cognition, affect, and social relations, Vol. 13* (pp. 165–196). Hillsdale, NJ: Erlbaum.

14

Comparing Pupil and Teacher Perceptions for Playful Fighting, Serious Fighting, and Positive Peer Interaction

Peter K. Smith, Rebecca Smees, Anthony D. Pellegrini, and Ersilia Menesini

Playfighting and chasing, or rough-and-tumble play (R&T), is a common form of peer interaction throughout the school years. Although often neglected in favor of a much more extensive research literature on pretend play, the last decade or two have seen a body of research that has established some basic facts about playfighting (Pellegrini, in press; Smith 1997). It takes up some 10 percent of children's recess time (Fry, 1987; Humphreys & Smith, 1987; Pellegrini, 1987). It is more frequent in boys, but present also in girls. It tends to increase through the preschool and early school years, peak in middle childhood, and decrease again in adolescence (Pellegrini & Smith, 1998).

Playfighting, although superficially similar to serious fighting, can be distinguished from it in a number of ways (Blurton Jones, 1967; Boulton, 1991; Fry, 1987; Humphreys & Smith, 1987; Pellegrini, 1988; Smith, 1989). These have been established by ethological observations, interviews with children (and adults), and video-based playback interviews with children (and adults), and are summarized in Table 14.1.

On school playgrounds, playfighting (c. 10 percent of time) is much more frequent than real fighting, which occupies approximately 1 percent of time (Schäfer & Smith, 1996). Occasionally playfighting leads to real fighting (maybe around 1 percent of playfighting bouts, though this percentage is higher for rejected children, and perhaps for adolescents; Pellegrini, 1988, 1994). This

Table 14.1
Main Ways in Which Playfighting and Real Fighting can be Distinguished

---

Circumstances leading to an encounter: Usually in a playfighting episode there is no conflict over resources.

Facial and vocal expression: Playfighting is usually preceded or accompanied by smiling and playful expression.

Self-handicapping: In playfighting, the stronger partner may allow another child to pin him or her during a wrestle, not using the maximum strength.

Restraint by participants: In playfighting, the contact between the partners is usually gentle and light.

Numbers of participants: In playfighting, there might be several partners involved.

Reaction of onlookers: Playfighting has little interest for nonparticipants.

Reversal of roles: Participants may take reciprocal roles during the encounter.

Relationship between participants immediately after a playfighting encounter: Children usually stay together.

---

transition from playful to real fighting might be due to either "honest mistakes" (a child mistakenly thinks that a playful action is aggressive) or "cheating" (a child deliberately misuses the play convention to inflict hurt on the partner).

Children themselves, when interviewed about playfighting, have fairly clear views (Smith, Hunter, Carvalho, & Costabile, 1992). Boys especially often report taking part in, and enjoying, playfighting; by 8 years old they feel confident in telling apart playfighting and real fighting, and can talk about some of the cues used in doing so. They recognize that playfights can sometimes turn into real fights, however with the risk being less if playing with a friend rather than a nonfriend.

Teachers and playground supervisors appear to view playfighting less positively than do children themselves. "It's the games boys want to play. For the most part this is fighting, violence, jumping on each other, and 'killing' each other. There's so much fighting in the name of play. . . . The children will tell you they're only playing, but it can move into a real fight" (Blatchford, 1989, p. 29, interview with junior school teacher). Teachers overestimate the proportion of "fighting," which is real fighting rather than playfighting; 30 primary school teachers estimated 37 percent (Schäfer & Smith, 1996) rather than a more realistic 5–10 percent, based on observational studies. Teachers also overestimate the proportion of playfights that turn into real fights; primary school teachers estimated 29 percent (Schäfer & Smith, 1996) rather than a more realistic 1 percent, based on the observational research. School teachers and supervisors are significant adults for pupils at school, so misperceptions of this kind might be cause for concern. It is not clear if these misperceptions are specific to playfighting, or are found in other areas of social behavior.

The aim of this study was to compare children's and teachers' perspectives on playfighting and real fighting in primary schools in England. We focused on boys, as they are more heavily involved in playfighting (Smith et al., 1992). We first report on the children's views on playfighting; these replicate and extend some of the earlier reports from Smith and colleagues (1992) with which we compare them. We then report some teacher views. Finally, we compare pupil–teacher agreement on playfighting, real fighting, and positive social interaction, to see if agreement is less regarding playfighting than the other two domains.

METHOD

Children and child interviews: All the boys who were regular attenders at a primary school, in a working-class area of a northern industrial city in the United Kingdom, were interviewed individually. They constituted 4 classes ($n = 44$), aged 5 to 8 years (mean 6.5 years). The interview asked about the following: the 3 classmates liked most and liked least, for social impact and preference; the 5 toughest children in the class, for dominance ranking; responses to 4 hypothetical situations (from Dodge & Frame, 1982) to give positive, neutral, or aggressive attributional scores; and perceptions and experiences of playfighting and real fighting (from Smith et al., 1992).

Teachers and teacher questionnaires: Each class teacher from the primary school ($n = 4$) was given a short questionnaire for each of the boys in their class, to assess the following: proactive aggression and reactive aggression (items from the teacher rating scale of Coie & Dodge, 1987); ratings of frequency with which each boy engaged in playfighting and serious fighting; and ratings of how well each boy interacted with other children, and of academic ability. A further questionnaire was given to 17 teachers from three neighboring primary schools (12 female, 5 male). These asked if the teacher could tell the difference between real fighting and playfighting, and how; if they ever had problems in telling real fighting from playfighting, and why; and why they thought boys playfight, and what costs and benefits it might have.

RESULTS

Child Interviews

The results from our sample ($n = 44$) are compared with those of Smith and colleagues (1992) for the boys interviewed at ages 5 ($n = 33$), 8 ($n = 24$), and 11 ($n = 24$) years, and summarized in Tables 14.2 and 14.3.

Most boys said yes in response to "*Do you ever playfight?*" and an even larger majority to "*Do you ever playchase?*"; and over half say yes in response to "*Do you like playfighting?*" (see Table 14.2). When asked "*Who do you playfight with at school?*" of 59 nominations, 50 (85 percent) could be categorized as friends: 25 were in the 3 nominations of best friends, and 25 were specifically identified as friends in the interview; only 9 (15 percent) were not identified as friends.

Those boys who said they *did* playfight were then asked, "*Why do you play-*

Table 14.2
Percentage Responses by Boys to Questions Regarding Playfighting for this Study, Compared with Smith and Colleagues (1992)

	Ever play-fight?	Ever play chase?	Like play-fighting?	Tell if play or real fighting?	Playfight lead to real fight?
5 yrs., $n = 33$ Smith et al. (1992)	70	91	58	82	79
5–8 yrs., $n = 44$ This study	70	81	56	93	88
8 yrs., $n = 24$ Smith et al. (1992)	50	83	50	75	79
10 yrs., $n = 24$ Smith et al. (1992)	58	83	67	96	79

Table 14.3
How Boys Said They Would Respond if Accidentally Hit Hard in a Playfight, either by a Friend or by Someone They did not Like

	TELL	HIT BACK	NOTHING	VERBAL
FRIEND	9	10	14	7
DISLIKED PEER	16	19	5	2

fight?" The most frequent response (38 percent) was *Fun* (also most frequent for 5-, 8-, 10-yr.-olds in Smith and colleagues 1992): "I enjoy it," "It's fun." Other common responses were *Similarity to real fighting*: "Because I like playing it, because it's like real fighting," "Better than real fighting, you can fight people," "Because if someone hits you, you can hit them back"; *Doesn't hurt*: "You don't usually get hurt in a playfight," "When you're pretending you don't get hurt"; and *Other reasons*: "If we're playfighting he might be winning, and then he might let me win," "It learns you how to get muscles. If anyone hits you you can hit them back."

Those boys who said they *did not* playfight were asked, "*Why do you not playfight?*" The most frequent response (37 percent) was *Injury* (also most frequent for 5-, 8-, 10-yr.-olds in Smith and colleagues 1992): "You might get hurt," "Because you get hurt in your back then you have to go inside and tell miss." Other common responses were *Dislike of physical characteristics*: "It's not very nice," "Because I don't like to get into fights"; *Boring*: "It's boring"; *Rules*: "You can't fight at school," "Because you're not allowed to"; and *Can lead to real fight*: "It leads to a real fight," "Because it gets real."

The great majority of boys said yes when asked, "*Can you tell if children are just playfighting rather than real fighting?*" and also when asked, "*Can a playfight lead to a real fight?*" (see Table 14.2). When asked how often a play fight led to a real fight, 23.7 percent replied "a lot," 57.9 percent "sometimes," and 18.4 percent "hardly ever."

We then asked, if a playfight did turn into a real fight, "*How might this happen?*" The main responses were (32 percent) *Hit too hard*: "It gets harder [the hitting] and they start to cry," "Because they are too rough and start punching and kicking," "They start punching and it changes into a real fight"; and (24 percent) *Accidental injury* (this was the most frequent category in Smith et al., 1992, for all ages): "When you play you might hurt him in the face and he'll start a fight." Other responses were (11 percent) *Deception*: One child deceiving the other into thinking it is playfighting when they intended to act aggressively from the start: "They think I'm pretending," "They do real fights but they don't know"; (5 percent) *Violation of the playfighting rules*: Doing something that wasn't accepted in a playfight, for instance one child said it could turn into a real fight if two children gang up against one; another said if children got each other on the floor it can change into a real fight; (5 percent) *Got carried away*: These few responses were quite explicit, "Because we get carried away and we start a real fight"; and (3 percent) because of name calling. In addition 21 percent did not know.

We then asked "*What would you do if one of your friends accidently hit you hard in a playfight?*" And "*What would you do if someone you didn't like accidently hit you hard in a playfight?*" The numbers of children responding in each category are shown in Table 14.3 (a few did not know). In the case of a friend, the most frequent response was "do nothing"; in the case of someone they didn't like, it was "hit back." The difference between the two categories of play partner was significant, $X^2_{(3)} = 11.75$, $p < .01$.

Finally, when asked, "*Have you ever had a serious fight?*" most (77 percent) replied yes.

In summary, this group of boys mostly reported taking part in and enjoying playfighting, which they thought of as "fun." They could discriminate between playfighting and real fighting. The majority thought that a playfight can lead to a real fight "sometimes," because of hitting too hard and risk of being hurt (either accidentally, or possibly deliberately).

Teacher Interviews

The next section of results is based on the views of 17 primary school teachers. When asked "*Can you tell the difference between playfighting and real fighting?*" 82 percent said yes, 18 percent no. For "*Do you ever have any difficulty telling playfighting from real fighting?*" 41 percent said yes, 59 percent no. Common reasons given for difficulty were: playfight turning into real fights, and playfights often accompanied by misleading body language such as an "intense look" or harsh vocalizations. When asked *"What percentage of all fighting bouts (play and real) are real fighting?"* the mean proportion given was 31 percent (range 10 to 80 percent).

We then asked, *"Why do you think boys playfight?"* The common responses were (41 percent) *Copying role models*: "They often see aggressive behavior performed by peers and adults and consider it the correct and normal way to behave. They also imitate aggression of models they look up to on TV, video, and film"; (32 percent) *Dominance*: "Children playfight because they are motivated by the natural desire to be top dog"; and (9 percent) *Natural behavior*: "It is the normal pattern of play when mixing with males."

Finally, we asked, *"What are the costs of playfighting?"* and *"What are the benefits of playfighting?"* The most common costs cited were (30 percent) *Leads to a real fight*; (23 percent) *Injury*; and (15 percent) *Aggression seen as acceptable*: "Aggression is seen as normal play." Regarding benefits, the most common response (33 percent) was *None*; this was followed by (28 percent) *Releases aggression/energy*: "It allows aggression to be channeled in what may be a not too harmful way"; and (19 percent) *Provides experiences*: "It teaches children what it is like to be hurt."

In summary, most teachers recognize a difference between playfighting and real fighting, but nearly one-half report difficulties in distinguishing them, often because playfights are seen as turning into real fights—nearly one-third, in their view. Many see this association with aggression and injury as a negative factor about playfighting, and one-third of teachers see no benefits at all—although one-fifth do see it as providing a useful experience.

Child and Teacher Views Compared

Many teachers do appear to see playfighting in a negative way. They overestimate the proportion of playfights turning into real fights (compared to observational studies), and many see no benefits to this form of play. Do teachers misperceive other aspects of children's behavior, or is it specific to playfighting? To address this question we used other data obtained from the child interviews and those with their class teachers ($n = 4$) in their school, regarding playfighting, real fighting, and social interaction. These were entered into a correlation matrix, and a cluster analysis was performed.

Twenty measures for each of the 44 children were entered into a correlation matrix: child's age; reported liking of playfighting; playfighting frequency; play-chasing frequency; total prosocial, neutral, and aggressive attributions; whether they had been in a real fight or not, and how often playfighting lead to real fighting; peer's scores for each child for dominance, like most, like least, social impact and social preference; teacher's ratings for each child of proactive aggression, reactive aggression, playfighting frequency, playchasing frequency, quality of interaction with peers, and academic ability.

A simple linkage cluster analysis (SLCA; McQuitty, 1957) was performed on the correlation matrix, and the result is shown in Figure 14.1, together with all correlations significant at $p < .01$ ($r = 0.39$ or greater; plus two correlations less than this, in clusters 5 and 6, which are significant at $p < .05$ and were in the original SCLA linkages).

Cluster One is a measure of peer liking and social preference, to which the teacher rating of quality of interaction with peers shows reasonable agreement; and to some extent, dominant children also tend to be liked. This cluster shows strong negative links to Cluster Two, which is mainly composed of teacher ratings of aggression and fighting; noticeably, this also has a strong link to the teacher's (but not the child's) estimate of playfighting frequency.

Cluster Three simply links (negatively) neutral and aggressive attribution scores. Cluster Four links (negatively) teacher's rating of academic ability to social impact with peers. Cluster Five shows that children who say they like playfighting also report often doing it. Cluster Six shows that children who think that playfighting often leads to real fighting more often get into real fights.

A child's reported playfighting frequency is not strongly related to aggression, or liking; teacher's estimate of a child's playfighting frequency is related to their estimates of child aggression and not getting on well with peers. Selected correlations for key variables are also shown in Table 14.4. The diagonal cells show child–teacher agreement for a particular type of behavior. This is low and nonsignificant for playfighting frequency. This discrepancy between teacher and child estimates is greater for playfighting than for other areas; agreement is better for general positive peer interaction and also better for actual aggressive behavior.

DISCUSSION

A majority of boys enjoy playfighting, thinking it is fun and doing it quite often. They know the difference from real fighting quite clearly; other research (Costabile et al., 1991) has shown that they can, by 8 years at least, also verbalize many of the cues found in observational research and given in Table 14.1. They do acknowledge that a playfight can lead to a real fight "sometimes." They think this is commonly because of someone "hitting too hard" and retaliation—a risk more associated with playing with someone not a friend; however, many children do preferentially playfight with friends (this study; Humphreys & Smith, 1987). The findings from our study broadly replicate those of Smith and colleagues (1992) and other relevant studies, confirming this general account.

Teachers have rather negative views of playfighting. They think that about one-third of playfights turn into real fights, and many cite this possibility as leading to a difficulty in distinguishing the two, and as a "cost" of playfighting, counteracted by few if any benefits. Again, our study here confirms the findings

Figure 14.1
Simple linkage cluster analysis of 20 variables describing pupils, from self, peers, and teachers.

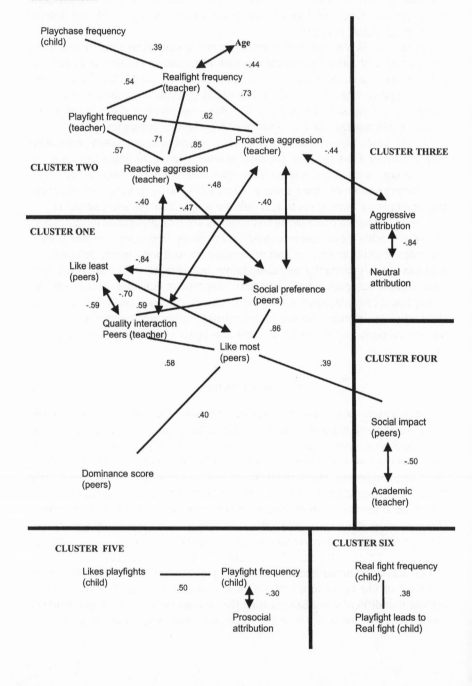

Table 14.4
Correlations Between Child and Teacher Estimates Regarding Playfighting, Real Fighting, and Social Interaction

	Playfight Teacher	Real Fight Teacher	Social Teacher
Playfight Child	.16	.30*	−.14
Real Fight Child	.04	.30*	−.07
Social Preference Peers	−.31*	−.37*	.59***

*$p < .05$ ***$p < .01$

of a previous study on teachers' views (Schäfer & Smith, 1996), in these respects.

It appears that teachers associate playfighting with real fighting, and the negative aspects of this, to a greater extent than might seem justified either by the observational evidence or by the views of children on the topic. In the final part of this study we sought to examine whether this discordance of views, or misperception, is something specific to playfighting. To do so we compared teacher's reports and children's self-rankings and peer nominations, on frequencies of playfighting and real fighting, and ratings of social interaction. The specificity hypothesis was supported. Teachers agreed with boys on ratings of positive social interaction, and (moderately) on frequency of aggression, but did not agree on frequency of playfighting; they confounded frequency of playfighting with frequency of aggression.

Why should teachers have some misperceptions of playfighting, compared to children's own views? We suggest here a number of reasons.

First, many teachers (especially in primary schools, as studied here) are female; playfighting tends to be a male activity and enjoyed more by boys than girls (Smith et al., 1992). Female teachers may underestimate the "fun" that many or most boys get from this activity.

Second, teachers are much older than children, and may have forgotten what playfighting was like, even though they did it as children themselves (just as many forget the details of children's games). This age factor has some support from Boulton's (1996) finding that lunchtime supervisors with longer service have less favorable views of playfighting. Johnson, Welteroth, and Corl (2001) found that adults with better memories of playfighting experiences as children had more favorable attitudes to it.

These two factors—older age and female gender—may "distance" teachers from their own memories of playfighting as children. In addition, there are the actual negative views of playfighting, which go beyond just "distancing" or "forgetting."

First, teachers may find playfighting noisy and intrusive when they prefer a quiet environment. Johnson and colleagues (2001) found that adults who are *not* teachers or parents express more tolerant attitudes to play aggression. Second, teachers may be particularly concerned about the costs of playfighting, through accidental injury. This might be seen as a legitimate concern, since a teacher or playground supervisor may be held responsible if a child is actually hurt in this way. Nevertheless, there is some degree of risk in any kind of play—play without risk or challenge will not appeal to many children. Also, the actual risk of accidental injury of any degree of seriousness is probably very slight, though further research on this is certainly called for.

A third factor leading to a negative view of playfighting was postulated by Schäfer and Smith (1996); this is the likelihood that teachers make their judgments about playfighting on the basis of the few children who *do* often turn playfights into real fights (and who may take up a lot of their time); Pellegrini (1988) found that for rejected children, about one-quarter of their playfights turn into real fights. Teachers may generalize this probability to pupils as a whole, for whom it is incorrect.

What can be done about such misperceptions? It does seem important that teachers, and trainee teachers, get more information on rough-and-tumble play and playfighting on the basis of the existing research. This might be incorporated into teacher training courses or in-service training for qualified teachers, in modules relating either to play and playground behavior, or to conflicts and conflict resolution. Playground supervisors (if not teachers—the roles are separate in the United Kingdom, for example) could also benefit from such training. Boulton (1996) found that a short training session using video, with 72 female lunchtime supervisors in the United Kingdom, improved their ability to discriminate playfighting and real fighting. Applications of research findings in directions such as this could help lead to a better appreciation of this kind of play from teachers, and a more accurate and balanced process of discrimination and supervisory action. At times, playfighting may need to be stopped; but if so, this should be done from a position of knowledge and informed decision making, rather than being strongly influenced by negative stereotypes of the activity.

REFERENCES

Blatchford, P. (1989). *Playtime in the primary school: Problems and improvements.* Windsor, England: NFER-Nelson.

Blurton Jones, N.G. (1967). An ethological study of some aspects of social behaviour of children in nursery school. In D. Morris (Ed.), *Primate ethology* (pp. 347–368). London: Weidenfeld & Nicolson.

Boulton, M.J. (1991). A comparison of structural and contextual features of middle school children's playful and aggressive fighting. *Ethology and Sociobiology, 12,* 119–145.

Boulton, M.J. (1996). Lunchtime supervisors' attitudes towards playful fighting, and ability to differentiate between playful and aggressive fighting: An intervention study. *British Journal of Educational Psychology, 66,* 367–381.

Coie, J.D., & Dodge, K.A. (1987). Social information processing factors in reactive and proactive aggression in children's peer groups. *Journal of Personality and Social Psychology, 53,* 1146–1158.

Costabile, A., Smith, P.K., Matheson, L., Aston, J., Hunter, T., & Boulton, M. (1991).

Cross-national comparison of how children distinguish playful and serious fighting. *Developmental Psychology, 27*, 881–887.

Dodge, K., & Frame, C. (1982). Social cognitive biases and deficits in aggressive boys. *Child Development, 53*, 620–635.

Fry, D.P. (1987). Differences between play fighting and serious fights among Zapotec children. *Ethology and Sociobiology, 8*, 285–306.

Humphreys, A.P., & Smith, P.K. (1987). Rough-and-tumble play, friendship, and dominance in school children: Evidence for continuity and change with age. *Child Development, 58*, 201–212.

Johnson, J., Welteroth, S., & Corl, S. (2001). Attitudes of parents and teachers about play aggression in young children. In *Play & culture studies, Vol. 3*. Westport, CT: Ablex.

McQuitty, L.L. (1957). Elementary linkage analysis for isolating orthogonal and oblique types and typal relevancies. *Educational and Psychological Measurement, 17*, 207–229.

Pellegrini, A.D. (1987). Rough-and-tumble play: Developmental and educational significance. *Educational Psychologist, 22*, 23–43.

Pellegrini, A.D. (1988). Elementary school children's rough-and-tumble play and social competence. *Developmental Psychology, 24*, 802–806.

Pellegrini, A.D. (1994). The rough play of adolescent boys of differing sociometric status. *International Journal of Behavioral Development, 17*, 525–540.

Pellegrini, A.D. (1995). A longitudinal study of boys' rough-and-tumble play and dominance during early adolescence. *Journal of Applied Developmental Psychology, 16*, 77–93.

Pellegrini, A.D. (in press). Rough-and-tumble play. In P.K. Smith & C. Hart (Eds.), *Handbook of social development*. Oxford: Blackwell.

Pellegrini, A.D., & Smith, P.K. (1998). Physical activity play: The nature and function of a neglected aspect of play. *Child Development, 69* (3), 577–598.

Schäfer, M., & Smith, P.K. (1996). Teachers' perceptions of play fighting and real fighting in primary school. *Educational Research, 38*, 173–181.

Smith, P.K. (1989). The role of rough-and-tumble play in the development of social competence: Theoretical perspectives and empirical evidence. In B.H. Schneider, G. Attili, J. Nadel, & R.P. Weissberg (Eds.), *Social competence in developmental perspective* (pp. 239–255). Dordrecht: Kluwer.

Smith, P.K. (1997). Play fighting and real fighting: Perspectives on their relationship. In A. Schmitt, K. Atswanger, K. Grammer, & K. Schafer (Eds.), *New aspects of ethology* (pp. 47–64). New York: Plenum Press.

Smith, P.K., Hunter, T., Carvalho, A.M.A., & Costabile, A. (1992). Children's perceptions of playfighting, playchasing and real fighting: A cross-national interview study. *Social Development, 1*, 211–229.

Part V
Adult Play

15

Play and Process: Adult Play Embedded in the Daily Routine

Erna Imperatore Blanche

The portrayal of what constitutes play during adulthood is controversial. For some, adult play is akin to leisure (Duzamazedier, 1974; Rojek, 1995). For others, adult play has specific characteristics that may or may not be associated with leisure (Apter, 1991; Huizinga, 1938/1955; Kerr, 1991). For still others, adult play is one form of leisure (Argyle, 1996; Gordon, Gaitz, & Scott, 1976). This study based its view of play on Huizinga's (1938/1950) germinal work, *Homo Ludens*, which places play at the core of civilization, in that "archetypal activities of human society are all permeated with play from the start" (p. 4). Central to Huizinga's argument is a view of play as different from the view of leisure as time off work, in that restricting play to leisure time (that is, time outside work) is to misunderstand and underestimate its importance in human life (Rojek, 1995).

This study also addresses play from the rhetoric of the self (Sutton-Smith, 1997). The rhetoric of the self focuses on individual subjective play experiences. The subjective experience of play has the characteristics of being fun, being intrinsically motivated, being voluntary, releasing energy, bringing arousal or excitement, being free, and being autotelic. Within the rhetoric of the self, play is seen as a state of mind that may promote self-actualization of one's potentials (Sutton-Smith, 1997). Although the present study did not originally intend to focus exclusively on autotelic or process-oriented experiences, as the study progressed, the importance of process-oriented activities became salient (Blanche, 1999). This study's original question was: How does the experience of play occur in daily life and in a variety of contexts as proposed by many authors? (Apter, 1991, 1992; Bowman, 1978, 1987; Cohen, 1987; Grover, 1992; Kerr, 1991, 1994; Schwartzman, 1978; Sutton-Smith & Kelly-Byrne, 1984a).

RESEARCH DESIGN

The design chosen for this study was naturalistic and involved the development of grounded theory. More specifically, the questions guiding this research were: How do individuals embed the characteristics of play described in the literature in their daily routine? And, what is the meaning of these experiences in their lives?

The data collection techniques utilized were participant observation, intensive interviewing, and survey methods. The participants consisted of 22 adults, 12 males and 10 females, aged 25 to 55 years, who were selected to portray diversity in income, educational level, lifestyle, and work situation. With the exception of one participant, each participant spent a minimum of 8 and a maximum of 18 hours with the researcher. The researcher spent a total of 244 hours with the participants.

Characteristics of Play Identified in the Literature

The first step in this study entailed a review of the existing literature on the characteristics of play and adult play. Based on this review, the characteristics of the experience of play were clustered into six groups. First, play is considered as free, nonserious, and not necessary for immediate survival and self-preservation (Lurker, 1991; Marcuse, 1955/1966; Vandenberg, 1978; Volkwein, 1991). Second, play is voluntary, intrinsically motivated, process-oriented, and engaged in for the purpose of enjoyment (Apter, 1991; Caillois, 1961; Huizinga, 1938/1955; Kraus, 1984). Third, play is spontaneous. Fourth, play may include a momentary suspension of reality as it lies outside ordinary life (Apter, 1991; Csikszentmihalyi, 1981; Kerr, 1991; Kraus, 1984; Marcuse, 1955/1966; Singer & Singer, 1990; Volkwein, 1991). In the adult this momentary suspension of reality may be a "momentary escape from instrumentally oriented activities" (Volkwein, 1991, p. 361) that creates the experience of being ambiguous or liminal (Bateson, 1955/1972; Turner, 1982, 1987) and may provide opportunity for creativity. Fifth, play is physically or mentally active (Kraus, 1984; Quarrick, 1989; Sutton-Smith & Kelly-Byrne, 1984a, 1984b), and sixth, play involves tension (Huizinga, 1938/1955), or a search for increased levels of arousal (Apter, 1991; Volkwein, 1991). These characteristics often overlap; however, the combination of these characteristics differentiates the experience of adult play from experiences derived from performing other occupations such as leisure, work, self-care, and ritual. In order to avoid the description of play as opposite to work

Table 15.1
Contexts (settings) in Which the Observational Data were Collected

Non-work-related observations	Work-related observations
Interviewing or observing at the participant's home, beach, park	Seeing clients at a physical therapist's, surgeon's, and lawyer's office
Participating in a belly dancing, yoga, acting, or language class	Teaching a yoga, dance, English, music, religion, or aerobics class
Doing gardening	Participating in a business meeting
Having a birthday party for participant's child	Coaching resident and operating on patient
Traveling and running errands	Representing cases in court
Having a pedicure	Participating in a sales meeting
Playing tennis or racquet ball	Conducting a religious service
Attending an art exhibit	Telemarketing
Rock climbing	Waiting tables
Having lunch with a friend	Conducting a dress rehearsal
Participating in a Super Bowl party	Answering phones
Doing aerobatics	Running a business
Painting	Building a structure with members of a church

Reprinted by permission from E. Blanche.

or similar to leisure, this study focused on the participant's experience of some or all of these characteristics regardless of whether or not they were labeled as "play," "leisure," "work," or "ritual."

Instruments

Participant Observation

In this study, participant observations provided the moment-to-moment accounts of play events and information about the initiation and termination of occupations or activities that were reported to have experiential qualities of play. The moment-to-moment accounts also provided a deeper understanding of enfolded occupations that were experienced as play but that were not perceived as meaningful enough to be reported in the survey completed at the end of the day. The participants were observed in at least two different settings; one was described as recreational and/or pleasurable, the other as work. Table 15.1 provides examples of the settings in which the observations and/or interviews were conducted.

Intensive Interviewing

Intensive interviewing is a basic mode of inquiry that utilizes guided conversation to develop an "understanding of the experience of other people and the meaning they make of that experience" (Seidman, 1991, p. 3). Intensive inter-

Table 15.2
Characteristics of Play and DOES Item Addressing Them

Characteristics of play	DOES item
Spontaneity	# 1 (spontaneous–planned)
Arousal seeking	# 2 (exciting–boring)
Use and release of energy	# 3 (stressful–relaxing); # 11 (energized–depleted)
Pleasure	# 4 (pleasurable–miserable)
Not necessary for survival	# 5 (a frill–necessary)
Related to creativity	# 6 (creative–customary)
Clear objectives	# 7 (clear purpose–unclear)
Physical activity	# 8 (physically active–not active)
Mental activity	# 9 (mentally active–not active)
Free	# 10 (free–restrained)
Intrinsic motivation	# 12 (for you–for someone else)
Fantasy	# 13 (know to be true–imagine)

Reprinted by permission from E. Blanche.

viewing was added to the proposed study because it gathers information about the meaning and function of play and focuses on the experience of play across different temporal cycles. The interviews focused on occupations or activities that possess the characteristics of play described in the literature or may have been regarded as play by the participant.

Survey: Daily Occupational Experience Survey (DOES)

Survey methods are useful in providing a "snapshot" of a particular day (Chapin, 1974) and are often used to identify activity patterns in their natural settings (Chapin, 1974, 1978). The survey instrument utilized in this study originated in a questionnaire previously developed for the pilot study. It was revised so it would include all of the experiential characteristics of play identified in the literature. By including the experiential qualities in this questionnaire, the participants described experiences rather than defining or categorizing an occupation or activity as work, play, self-care, or leisure. The characteristics of play described in the literature and explored in the DOES are listed in Table 15.2.

The DOES resembles a time diary in that the participants group their actions into meaningful activities or occupations and then report on the experiential qualities of these occupations. The participants were asked to complete one questionnaire per activity performed during the sample day. The experiential qualities were presented in dichotomous pairs (see Table 15.2).

In addition to completing one questionnaire per activity performed during that sample day, the participants were asked to complete additional questionnaires on activities that they considered a passion, or looked forward to during the day or the week. For the purpose of brevity, these activities are named extraordinary experiences. The term "extraordinary experiences" was borrowed from Abrahams (1986), who defines them as experiences that break the daily routine, providing a baseline against which other activities are judged and the fullness of one's life is measured. Extraordinary activities were singled out in an attempt to identify experiences during which the characteristics of play described in the literature might occur and to explore the existence of these characteristics in the adult. These activities were analyzed separately. An explanation of why these activities were later labeled "process-oriented" is provided in the next section.

The DOES focused on the experiential qualities of the participants' primary and enfolded occupations. Primary occupations or primary activities were defined as those occupations that created the need for a person to be in a specific place at a specific moment in time. Secondary or enfolded occupations were defined as those activities that were performed simultaneously with the primary activity. The data gathered by the DOES provided a sampling of the participants' identification of primary and enfolded occupations during the daily cycle, experiential qualities of the occupations engaged in during the day, tendency to engage in primary and/or enfolded occupations that are experienced as having the characteristics of play, and the embeddedness of the characteristics of play in daily life.

DATA MANAGEMENT AND ANALYSIS

The data gathered by all three methods were analyzed qualitatively because qualitative methods allow the researcher to view action as embedded in the constraints of everyday life (Denzin & Lincoln, 1994). The steps of data analysis for the fieldnotes and interview transcripts followed the naturalistic methods of inquiry as described by Lincoln and Guba (1985), Miles and Huberman (1994), and Polkinghorne (1991). The analysis of the information derived from the DOES followed a similar process.

The information was organized in spreadsheets, which were utilized to help analyze the information provided by all participants and to examine themes that ran through the activities reported in the DOES. Following qualitative data analysis methods, the researcher organized both sets of data and continued categorizing, synthesizing, searching for patterns, and interpreting the data (Glesne & Peshkin, 1992). The Ethnograph Version 5.0 assisted in the process of data analysis. Microsoft Excel Version 5.0 assisted in the analysis of the DOES. A detailed explanation of the procedure is provided next.

Analysis of the DOES

The analysis of the information derived from the DOES followed the following process. First, the information was organized in spreadsheets according to the categories of primary and secondary occupations performed by each individual during the sample day and according to the experiential qualities identified by each participant in relation to the occupations that he or she listed.

One spreadsheet (Appendix A) was generated per participant. Each row represents one activity reported in the DOES questionnaire. The letter "a" is used for all primary occupations; the letter "b" is used for the secondary or enfolded occupations. Each column represents one experiential quality of each activity reported by the individual. The characteristics of primary occupations are portrayed in shaded columns and the characteristics of secondary occupations are portrayed in nonshaded columns. The number "1" is used to identify the participant's choice. The participants were not initially provided with third choices beyond each pair of alternatives; however, while completing the questionnaires, some wrote in a third alternative. The proposed third alternative was either *both* or *neither*. To accommodate those answers, the researcher allowed the participant to define his or her experience as *both* or *neither* in addition to the provided alternatives. If the participant could report the experience to be *both* alternatives, a "1" was entered under both characteristics when the data were entered into the Excel spreadsheet. If the participant reported an activity to be *neither* alternative provided, the spaces were left blank. Therefore, the totals are not perfect sums of paired characteristics. For the purpose of brevity, Appendix A represents a section of a spreadsheet with only four experiences and eight possible activities (four primary and four secondary). Each original spreadsheet consisted of 52 columns (13 pairs of experiential qualities reported as primary and secondary experiences). The number of rows depended on the number of activities reported during the sample day. The analysis was started with a total of 22 spreadsheets (one per participant).

At the bottom of each participant's spreadsheet is the total number of primary and secondary occupations reported by the participant, and the total number of times that each characteristic was reported. Based on the results of the pilot study, each participant was expected to complete between 15 to 30 DOES questionnaires, representing 15 to 30 occupations performed in one day. The participants in this study completed between 15 and 31 DOES questionnaires, meaning that they described between 15 and 31 primary activities. The reported secondary activities varied in number from 2 to 26. The experiences of a total of 690 activities were analyzed.

Total 1 + 2 at the bottom of the page in Appendix A represent the total number of activities reported. *Total 1* represents the total number of primary activities and the number of times that each experience was reported to occur during the performance of primary activities. *Total 2* represents the total number of secondary activities and the number of times that each experience was reported to occur during the performance of secondary activities. In Appendix A *% of each* represents the percentage of times that each characteristic was experienced during the performance of a primary activity (15 primary activities in the example provided) or during the performance of a secondary activity (8 secondary activities in the example provided). The row *% of total* represents the percentages that each characteristic was experienced from the total of primary and secondary activities reported (in this example, 23 activities).

Each of the participant's totals were entered into a second spreadsheet presented in Appendix B. In this spreadsheet, each row represents one participant. The bottom numbers represent the total number of times and the percentage of times that each experience was reported by all the participants combined. For the purpose of brevity, this spreadsheet has also been reduced to four experiences. Appendices A and B are sections of spreadsheets utilized to illustrate one method of data analysis; therefore, the totals are not representative of the data provided. All spreadsheets were utilized as a data management technique to help analyze the information provided by all participants and to examine themes that ran through the activities reported in the DOES.

In addition, a spreadsheet was generated with the activities reported by the participants to be extraordinary, in that they either considered them passions or looked forward to them during the day or week. This information was utilized to explore the relationship between the characteristics of activities that were performed during the sample day and activities that are identified as extraordinary activities.

The extraordinary activities were reported to be intrinsically motivated, were performed for the pleasure derived from engaging in them, and occurred in a variety of contexts including work.

Synthesizing Data from Fieldnotes, Interviews, and DOES

The steps of data analysis for the fieldnotes and interview transcripts followed the naturalistic methods of inquiry as described by Lincoln and Guba (1985), Miles and Huberman (1994), and Polkinghorne (1991). First, the researcher entered the fieldnotes and interview transcripts into the Ethnograph database. Second, data were reviewed, coded/labeled, and relabeled into categories and patterns until they reached a comprehensive theme. Following a naturalistic method of data analysis, the data were displayed in tables arranging the information into focused topics, which facilitated drawing conclusions from them (Huberman & Miles, 1994). The information derived from the interviews and observations was compared to the information derived from the DOES.

One theme that emerged from this analysis was the prevalence of the experiential characteristics of play during the sample day and during extraordinary experiences (see Table 15.3). This analysis indicated that experiential characteristics such as spontaneity, excitement and increased energy, relaxation, pleasure, frill, creativity, physical and mental activity, freedom, and being performed for the person or intrinsic motivation occurred more often during the participation in extraordinary activities. This data supports the existing literature describing these experiential characteristics as related to play. This information will be published elsewhere.

In order to explore the existence of patterns of experiences, all the participants' entries were sorted by play characteristic (for example, all activities with the characteristic of being spontaneous) and by grouping of characteristics (for example, all activities with the characteristics of being pleasurable and intrin-

Table 15.3

Comparison of the Rate That Each Experiential Characteristic of Play Described in the Literature Was Reported to Occur—during the Extraordinary Activities and during the Sample Day

Paired characteristics	% experienced in everyday activities	% experienced in activities reported to be play, passions, or looked forward to
Spontaneous/planned	42% / 53%	52% / 56%
Exciting/boring	36% / 15%	86% / 0%
Stressful/relaxing	23% / 46%	20% / 86%
Pleasurable/miserable	53% / 12%	96% / 0%
Frill/necessary	33% / 65%	74% / 32%
Creative/customary	38% / 57%	80% / 21%
Clear purpose/unclear	78% / 21%	74% / 26%
Physically active/not active	35% / 65%	64% / 10%
Mentally active/not active	68% / 31%	92% / 6%
Free/restrained	58% / 32%	86% / 10%
Energizing/depleting	52% / 26%	82% / 14%
For you/for someone else	75% / 42%	94% / 34%
True/imaginary	85% / 14%	76% / 22%

Reprinted by permission from E. Blanche.

sically motivated). When this analysis was performed with the experience of unclear purpose, the data revealed that although the rate of this characteristic did not significantly increase during engagement in extraordinary activities, unclear purpose associated closely with other characteristics of play described in the literature. This relationship is presented in Table 15.4. This level of analysis suggested that unclear purpose needed further attention.

Third, the researcher examined the presence of patterns (grouping of experiences) among the activities described as having the characteristic of unclear purpose by using information derived from the DOES in conjunction with the information derived from the interviews and the participant observations. Results of this analysis suggested that the characteristic of unclear purpose might have indicated that the activity was geared toward the process rather than the goal of the activity. When this interpretation was evaluated by asking the participants to describe the purpose of some of the extraordinary activities they had previously reported as having a clear purpose, they often answered "to have fun" or "to release tension," thus suggesting that the activity was being performed for the pleasure derived from the process or their state of mind.

The extraordinary activities were later labeled "process oriented" because they occurred in a variety of contexts, did not have all of the characteristics of play, were mainly directed toward the pleasure derived from the process of engaging in them, and were reported to be performed for themselves (rather than for others); this was also done to avoid a semantic confusion with play as a category of activity. Most if not all of these activities appeared to be geared toward

Table 15.4
Correspondence between the Experiential Qualities of Activities Reported to Be Experienced as Having an Unclear Purpose

Set of characteristics	Primary occupations reported to have an unclear purpose	Secondary occupations reported to have an unclear purpose
Spontaneous/planned	75% / 20%	73% / 17%
Exciting/boring	44% / 9%	45% / 6%
Stressful/relaxing	18% / 69%	9% / 69%
Pleasurable/miserable	73% / 9%	70% / 3%
Frill/necessary	64% / 35%	85% / 9%
Creative/customary	78% / 13%	65% / 32%
Clear purpose/unclear	0% / 100%	0% / 100%
Physically active/not active	20% / 80%	2% / 98%
Mentally active/not active	73% / 27%	54% / 46%
Free/restrained	69% / 25%	82% / 9%
Energizing/depleting	56% / 16%	70% / 8%
For you/for someone else	80% / 53%	93% / 22%
True/imaginary	62% / 44%	71% / 24%

Note: A total of 55 primary and a total of 96 secondary occupations were described as having an unclear purpose.
Reprinted by permission from E. Blanche.

acquiring a state of mind that is consistent with the rhetoric of the self described by Sutton-Smith (1997). As previously stated, this rhetoric focuses on the individual's subjective experience. This subjective experience may promote self-actualization of one's potentials, and has the characteristics of being fun, intrinsically motivated, voluntary, releasing energy, bringing arousal or excitement, is free, and is autotelic (Sutton-Smith, 1997). The grouping of these experiences into patterns is presented in the findings.

The patterns of experiences that emerged from this analysis are presented in Tables 15.5 and 15.6. The initial dimensions presented in Table 15.6 emerged from the data and were used to organize the experiential characteristics of each pattern and explore how they differed from each other. The patterns of experiences were later labeled mastery, restoration, heightened self-awareness, adventure, creation, and ludos. Further analysis of these tables revealed that these patterns could be organized along a continuum of novelty and intensity. The findings presented in Tables 15.5 and 15.6 are described in the next section.

Fourth, the researcher searched for contradictory data and for alternative explanations of the data (Polkinghorne, 1991). The patterns presented in Table 15.5 were organized along different continuums. For example, at first they appeared to relate to intensity of external sensory experience, then they appeared to be all related to the need for others to be part of the activity; however, when contradictory data provided an alternative explanation, these choices were dropped, until the continuum of novelty and intensity organized the data into a

Table 15.5
Dimensions of Process-oriented Experiences

			Patterns of Experiences			
Dimension	*Restoration*	*Ludos*	*Heightened self-awareness*	*Mastery*	*Adventure*	*Creation*
Pleasure derived from the activity	Letting go; removal of a situation	Ambiguity of suspending judgment	Immersion, sense of self	Control	Exposure to novel information	Creation, establishing a new order
Physical and/or mental engagement	Low	Momentary high	High	Some activity needs to be present		
Novelty in the task	May or may not be present			Skilled activity, little novelty	Exposure to novelty	Creation of novelty
Level of energy and excitement	Low, restores energy	Momentary high, feels excited	Can be high, spends energy, feels energized	May spend energy	Exciting, may not spend much energy	Can be exciting, stressful, and depleting
Perceived challenge involved in the task	Low	Fun, perceived as not crucial	Can be perceived as challenging	Challenge is controlling the task	Challenge of exposing oneself to new information	Creation of challenge
Perceived necessity	Restoring energy	Fun, not clear	Perceived as necessary, growth	Perceived as necessary or frill		

Reprinted by permission from E. Blanche.

figure. These steps were repeated until all experiences reported by the participants fit with the existent descriptions (Polkinghorne, 1991).

The strength of the conclusions was evaluated by addressing dependability, confirmability, credibility, transferability (Lincoln & Guba, 1985), and application (Miles & Huberman, 1994). Dependability and credibility in this study were addressed by having more than one method of data collection that allows for triangulation across data sources, by using peer reviews when coding the data, and by asking chosen informants for their reactions to some of the researcher's understandings and basic conclusions. Transferability refers to ability to generalize the findings. Guba (1981) refers to generalizations as "enduring; that is, unchanging over time, truth statements that are context-free—that hold in any context" (p. 80). This study addressed transferability by comparing the findings with existing theories on adult play. The data collected confirmed some of the assumptions made by the literature on adult experiences and adult play.

THE FINDINGS

Recurrent analysis of the data revealed three sets of findings. The first set addresses the characteristics of play reported to be experienced during the day. These characteristics included spontaneity and freedom in the decision and/or during the performance of the activity; a sense of excitement or increased energy while being considered relaxing, pleasurable, and novel; a mental and/or physical activity; and one that had the primary purpose of fun or satisfying the self in the process.

The second set of findings focused on analyzing patterns of extraordinary experiences that had emerged from the data. This set of experiences included what was later described as process-oriented experiences or process-oriented occupations. Process-oriented experiences were enjoyable, intrinsically motivated, and primarily process oriented. Six patterns of these experiences emerged from the data. The remainder of this chapter focuses primarily on this level of analysis. It will describe process-oriented occupations and the six patterns of process-oriented occupations that emerged from the data.

The characteristics of process-oriented activities, as described by the participants, fell into six patterns of experiences. These were: relaxing and restoring energy, frolicking, gaining self-awareness, mastering a task, adventuring into something new, or creating something. These patterns can be understood as predominant themes that emerged from the data, although process-oriented occupations were often motivated by more than one pattern of experience, and the nature of the experience fluctuated over time. For the discussion that follows, these themes will be titled restoration, ludos, self-awareness, mastery, adventure, and creativity.

Restoration

Restoration describes a group of activities in which the participants engage in relaxation to reduce the number of activities being performed or reduce stress.

Seeking activities that reduced stress in a certain area led to decreasing the individual's arousal level. The stress often included intellectual, physical, and emotional demands. For example, one participant reported that one of the most enjoyable activities performed during the day was driving. When further questioned, he explained that he had recently bought a convertible antique car, which made driving more enjoyable. Further, while driving, he enjoyed listening to music or just being away from the telephone.

Unwinding activities were often reported to be less physically or mentally active than what was done during the rest of the day. Bob, a participant, viewed these unwinding experiences as "imposing themselves" on the individual because they occurred as a result of exhaustion. He reported not seeking these activities per se, but having to stop what he was doing in order to rest. The following excerpt supports the motivation to perform these restorative activities:

Sometimes I get to the point where I'm a little overwhelmed, and what I need to do is relax. . . . So even though I have a busy schedule I will stop. Get in the car. And I go down to the Marina, because it's one of the closest places, and I'll take the channel that goes into the Marina. I'll go down and there are a series of parking places there. I'll park there; I'll drink my soda and will get something to eat there. And I'll just sit and watch the boats come in and out and watch the water. And it relaxes me because it is very therapeutic. And sometimes when I'm really, really stressed out I do that because it's a way that I can find some inner peace and put things into perspective.

Occupations that offered a restorative experience did not necessarily require stopping all activity but did require decreasing external demands, changing focus, and gaining control over oneself. Occupations performed because of their value in gaining control over oneself did not necessarily increase the person's level of self-awareness. Rather, they decreased the number of demands placed by the environment, and as a result individuals could restore control over themselves. The following dialogue illustrates this point:

Q: What do you do to cut stress at the end of the day?
A: Well, if I get home from work, I'll sit on the couch, look at the mail, and put my feet up and just relax for about 20 minutes.

These dialogues illustrate how the participants needed to remove themselves from excitatory stimuli and external demands and regain control over themselves or center themselves. Restorative occupations often served as a passage from activities that were externally imposed to activities that were performed for their enjoyment. Paloma, a pilot learning to do aerobatics, provides an example of the need to unwind or center herself before engaging in other, more energy consuming, process-oriented occupations. When asked if she could fly immediately after her regular job as a driver delivering packages, she responded:

A: No, not at all. Never. During the summer getting off at 6, it was still light until 8, still, I would never go flying after that.

Q: Why?

A: I was exhausted mentally and physically. The job I was doing. I was doing other peoples routes, like when they were out sick or whatever. So, I was always in a new area trying to find places and delivering packages. So it was kind of a mental and a physical thing. It was very draining.

Q: And when you came home during that time, that is when you watched TV or vegged out?

A: Yeah. I would basically collapse on the couch and that is where I would end up. I usually would fall asleep as soon as I got horizontal, I would be asleep.

Q: What about the running? . . .

A: Basically, I wouldn't run.

In some cases, the activities performed during the regaining of energy included watching television, having a pedicure, leafing through magazines, taking a bath, or being in touch with nature. In some cases, the transition was short in duration; in others, it took more time. For one person, removing herself from the situation and regaining energy required sleep, whereas for another participant, it required putting her feet up and having a drink after work. The combination of unwinding with other types of process-oriented experiences will be discussed later in this section. This type of unwinding experience mirrors some descriptions of leisure activities encountered in the existing literature.

In summary, restorative experiences are derived from removing oneself from the demands placed by the environment and engaging in low-intensity physical, intellectual, or spiritual tasks. These activities are sought to regain energy, are often customary activities, include a feeling of freedom from external demands, and may occur spontaneously.

Ludos

Another type of experience reported by the participants in this study were lighthearted, nonserious forms of diversion, termed "ludos" by this researcher. These forms of diversion included teasing, joking, gossiping, flirting, and "horsing around." When performing process-oriented occupations that provided these lighthearted experiences, the participant did not express a conscious motivation to perform the activity for any reason other than that it appeared to be fun. In most cases, the context of the activity was recognized as having the potential to be enjoyable, but it did not guarantee it. Lighthearted experiences occurred spontaneously as an interlude within other occupations. The following excerpt illustrates this point:

It's really, it's nice to be all up there on the farm. I mean, we're talking they've got 50 acres with cows and sheep and, you know, all them animals. Oh, it's great. It is really great. One year it was raining and it was all mud . . . and we got the football out. We all got out there and played football in the mud. By the time we got in, my grandma had to get the hose and hose us down before we came in her house. We had mud from our head to our toes, you know, 'cause out there in the mud, and the slosh, and we just like fell on the ground, you could slide.

Another example is provided by Nancy's description of a softball team she was invited to join.

My friend Pete was a bartender, and they started a league. And Pete told them that he knew a girl who could play 'cause they needed to have so many girls on the team. So then I got on the team that way. So all the guys, you know, they go to the bar before the game, and they drink a little, they come out and play. They're really good players, so they can actually play drunk. Sometimes it's funny to watch them. They're drunk and they're out there playing. They think they're doing good, and they're not [*laughing*].

In both excerpts, the participant recognized the context as having the potential to be fun. In the first excerpt, the mud prompted the motivation to get the ball and play football. In the second, it was belonging to a team that went out drinking before they played ball. When the participants described these situations, they often became animated, talked faster, and laughed, suggesting an increase in the level of energy and excitement.

Roland provides another example. Roland worked in an office where spontaneous jokes and witty, humorous comments were made on a constant basis. The office appeared to be like a "sitcom." The three male lawyers and their male receptionist who shared the office moved quickly from one activity to the next, tending to enfold one occupation into the other on a constant basis. Their dry humor appeared to release tension and bring lightness to their intense activity.

Lighthearted experiences are often described in the literature as play. For example, Bateson's (1955/1972) descriptions of play as involving conscious or unconscious awareness of the message "this is play" corresponds to the description of ludos. In all of the examples provided, there needed to be a message shared among the participants that the interaction was bracketed as play.

In summary, ludos encompasses lighthearted, spontaneous activities that include a momentary increased level of excitement and a suspension of reality judgment, require some mental and/or physical energy, are performed for the purpose of fun, release unconscious tension, and focus on the feeling derived from the activity, not the outcome. Ludos often included interaction with others and could include activities that require physical, intellectual, and emotional engagement. Some activities included in ludos are joking, teasing, the process of playing games, and sometimes daydreaming. In ludos, the messages "this is play" and "is this play?" have an important role.

Heightened Self-Awareness

The participants also performed process-oriented occupations as a way to heighten self-awareness physically, intellectually, or spiritually. These occupations require intense focus and deep immersion in an experience that could lead to growth. Maslow (1954) first described this need to fulfill one's potentialities as self-actualization. The occupations that are performed may not always appear to be pleasurable or relaxing, but on further inspection, they are reported to be. The satisfaction derived from newly attained self-awareness could be planned or spontaneous.

Heightening awareness was reported to occur in the intellectual, physical, and/ or spiritual/emotional areas. One participant provided an example of increased intellectual and emotional awareness through music. When playing music, Ian reported to be learning about the world and about himself.

... doing an activity when I'm learning something, I think it is not only learning about the world, but learning about myself too ... and that's why I say something that could be either intellectually engaging or emotionally engaging. And I could sit down and play a piece and it could be a lot of fun, but it's even a more valuable activity to me if it is something that could get me to feel something that I really want to feel or need to feel, whether it's sad or happy.

Heightening self-awareness can also occur through religious or mystical ceremonies. Other participants described attaining the experience of heightened awareness through yoga, meditation, and/or the use of drugs. These occupations were experienced as transformative in that the person gained awareness of an aspect of his or her life. For example, for one participant, an intense yoga session was an activity he looked forward to doing during the week. He described these sessions through phrases as: "getting a rush," "climbing a mountain," or "the closest one could get to God." For him, yoga is about increased awareness, as it teaches people to focus and have a deep sense of awareness about everything. Heightened self-awareness in the spiritual area helped some participants restore and/or challenge their sense of well-being.

Heightened self-awareness could also be gained in the physical body through sensory and motor activity. For example, Paloma described aerobatics as a necessary activity. When further probed as to whether aerobatics really was necessary, she explained that her body did not feel the same when she was unable to fly for an extended period of time. Paloma "knew" as an 8-year-old that she wanted to do aerobatics when she grew up, even when she had only watched it performed. Both Paloma and her husband engaged in aerobatics. They pursued their lifelong dream of becoming pilots and making a living doing aerobatic air shows. Both described aerobatics as an activity that fulfilled a need because their bodies did not feel like theirs when they did not fly.

Other occupations that were described as providing a sense of heightened self-awareness were rock climbing, running, playing tennis, and being exposed to a stimulating environment, such as a rock concert. When an experience of heightened self-awareness was pursued through activities that provided novelty, they could sometimes be risky.

In summary, the pleasure of heightened self-awareness was derived from the experience of immersing oneself in an activity and increasing the sense of self, physically, mentally, or spiritually. These experiences were often intense and required a high level of personal involvement.

Mastery

Other activities performed by the participants were motivated by the enjoyment derived from engaging in a skilled activity that was perceived as controllable. These activities were often planned and included mastering physical and/or intellectual challenges. If the performance also led to success, then the enjoyment was twofold. In the literature, the experience derived from this type of process-oriented activity has been described as "flow" (Csikszentmilhalyi, 1975, 1988, 1990, 1993). The motivation underlying flow is described as achievement motivation, mastery motivation, or a need to feel competent.

Csikszentmilhalyi (1988) describes the dimensions of flow as occurring when the activity being performed has relatively clear goals and unambiguous feedback, the activity is under the person's control, the person reports focused concentration on the activity, the person temporarily loses the awareness of self, and the person's skills match the demands of the task. Mastery is similar to flow in that the activity is under the person's control, the person focuses on the task, and the person's skills match the demands of the task. Mastery and flow share many elements with play, such as the pleasure derived from the activity, the person's control over the activity, and the temporary loss of awareness of self, derived from entering a private world. Yet in order to acquire flow, the activity requires clear goals, unambiguous feedback, and focused concentration and skills that match the demands of the task. In comparison, play allows for ambiguity and the goals can be changed at any time (Csikszentmilhalyi, 1981). According to Csikszentmilhalyi (1981), play differs from flow in that play provides the possibility of changing goals and restructuring reality. He adds that flow describes a process of involvement in reality, whereas playfulness is an attitude toward that reality. Csikszentmilhalyi's (1990, 1993) descriptions of flow highlight the contrast between lighthearted ludos and mastery.

The analysis of the data in this study suggests that process-oriented activities, such as those identified by Csikszentmilhalyi (1981, 1990, 1993) as involving flow, were often framed within product-oriented parameters. The experiences of flow described by the participants in this study reflected the enjoyment derived from mastering an activity, which may not necessarily have included a focus on the outcome, and thus are considered to be motivated by the process. In mastery, the participants were confident that they could succeed because they had the necessary skills. The following excerpt illustrates this point. Arnold likes doing depositions for medical cases. He explains the challenge of being in court.

I went to court to testify. That really increases your level of adrenaline 'cause you're in front of the jury and . . . there is wit and knowledge, and the lawyer is trying to trip you . . . I understand that this is the way the game is played, and you have to play the game and play it well, so I try to do that very well. A lot of fun, the preparation, the hours of reading the chart.

In the above excerpt, there is a certain amount of uncertainty that borders on adventure. However, Arnold perceives himself to be in control, and to have the skills to do a good job. The success of performing the activity adds to the pleasure derived from performing the activity. However, the process of meeting the challenge is what draws the person to perform it. Experiences of mastery are closely related to process- and outcome-oriented occupations because the person has performed the task before and therefore knows the satisfaction derived from its accomplishment. Herman provides another example. He enjoys taking charge of charitable organizations during his leisure time. When asked why he does it, he answered:

You know, you can do a better job than they're doing. You do it, you do a better job. That's why. I'm not the kind of guy that can see a job being done not as good as it can be. The only way it's going to get done, what I consider a better way, is do it myself, so I do it. The challenge is to get in charge and write the show, make it more productive, more interesting, more fun. In any organization I've ever belonged to, I did well when I was in charge. I mean . . . any organization I've ever been a part of, or I've been in charge of it, has done well . . .

The following excerpt illustrates another participant's enjoyment derived from performing a challenging task that has been mastered, rather than from mastering a more advanced level of a task.

At first it was just a job. I thought it was something I was going to do until I decided to go back to school and it got to be 5 years becoming 10, 10 becoming 20. The better I got at that the more I enjoyed it because it has been such a challenge. I enjoyed the challenge.

Participating in challenging activities can also lead the person to perform activities that may be risky and test the person's limits, either physically or intellectually. Performing activities that are risky but have a degree of skill may provide the experience of mastery and novelty. These experiences will be described under "Adventure."

In summary, the participants in this study derived the experience of mastery from performing occupations they were skilled at and in which they felt confident about success. In the experience of mastery, there was little or no uncertainty, the challenge was controllable, and the pleasure of performing the occupation was derived from the control exercised over it. Occupations that provide a sense of mastery have clear goals, are customary but not routine, and require active engagement. The experience of mastery can be closely related to outcome-oriented occupations and flow, in that in mastery, as in flow, the person's enjoyment is derived from knowing that he or she can control the activity. The experience of mastery may often be related to knowing the outcome, which would make it more of an outcome-oriented experience; however, when mastery moves into adventure, the outcome is less controlled.

Adventure

Some participants performed activities that were prompted by novelty or a desire to experience a new aspect of the world or a new activity. For example, at least two participants described the need for newness and change as important aspects of their lives. The following excerpt illustrates the need for novelty:

I get energy from new events, from new information, from getting things I don't know about. I find that neat, energizing. When you use the word energizing, it's fascinating, it's intriguing, it's a combination of all those things. It's not getting on a high like some people do after jogging, it's not doing that. . . . It's not physiological. For me, to get energized is definitely mental. I get something out of either getting new information, a new event, or a new circumstance. . . . With me, wanting to do more of the same is not something that is necessarily a good thing. I would like to do more of similar events under new circumstances.

The above excerpt illustrates how novelty in the context of an occupation is deliberately sought; however, the outcome and/or the experience derived from the activity cannot be planned. In some cases, seeking a specific context provided the novel experience; in other cases, it did not. Novel experiences include being exposed to something to which one is usually not exposed, such as beauty in nature, a random walk in an unknown city, having a philosophical conversation, or gauging rare coins.

Father Pat Sullivan provided another example. Pat was in a transitional period in his life. He had decided that he needed to search for himself. As a result, he deliberately engaged in new occupations. He described his tendency to seek novel experiences in the following way:

A: One thing that is a way to alleviate stress recently . . . is getting into a car and driving to a different part of [the city] and walking. Seeing the different parts of the city.

Q: But when you do that, do you go into a map and look where you are going?

A: No, I just often go to different parts of the city, but ordinarily it's, I don't plan that much. It's more a spontaneous kind of thing.

The experience was not derived from conquering a challenging task but from being exposed to a situation and exploring it. Seeking novelty may relate to the childhood urge to explore. In the adult, the exploration leads to an experience of adventure.

The analysis of the data suggests that the experience of adventure can be derived from an activity that may require either physical, intellectual, or spiritual exploration. The activity is often energizing or invigorating and can be motivated by a need for change.

Some participants mentioned a sense of adventure within mastered occupations in an attempt to increase the excitement derived from the task. For example, Molly reportedly enjoyed bringing variety to her habitual occupations. She looked for new speakers to come to her class, she changed the dinner routine by making it a picnic, and she liked to add different styles of clothes to her wardrobe. Arnold provides another example. When asked what was the satisfaction he derived from surgery, he answered:

I have a theory that every patient's problem is different from the next guy's and you have to solve the problem for that patient so that it will turn out to be successful. You have to unlock the problem, and I look at it that way and, in each case I say, "Oh, I solved that problem. It was such a difficult problem, I solved it." Each patient is different. They have their own problem that makes it anything but a routine problem. I enjoy finding what it is ... I enjoy the actual puzzle solving. And then, of course, the gratification you get at the end when you have solved it. There is a more one-to-one correlation because you realize, as you are doing it, that you are going to reach a successful goal. You know that the solution is in sight. And you have to reach the solution or you are not going to help that patient.

The above excerpt illustrates the experience of mastery derived from conquering a task. These experiences are often a combination of mastery and adventure. In the above excerpt, Arnold chose to highlight the differences in each patient, so the novelty would provide excitement to his interaction with the task. There might not have been real novelty but, rather, a desire to include novelty to increase the excitement of a profession that he had practiced for over 20 years.

The search for novelty in the physical area could contribute to the performance of risky occupations. These risky occupations included the performance of novel physical activities or pushing the limits of mastered occupations to increase novelty and a sense of adventure.

I had a mountain biking accident earlier this March. It took 22 stitches to sew it [his leg] up. I was very lucky not to have more damage. But, the thrill of going down a mountain road, or a single track mountain trail on my mountain bike, it's fun. It is an adrenaline kick actually.... I was doing 30 miles an hour when I did that.... There is a 5,100-foot climb and we did it all day and we rode down it in about a half hour. Took us about six hours to climb up and took us about a half an hour to get down it.... It is a balancing act. . . . I had a good time. It was good workout, it killed the day and I had fun. That is what I like.

In this excerpt, the participant describes the satisfaction he derived from performing an activity, for which he had been training. This excerpt illustrates the combination of mastery and adventure, in that first there was the adventure of learning to mountain bike and then the occupation of going down and relying on his acquired skills.

The experience of adventure was often combined with lighthearted occupations. Ludos has many of the characteristics of adventure in that a novel aspect is introduced into a common situation. In ludos, the novel aspect is introduced tentatively in an *as if* context, minimizing the importance of the activity and diluting the consequences. The person often suspends judgment and reality is turned around. In comparison, the experience of adventure also can occur in a serious mode, as when climbing a new mountain, traveling to an unknown city, experimenting with drugs, or learning a new skill.

Berlyne (1969), Hutt (1978), and Day (1981) propose a play typology in which one type of play is diversive play and the other is exploratory play. Diversive play is initiated by boredom, has the characteristics of being aimless, is easily disrupted, is fun and relaxed, and has pleasure as the goal (Day, 1981). Ludos has these characteristics in that it may be initiated by boredom or a decrease in the level of arousal. In comparison, Day describes exploratory play as being initiated by novelty, uncertainty, and curiosity. The adult's search for newness and adventure has some of the characteristics of exploratory play, but is not prompted by the environment. Instead it is initiated by the person's curiosity or desire to find novelty and uncertainty, and could be initiated by boredom.

In summary, the experience of adventure is derived from performing occupations that expose one to novelty. Adventure is physically or mentally active, and the excitement derived from the activity is related to the novelty in the task. The experience of adventure can be derived from exposing oneself to novelty through sensory-motor exploration and intellectual exploration. Sensory-motor exploration includes activities such as bungee jumping, having a massage for the first time, and having an unusual sexual encounter. Intellectual exploration is included in activities such as watching a movie for the first time and engaging in a discussion for the pleasure of exploring different points of view.

The experience of adventure differs from the experience of heightened self-awareness in that in adventure the person focuses on the interaction and exploration in the world, and in heightened self-awareness the person focuses on the exploration and awareness of the self. In the experience of heightened self-awareness, the person does not necessarily engage in a novel activity, although he or she may allow novelty to be part of it, while in the experience of adventure, the person seeks novelty for the sake of novelty.

Creativity

Creativity also can be a process-oriented activity as long as the goal is the creation itself rather than the product. In other words, creativity is process oriented when motivated by the need to express and discover order rather than by the need to produce. Father Sullivan describes this process:

Yes, that's why in a school like this one, it's as important for a child to develop his ability to write and create a writer as it is for him to memorize and learn a lot of religious rules and beliefs. Not to say that religion is not important, but the creativity, you can't and it is how God is, the gift from God and it's how he is God-like in that he is created. He is taking chaos, words, and imposing order on them and creating something beautiful. That's a Godly experience. That's a sacred experience.

The experience of creating differs from the experience of mastery in that in mastery, the pleasurable experience is derived from controlling the activity, and in the creative experience, the pleasure is derived from consciously organizing events or elements to produce novelty or novel solutions.

The enjoyment of creating also can center on the production of an object such as a painting, an arts and crafts project, or a sculpture. However, when creating is a process-oriented activity, the focus and enjoyment lies in the act of creating, rather than in the product of the creative process. Often, the pleasure derived from creating is evidenced when a person enjoys the entire process of producing a specific object and does not shortcut the process in order to attain the product. For example, Eli liked engaging in the entire process of a creative project. When she cooks, she enjoys choosing the ingredients that she will need, buying the food herself, and then producing the meal. When she sews a costume, she likes going to the fabric store, buying the material, and then sewing it from scratch; when she does photography, she likes developing the film herself. She described the process of developing film in the darkroom in the following way:

. . . in the dark and then like these images just pop up. And sometimes, you'll take a picture and then you get to see what it looks like and a lot of things are there that you instinctively knew you were feeling and then to see them right there, and you go, "gosh I did all that. I captured that." You know, one person like this and one person like that, and you're actually seeing a story. And then see it there, it's really neat. Because sometimes you really don't even know what you did and then you see it and it's really nice. And then you can manipulate things in the darkroom to make them darker or lighter or crop the image. Pulling certain things out. . . . I really liked it. . . . You see, I used to stay there, this is where I get fanatical.

An important distinction between the process-oriented creative experience and the creation of a product is that in process-oriented occupations, the person does not know where the creation is going to end and he or she is flexible during the process. When Bob, a painter, was asked if he had an idea about how the painting was going to look after he finished it, he replied:

It will be perfect when it is finished. But visually, how to describe it, I discover along the way. But there's no, I, it's not goal oriented in that sense so I'm not trying to manifest a vision at all. I just know it will be perfect when I'm finished. But I haven't got a clue what it's going to look like.

Another participant described how, as he became freer, the process of painting became more important than the product. He related his evolution in painting to his spontaneity and freedom in allowing his paintings to develop.

Day (1981) describes play is stimulus oriented, free, undirected, symbolic, includes fantasy, and the goals are mastery and integration. Ann's remarks demonstrate these ideas:

This is primarily for a creativity outlet and fun. This is not, when I go to boxing that is mostly exercise. But when I dance its for creative pleasure more than anything else. . . . When I'm dancing, it's like a totally different world. It's kind of like acting. It's like just a total release of everything that is going on around me. Just focusing on the dancing, there are so many things to concentrate on when you're dancing. Every way that your body is placed and every position of your leg and your foot and pelvis and your head and your eyes. Its like, there's so many things to think about, your brain does not have enough room to think about.

Creativity does not need to occur in artistic occupations; some participants manifested it in their daily activities. For example, when Molly was asked about creative activities in her life, she responded that she used to write, but now channels her creativity in other ways.

. . . writing or something. But not any more. But I did that for quite a while, and I'm always creative in my dress. And that really is a kind of creativity for me. And even in cooking. Sometimes my husband will say, "Why did you make it this way. Didn't you know that I liked it the other way?" I get tired of making the same thing all the time. . . . But I think I'm a creative person even though I'm not a great guitarist or artist or something, I think I am creative. I am a good baker. And I love to create in that way.

Creativity occurred often throughout the day. The participants reported the experience of creativity in 38 percent of primary occupations and 50 percent of secondary occupations; however, from these reported activities only a small percentage can be considered to be process oriented. When creativity was reported as a secondary occupation, it was correlated more often with occupations that were also reported to be process oriented (free, a frill, and have an unclear purpose). It is important to note that the characteristics of play also occurred more often during secondary occupations, suggesting that non-goal-oriented creativity may relate to play rather than creativity at large.

Creativity often served as a medium to gain heightened self-awareness. Some participants reported being creative as a way of nourishing their souls. They often described a feeling of losing themselves in the act of creation and later emerging from it having learned something extremely valuable about their most intimate self.

In summary, the experience of creating was derived from bringing something into existence or giving a new order to existing data. The experience of creating is derived from occupations that focus on the process of creating rather than the product. Process-oriented, creative occupations were often reported to have an unclear purpose, provide a sense of freedom, provide room for spontaneity, and be unnecessary.

The analysis of the data revealed six themes or types of process-oriented experiences. These themes are restoration, ludos, heightened self-awareness, mastery, adventure, and creation. Table 15.6 summarizes the characteristics of each type of experience.

A CONCEPTUAL MAP OF PROCESS-ORIENTED
OCCUPATIONS

This section organizes the above information into a conceptual map that depicts the relationship between the different types of process-oriented occupations and adult play. The six process-oriented occupations can be organized according to the presence of novelty in the external environment and the intensity of the person's involvement in the task. The experiences of mastery, adventure, and creation can be laid out in a continuum when organized in relation to novelty in the environment (see Figure 15.1). The experience of mastery occurs during the performance of skilled occupations that have little or no novelty, the experience of adventure occurs when the person exposes himself or herself to novelty, and the experience of creation occurs when the person creates novelty.

In comparison, when experiences are organized according to the intensity of the person's involvement in the task, the experiences of restoration, ludos, and self-awareness can be laid out in a second continuum (see Figure 15.2).

Restorative experiences are less intense in personal involvement than ludos or heightened self-awareness. Experiences of ludos occur during occupations in which intensity is either temporary or bracketed as outside the judgment of ordinary life. One existing classification of discretionary activities is the one by Gordon and colleagues (1976), who classify these according to the level of expressive involvement required. In this classification, play experiences that occur during work are described as requiring a high medium level of expressive involvement. Gordon and colleagues' descriptions of what constitutes play at work match descriptions of ludos and, therefore, lend support to situating ludos between restoration and heightened self-awareness. The experience of height-

Table 15.6
The Characteristics of Each Pattern Type of Process-oriented Experiences

Patterns	Characteristics
Restoration The pleasure or satisfaction derived from relaxation, decreased active performance.	Requires one's removal from ongoing activity Helps regain energy Often physically not active, may be somewhat mentally active Excitement may decrease Often customary Provides a feeling of freedom from ongoing pressures May be described as "imposing itself" on the individual Includes passive entertainment
Ludos The enjoyment derived from lighthearted active participation in an occupation that may take brief moments of time.	Spontaneous Short duration Perceived as nonstressful Momentary increased level of arousal Active physically and/or mentally Perceived as having an unclear purpose Perceived imagination and creativity in creating the situation Produces sense of well-being Appears as lighthearted The participants suspend judgment during its performance
Heightened self-awareness The pleasure and satisfaction derived from increased sense of self (physical, intellectual, and/or spiritual).	Physically and/or mentally intense Person might describe it as necessary nourishment for the body, mind, or spirit Requires intense focus and immersion in an activity May be perceived as stressful
Mastery The pleasure and satisfaction derived from the interaction with known occupation and the challenge of controlling the process of the performance.	May have a clear purpose Mentally active Physically active Customary and skilled May be perceived as necessary Some stress when it includes novelty and challenge (adventure)
Adventure The pleasure and satisfaction derived from being exposed to novel experiences (physical or intellectual).	Exciting Mentally active Includes novelty
Creativity The pleasure and satisfaction derived from bringing something into existence or giving original order to existing data.	Creative and often imaginative May include stress, and is often depleting May be perceived as necessary Reported as having a clear purpose Mentally active

Reprinted by permission from E. Blanche.

Figure 15.1
The continuum of novelty.

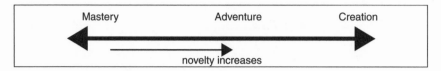

Figure 15.2
The continuum of intensity of involvement.

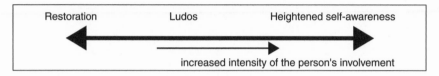

Figure 15.3
The circle of intensity of involvement.

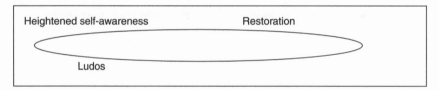

ened self-awareness occurs during occupations that require intense involvement with the task. These conceptual maps depict the fluidity of the experiences, plotted as moving dots or lines, as they are organized in a continuum that allows transitioning from one to the other. Experiences are fluid and change over time. Although the continua are depicted in straight lines, an experience is not exclusively in one direction or another, nor is it in segmental stages. Rather, an experience can be transformed from heightened self-awareness to restorative. A person can increase the level of involvement and can move from restoration into heightened self-awareness and then abruptly stop, without going back down through ludos to decreased intensity. Therefore, the cyclical nature of such experiences might be better depicted as a circle (see Figure 15.3).

In the same manner, the same experience of playing tennis can be understood as transforming according to the amount of novelty. At first, the players may experience some degree of novelty because neither can completely control the movements of the other player. However, if one player has inferior tennis skills, then mastery would dominate the experience for the other. When two players are matched in skills, there is novelty in the task, and some creativity is needed to outsmart the other player. In every act of process-oriented creation, there is

Figure 15.4
The circle of novelty.

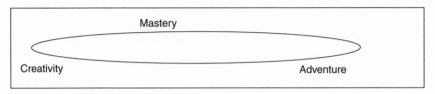

Figure 15.5
A conceptual map of process-oriented experiences.

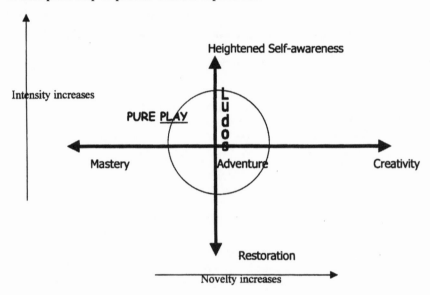

a certain degree of mastery involved in that the person rests his or her creativity on mastered skills. Figure 15.4 depicts this continuum.

Because most occupations can be viewed as situated in a dimension of intensity of involvement, as well as a dimension of novelty, these continua of experiences can be depicted simultaneously as intersecting axes (see Figure 15.5). Each axis represents one continuum of experiences. The transformational process occurring during the performance of a process-oriented occupation can be plotted according to the two dimensions.

In this diagram, pure play—having most of the characteristics of play described in the literature and supported by the findings in this study—falls into the intersection of adventure and ludos. However, there are elements of play present in all process-oriented occupations and throughout all the axes points.

A pure expression of play is positioned in the intersection of seeking novelty and increasing the intensity of involvement. Ludos is one expression of play; however, ludos can occur without seeking novel stimulation in the environment. Therefore, in this study the most pure form of play, an improvisation class, includes both exposing oneself to novelty and moving into creating novelty at the same time as involvement increases and becomes ludos. Nonetheless, elements of play permeate throughout all process-oriented occupations.

Forms of play fall at different points on the conceptual map. For example, instances of deep play could be depicted as falling in the transformation of mastery into adventure in the continuum of novelty. Concurrently, the intensity of a person's involvement increases, providing the experience of heightened self-awareness. Certain risky experiences fall where adventure moves into creativity, because there is no mastery involved, yet they heighten self-awareness by making the person aware of his or her mortality.

In summary, this diagram represents enjoyable, process-oriented experiences. These experiences have been previously described in the literature; however, this model lends itself to representing the fluidity of the experiences, the transformative nature of process-oriented experiences, and the individual's styles in incorporating play in their daily routines.

CONCLUSION: ADULT PLAY

The findings in this study revealed that process-oriented occupations were fluid and transformative, and thus provided meaning in the lives of the participants. Sometimes they were *the* meaning. The experiences were fluid in that the participants often made a transition from one type of experience to another while performing an occupation. These experiences were also mood transformative. Abrahams (1986) states that extraordinary experiences arise spontaneously during the day and break the daily routine, providing a baseline against which other activities are judged and the fullness of one's life is measured. Process-oriented occupations offer the possibility for those extraordinary experiences to occur.

Six patterns of process-oriented experiences emerged from the data: mastery, adventure, creativity, restoration, ludos, and heightened self-awareness. These patterns can be organized according to the level of intensity and the amount of novelty.

ACKNOWLEDGMENT

The author would like to thank Diane Parham for her assistance in developing these ideas during the dissertation process. The paper is based on *Play and Process: The Experience of Play in the Life of the Adult* (Blanche, 1999).

APPENDIX A: Section of Spreadsheet Utilized to Analyze the Experiential Characteristics of One Participant

Activities Performed by One Participant During the Sample Day

Activities

Activities		1 Ex	1 Bo	2 Ex	2 Bo	1 St	1 Re	2 St	2 Re	1 Pl	1 Mis	2 Pl	2 Mis
1a. talk to husband										1			
1b. none													
2a. get up						1							
2b. feed cats/dogs								1					
3a. shower/dress							1			1			
14b. talk								1				1	
15a. go to bed													
15b. none													
Total 1	15	3	6			7	5			10	0		
Total 2	8			2	1			3	3			5	1
% of 1		20%	40%			47%	33%			67%	0%		
% of 2				25%	13%			38%	38%			63%	13%
Total 1 + 2	23												
% of total		22%	30%			43%	35%			65%	4%		

Note: Ex = exciting; Bo = boring; St = stressful; Re = relaxing.

APPENDIX B: Section of Spreadsheet Utilized to Analyze the Experiential Characteristics of the Activities Reported by All the Participants

Total Reported Characteristics by Each Participant and Total Percentage

Participants	# of activities			Characteristics							
Particpants				Experiential Qualities							
				1	1	2	2	1	1	2	2
				SPONTANEOUS/PLANNED				EXCITING /BORING			
	1	2	1+2	Sp	Pl	Sp	Pl	Ex	Bo	Ex	Bo
Ian	15	11	26	2	13	9	2	6	9	8	3
Herman	19	10	29	7	5	4	1	2	2	0	1
Leo	22	6	28	10	12	4	2	16	0	4	0
Anthony	18	8	26	6	10	5	3	0	0	1	0
Jane	24	21	45	3	20	5	13	2	2	6	4
Paloma	15	8	23	9	6	6	1	3	6	2	1
Ann	21	8	29	5	16	4	4	14	2	6	0
Totals of 1	134			42	82			43	21		
Totals of 2		72				37	26			27	9
TOTALS											
% primaries											
% secondaries											

Note: Sp = spontaneous; Pl = planned; Ex = exciting; Bo = boring.

REFERENCES

Abrahams, R. (1986). Ordinary and extraordinary experience. In V. W. Turner & E. M. Bruner (Eds.), *The anthropology of experience* (pp. 45–72). Urbana: University of Illinois Press.

Apter, M. (1991). A structural-phenomenology of play. In J. Kerr & M. Apter (Eds.), *Adult play: A reversal theory approach* (pp. 13–30). Amsterdam: Swets & Zeitlinger.

Apter, M. (1992). *The dangerous edge: The psychology of excitement.* New York: Free Press.

Argyle, M. (1996). *The social psychology of leisure.* London: Penguin Books.

Bateson, G. (1972). A theory of play and fantasy. In G. Bateson (Ed.), *Steps to an ecology of mind* (pp. 177–193). Toronto, Ontario, Canada: Chandler. (Original work published 1955)

Berlyne, D. E. (1969). Laughter, humor and play. In G. Lindsey & E. Aronson (Eds.), *The handbook of social psychology* (Vol. 3, pp. 795–851). Reading, MA: Addison-Wesley.

Blanche, E.I. (1999). *Play and process: The experience of play in the life of the adult.* Ann Arbor: University of Michigan.

Bowman, J. (1978). The organization of spontaneous adult social play. In M. Salter (Ed.), *Play: Anthropological perspectives* (pp. 239–250). Champaign, IL: Leisure Press.

Bowman, J. (1987). Making work play. In G. A. Fine (Ed.), *Meaningful play, playful meaning* (pp. 61–71). Champaign, IL: Human Kinetics.

Caillois, R. (1961). *Man, play, and games.* New York: Free Press of Glencoe.

Chapin, F. S. (1974). *Human activity patterns in the city.* New York: Wiley.

Chapin, F. S., Jr. (1978). Chapter 1: Human time allocation in the city. In T. Carlstein, D. Parkes, & N. Thrift (Eds.), *Timing space and spacing time: Vol. 2. Human activity and time geography* (pp. 13–26). New York: John Wiley & Sons.

Cohen, D. (1987). *The development of play.* New York: New York University Press.

Csikszentmilhalyi, M. (1975). *Beyond boredom and anxiety.* San Francisco: Jossey-Bass.

Csikszentmilhalyi, M. (1981). Some paradoxes in the definition of play. In A.T. Cheska (Ed.), *Play as context.* West Point, NY: Leisure Press.

Csikszentmilhalyi, M. (1988). The flow experience and its significance for human psychology. In M. Csikszentmilhalyi & I.S. Csikszentmilhalyi (Eds.), *Optimal experience: Psychological studies of flow in consciousness* (pp. 15–35). New York: Cambridge University Press.

Csikszentmilhalyi, M. (1990). *Flow: The psychology of optimal experience.* New York: Cambridge University Press.

Csikszentmilhalyi, M. (1993). *The evolving self.* New York: HarperCollins.

Day, H.I. (1981). Play: A ludic behavior. In H.I. Day (Ed.), *Advances in intrinsic motivation and aesthetics* (pp. 225–250). New York: Plenum Press.

Denzin, N. K., & Lincoln, Y.S. (1994). Entering the field of qualitative research. In N. K. Denzin & Y. S. Lincoln (Eds.), *Handbook of qualitative research* (pp. 1–17). Thousand Oaks, CA: Sage.

Duzamazedier, J. (1974). *Sociology of leisure.* Amsterdam: Elsevier.

Glesne, C., & Peshkin, A. (1992). *Becoming qualitative researchers: An introduction.* White Plains, NY: Longman.

Gordon, C., Gaitz, C. M., & Scott, J. (1976). Leisure and lives: Personal expressivity across the lifespan. In R.H. Binstock & E. Shanas (Eds.), *Handbook of aging and the social sciences* (pp. 310–341). New York: Von Nostrand-Reinhold.

Grover, K. (1992). *Hard at play: Leisure in America, 1840–1940.* Amherst, MA: University of Massachusetts Press.

Guba, E. G. (1981). Criteria for assessing the trustworthiness of naturalistic inquiries. *Educational Communication and Technology Journal, 29*, 75–92.

Huizinga, J. (1955). *Homo ludens: A study of the play-element in culture.* Boston: Beacon Press. (Original work published 1938)

Hutt, C. (1978). Exploration and play in children. In D. Muller-Schwarze (Ed.), *Evolution of play behavior* (pp. 328–348). Stroudsburg, PA: Dowden, Huchinson & Ross.

Kerr, J. (1991). A structural phenomenology of play in context. In J. Kerr & M. Apter (Eds.), *Adult play: A reversal theory approach* (pp. 31–42). Amsterdam: Swets & Zeitlinger.

Kerr, J. (1994). *Understanding soccer hooliganism.* Buckingham, England: Open University Press.

Kraus, R. (1984). *Recreation and leisure in modern society* (3rd ed.). Glenview, IL: Scott, Foresman.

Lincoln, Y. S., & Guba, E. G. (1985). *Naturalistic inquiry.* Newbury Park, CA: Sage.

Lurker, E. (1991). Zen and the art of playing. *Play and Culture, 4*, 75–79.

Marcuse, H. (1966). *Eros and civilization.* Boston: Beacon Press. (Original work published 1955)

Maslow, A. H. (1954). *Motivation and personality.* New York: Harper & Brothers.

Miles, M. B., & Huberman, A. M. (1994). *Qualitative data analysis.* Thousand Oaks, CA: Sage.

Polkinghorne, D. E. (1991). Qualitative procedures for counseling research. In *Research and counseling* (pp. 163–204). East Brunswick, NJ: Falco & Falco Inc.

Quarrick, G. (1989). *Our sweetest hours: Recreation and the mental state of absorption.* Jefferson, NC: McFarland & Company.

Rojek, C. (1995). *Decentering leisure.* London: Sage.

Schwartzman, H. (1978). The dichotomy of work and play. In M. Salter (Ed.), *Play: Anthropological perspectives* (pp. 185–187). Champaign, IL: Leisure Press.

Seidman, I. E. (1991). *Interviewing as qualitative research.* New York: Teachers College Press.

Singer, D., & Singer, J. (1990). *The house of make-believe.* Cambridge, MA: Harvard University Press.

Sutton-Smith, B. (1997). *The ambiguity of play.* Cambridge, MA: Harvard University Press.

Sutton-Smith, B., & Kelly-Byrne, D. (1984a). The masks of play. In B. Sutton-Smith & D. Kelly-Byrne (Eds.), *Masks of play* (pp. 184–197). New York: Leisure Press.

Sutton-Smith, B., & Kelly-Byrne, D. (1984b). Introduction. In B. Sutton-Smith & D. Kelly-Byrne (Eds.), *Masks of play* (pp. 76–77). New York: Leisure Press.

Turner, V. (1982). *From ritual to theatre: The human seriousness of play.* New York: PAJ Publications.

Turner, V. (1987). *The anthropology of performance.* New York: PAJ Publications.

Vandenberg, B. (1978). Play and development from an ethological perspective. *American Psychologist, 33*, 724–738.

Volkwein, K.A.E. (1991). Play as a path for liberation: A Marcusean perspective. *Play and Culture, 4*, 359–370.

Author Index

Subject Index

About the Contributors

DORIS BERGEN is Professor of Educational Psychology at Miami University in Oxford, Ohio. Her research interests include the study of play and humor in early and middle childhood, social interactions of children in inclusive settings, and effects of early phonological awareness levels on later reading skills. She is Director of Miami's Center for Human Development, Learning, and Teaching.

ERNA IMPERATORE BLANCHE is on the faculty in the Department of Occupational Science and Occupational Therapy, University of Southern California.

ROSEMARY BOLIG is an Associate Professor of Education in the Department of Education, the University of the District of Columbia, on the faculty of Walden University, and an independent consultant.

JAMES F. CHRISTIE is Professor of Curriculum and Instruction at Arizona State University. His research interests include children's play and early literacy development.

MELLISA A. CLAWSON is Assistant Professor of Early Childhood Education and Special Education at the University of Maine at Farmington. Her research interests include early childhood education practices, play and development, and peer and parent–child relationships.

AMY CLAYTON was an undergraduate student in Psychology at Elon University.

REBECCA DEUTSCHER has been working as a Psychometrician at KnowledgePlanet, making learning more individualized for people by incorporating assessment techniques into an adaptive learning system.

CHRISTINE J. GEIGER is currently a substitute teacher in New Jersey.

THOMAS HENRICKS is Danieley Professor of Sociology at Elon University. His interest in play studies stems from a wider concern with the organization of expressive culture in modern societies, such as the ways in which people's vision of enjoyment is framed by social and cultural forms. Among his writings is *Disputed Pleasures: Sport and Society in Preindustrial England*, published by Greenwood Press.

MINDI HOLT was an undergraduate student in Psychology at Elon University.

ROBYN M. HOLMES is Associate Professor of Psychology at Monmouth University. She received her Ph.D. from Rutgers University. Her research interests are children's play and social cognition and qualitative methods. She is the author of numerous articles and two books—*Fieldwork with Children* and *How Young Children Perceive Race*.

CATHERINE KING is on the faculty of Psychology at Elon University.

KRISTEN KURTZ was an undergraduate student in Psychology at Elon University.

DAVID F. LANCY is Professor of Anthropology at Utah State University. His research and teaching interests span anthropology and developmental psychology and public schooling. He is the author of *Playing on the Mother Ground: Cultural Routines for Children's Development*, an analysis of child development in non-Western societies (particularly the Kpelle society) and *Whose Mummy Is It?* an interactive adventure that introduces students (playfully) to the field of Egyptology.

LISA MAESTRI was an undergraduate student in Psychology at Elon University.

ERSILIA MENESINI is Lecturer at the Department of Psychology, University of Florence, Italy.

ERICA MORRIS was an undergraduate student in Psychology at Elon University.

PHYLLIS NEVES has taught in public schools, where she currently is assigned to a pre-kindergarten classroom. Her interests in early literacy were enhanced through graduate study at the University of Texas at Austin.

PEGGY O'NEILL-WAGNER began her studies of nonhuman primates as an undergraduate and then graduate student under Dr. Harry Harlow at the University of Wisconsin. After thirteen years working with monkeys in laboratory and field settings, she joined the NICHD Laboratory of Comparative Ethology staff at the NIH Animal Center in Poolesville, Maryland, in 1984. Since then she has received numerous awards and acknowledgments for her research and dedication toward developing innovative techniques for enriching the lives of captive primates.

ANTHONY D. PELLEGRINI is Professor of Educational Psychology at the University of Minnesota, Twin Cities campus. He has studied many aspects of children's play across his career, beginning with the language of preschoolers' symbolic play and how it relates to subsequent literacy and moving on to children's play behaviors during recess. Most recently he is studying children's games during their first year of school.

CHRISTOFER S. PRICE is employed as a statistician for a government contractor located in the Washington, D.C. area. One of his many assignments involves analysis of the student test scores for publicly supported education required testing. Prior to his current position he spent many years dedicated to the study of nonhuman primates in the wild and in captivity.

STUART REIFEL is a professor at the University of Texas at Austin, where he teaches in the Early Childhood Education Program. His research interests are in play and the curriculum. He was series editor for the first three volumes of *Play & Culture Studies*.

DOROTHY JUSTUS SLUSS is Professor of Early Childhood Education at Clemson University, Clemson, South Carolina.

REBECCA SMEES is a researcher at the Institute of Education, University of London.

PETER K. SMITH is Professor of Psychology at Goldsmiths College, University of London, and Head of the Unit for School and Family Studies there. He has researched extensively on children's play, bullying in school, family relationships, and grandparenting. He is co-editor of *The Family Systems Test* (FAST) (in press, Psychology Press).

SANDRA J. STONE is an Associate Professor at the Center for Excellence in Education at Northern Arizona University. She teaches courses in literacy, multiage education, and early childhood education. Her research interests include mixed-age groupings, children's play, and literacy. She is the director of the National Multiage Institute and is also editor of the *Journal of Research in Childhood Education*. She has authored several books including *Creating the Multiage Classroom* (1996), *Playing: A Kid's Curriculum* (1993), and *Powerful Ways to Use Literacy-Based Centers* (2001).

BRIAN SUTTON-SMITH is Professor Emeritus at the University of Pennsylvania. He is an internationally renowned scholar who has published extensively in the area of play. One of his most recent books is *The Ambiguity of Play*, Harvard University Press.

MAUREEN VANDERMAAS-PEELER is currently an Assistant Professor of Psychology at Elon University. She received her Ph.D. in Developmental Psychology from North Carolina State University. Her research interests concern children's development in sociocultural contexts, with an emphasis on the influences of parent–child interactions on cognitive and social development in young children.

SUSAN J. WELTEROTH is the Principal at Watsontown Elementary School, Warrior Run School District, Washingtown, Pennsylvania. She is also an Adjunct Instructor in Early Childhood Education at Susquehanna University.

EMILY WOODY was an undergraduate student in Psychology at Elon University.